Failed Sanctions

CONTEMPORARY CUBA

UNIVERSITY PRESS OF FLORIDA

Florida A&M University, Tallahassee
Florida Atlantic University, Boca Raton
Florida Gulf Coast University, Ft. Myers
Florida International University, Miami
Florida State University, Tallahassee
New College of Florida, Sarasota
University of Central Florida, Orlando
University of Florida, Gainesville
University of North Florida, Jacksonville
University of South Florida, Tampa
University of West Florida, Pensacola

Paolo Spadoni

FAILED

University Press of Florida

Gainesville

Tallahassee

Tampa

Boca Raton

Pensacola

Orlando

Miami

Jacksonville

Ft. Myers

Sarasota

SANCTIONS

Why the U.S. Embargo against Cuba Could Never Work

Copyright 2010 by Paolo Spadoni

Printed in the United States of America. This book is printed on Glatfelter Natures Book, a paper certified under the standards of the Forestry Stewardship Council (FSC). It is a recycled stock that contains 30 percent post-consumer waste and is acid-free.

15   14   13   12   11   10   6   5   4   3   2   1

Library of Congress Cataloging-in-Publication Data
Spadoni, Paolo.
Failed sanctions : why the U.S. embargo against Cuba could never work /
Paolo Spadoni.
p. cm.
Includes bibliographical references and index.
ISBN 978-0-8130-3515-4 (alk. paper)
1. Economic sanctions, American—Cuba. 2. Embargo. 3. United States—Foreign economic relations—Cuba. 4. Cuba—Foreign economic relations—United States. 5. Cuba—Economic conditions. I. Title.
HF1500.5.U5S63 2010
327.1'17—dc22   2010023260

The University Press of Florida is the scholarly publishing agency for the State University System of Florida, comprising Florida A&M University, Florida Atlantic University, Florida Gulf Coast University, Florida International University, Florida State University, New College of Florida, University of Central Florida, University of Florida, University of North Florida, University of South Florida, and University of West Florida.

University Press of Florida
15 Northwest 15th Street
Gainesville, FL 32611-2079
http://www.upf.com

To my wife, Inés Avilés-Spadoni, my brother,
Mirco, my parents, Luigino and Maria Pia,
and my friend Luca Gaudenzi

Contents

Figures

Tables

Acknowledgments

I extend my sincerest gratitude to the many people who provided help with this study. I owe an enormous debt to the Center for Inter-American Policy and Research (CIPR) at Tulane University for granting me a generous research fellowship from August 2008 to July 2010 that greatly facilitated the completion of this work. The CIPR's director, Ludovico Feoli, offered me guidance and constant support, which I appreciate.

In working on the book, I benefited from critical reading of the material by scholars and leading experts on Cuba and U.S.-Cuba relations. Susan Eckstein and Peter Schwab deserve a special note of thanks for their valuable comments and suggestions, which helped me write a much better book in the end. I wish to acknowledge an anonymous reviewer for insightful observations on key aspects of U.S. foreign policy toward Cuba.

I also owe a great deal to John Kirk, editor of the Contemporary Cuba series for the University Press of Florida. John believed in this project from the beginning and provided exceptional assistance throughout the whole process. Much appreciation is due to Amy Gorelick, acquisitions editor at the Press, for her efficiency and professionalism.

My heartfelt thanks go to Terry McCoy, Philip J. Williams, Leann Brown, and Ido Oren for their encouragement and useful inputs. I acknowledge a major debt to William A. Messina Jr. for his enthusiastic support, kind words, and valuable help.

I would like to express my profound gratitude to several Cuban scholars and analysts at various research centers in Havana and to local journalists and foreign correspondents posted in Cuba. Their knowledge, willingness to help with the research, and friendliness made it possible for me to carry out such a stimulating study.

I particularly thank my good friend Luca Gaudenzi for nurturing my interest on Cuban issues and providing thoughtful suggestions. I will always cherish our great conversations in Cattolica and Gradara, Italy, and the memories of our trips to many Latin American countries during the 1990s.

I would like to thank my father, Luigino, and my mother, Maria Pia, for their love and generosity, and my brother, Mirco, for always being supportive and good to me. I am also grateful to my parents-in-law, Alberto Avilés and Lucy Avilés, for treating me as their own son and for their matchless hospitality. My father-in-law sadly passed from this life in October 2006.

Last, but certainly not least, I am especially grateful to my beloved wife, Inés, for believing in me and for being such an amazing partner and friend. Her unconditional love, loyalty, patience, and support gave me the strength to write this book.

Introduction

For almost five decades, the United States has maintained a comprehensive economic embargo on Cuba that severely restricts U.S.-based travel to the island and makes most financial and commercial transactions with Cuba illegal for U.S. citizens. During the cold war, the Castro government weathered the economic impact of the embargo in large part because of generous subsidies offered by the former Soviet Union, mainly through cheap oil supplies in return for overpriced Cuban sugar. But when the special relationship between Havana and Moscow ended abruptly in the early 1990s, Cuba became much more vulnerable to U.S. economic pressures.

Since the early 1990s, Cuba has suffered debilitating blows that resulted from the demise of the Soviet Union and the disappearance of the economic and financial system in which the island was inserted, the Council for Mutual Economic Assistance (CMEA). At the end of the 1980s, some 81 percent of Cuba's external commercial relations were with countries that were members of the CMEA. In 1989, Cuba exported 63 percent of its sugar, 73 percent of its nickel, and 95 percent of its citrus to these countries. Similarly, imports from CMEA countries represented around 85 percent of Cuba's total imports: 63 percent of food, 86 percent of raw material, 98 percent of fuel and lubricants, 80 percent of machinery and equipment, and 57 percent of chemical products (Alvarez González and

Fernández Mayo 1992, 4-5). The termination of traditional trade partnerships with the Soviet bloc proved disastrous for the Cuban economy. Between 1989 and 1992, the total value of Cuba's exports fell by around 61 percent while the same figure for imports dropped by approximately 72 percent (Mesa-Lago 1994, 223).

Furthermore, Cuba lost the favorable and stable terms under which most of its trade took place. In addition to "coordinated supply plans" and exports, Soviet subsidies and aid to Cuba averaged $4.3 billion a year from 1986 through 1990 (Hernández-Catá 2001, 4). It should be emphasized that the Cubans did not consider Soviet subsidies as financial aid but simply as credits and assistance to development. The extent of Soviet aid is also debatable because a substantial share of it was "tied aid" that kept Cuba committed to exports of sugar in exchange for relatively inexpensive Soviet oil and uncompetitive industrial machinery and technology. Whatever the interpretation of the preferential relationship between Cuba and the Soviet Union, it is clear that because the island lost the external support that had sustained its economy, it was forced to develop a new strategy for reinsertion into the global market economy.

After 1989, the Cuban economy went into recession, with the real gross domestic product (GDP) decreasing by a cumulative 34.8 percent from 1990 through 1993. The beginning of what the Cuban government called the "special period in time of peace" (established in September 1990) stimulated a more pragmatic stance toward economic policy. Cuba gradually moved away from strict central planning to a more mixed economy and opened the door to selected aspects of capitalism, to foster a recovery, while at the same time ensuring the survival of the social system and the major accomplishments of the revolution (Haines 1997).

Cuba's opening to foreign investment in the early 1990s was perhaps the most significant change for a socialist country whose economy had previously been under exclusive state control and ownership. The island's authorities resorted to foreign investment as a way to assure the diversification and promotion of exports, acquisition of raw materials, insertion into new markets, acquisition of technology and capital, and introduction of modern practices of management (Pérez Villanueva 1998, 98). Other measures were adopted: the promotion of international tourism (1991); limited capitalist-style reforms such as the legalization of the possession and circulation of U.S. dollars (August 1993), featuring remittances from Cubans living abroad and state-owned dollar stores and exchange houses open to the public; authorization of self-employment and the breakup of the state monopoly on land to set up agricultural cooperatives (September 1993); reorganization of the central administration of the state and reduction of bureaucracy with the establishment of a new structure of ministries and institutes for both horizontal and vertical functions (April 1994); and the creation of free farmers' markets (September 1994).

Considering the emergency conditions of the Cuban economy, the end of Cuba's active support of revolutionary forces in Africa and Latin America, and the end of its close ties with the Soviet Union, one might have expected the beginning of friendlier relations between Washington and Havana. However, just when Cuba was trying to reactivate its economy in the wake of the events that had taken place in Eastern Europe, the Cuban exile community in the United States successfully pressured the U.S. Congress to adopt a new set of economic sanctions against the island. The United States tightened its long-standing embargo by enacting first the Torricelli law in 1992 and subsequently the Helms-Burton law in 1996, in an attempt to undermine the Cuban government with additional economic sanctions. As Domínguez (1997, 49) observed, "The Cold War had turned colder in the Caribbean. Cuba was the only country governed by a communist party whose domestic political regime the United States was still committed by law and policy to replace, albeit by peaceful means."

The U.S. Embargo against Cuba in the Post–Cold War Era

At a time when the Cuban government was struggling for survival and opening the island to foreign investment, international tourism, and remittances to stimulate the ailing economy, the United States reinforced its economic sanctions against Cuba. In October 1992, President George H. W. Bush signed the Cuban Democracy Act (CDA), also known as the Torricelli law. The bill prohibited foreign subsidiaries of U.S. companies from dealing with Cuba, barred any ship that had docked in Cuban harbors from entering U.S. ports for a period of six months, and called for a termination of aid to any country that provided assistance to Cuba. In order to encourage democratic changes on the island, the Torricelli law also permitted a calibrated reduction of certain sanctions in response to positive developments in Cuba.

On March 12, 1996, President Bill Clinton signed the Cuban Liberty and Democratic Solidarity Act, better known as the Helms-Burton law. Besides codifying the existing restrictions that collectively formed the U.S. economic embargo against Cuba, the Helms-Burton law aimed to disrupt the flow of foreign investment into Cuba by creating a riskier and more uncertain business environment, and complicate Havana's access to external financing. The rationale for the legislation was that this plan might ultimately lead to the collapse of the Cuban government or at least seriously undermine the process of slow but constant economic recovery witnessed by the communist island since its lowest point in 1993. The attempt to undermine Cuba's opening to foreign investment was linked to the possibility of lawsuits and the imposition of travel restrictions against foreign companies or other entities that "traffic" in U.S. properties expropriated during the early days of the Cuban Revolution. The right to sue foreign companies was also granted to Cubans who became U.S. citizens after the expropriation occurred, in an attempt to further increase the potential impact of the legislation.

Since the late 1990s, economic sanctions against Cuba have been under fire in the U.S. Congress. An increasing number of lawmakers have pushed for a rapprochement with the Castro government and the lifting of restrictions on travel to and trade with the island. In October 2000, the U.S. Congress passed a resolution allowing direct commercial exports (on a cash basis) of food products to Cuba for the first time in almost four decades. In June 2004, however, the White House again intensified economic pressure on its communist neighbor by implementing more stringent rules on remittances, family visits, and U.S.-based educational travel to Cuba. It also said it would increase financial support of anti-Castro groups on the island.

There has been considerable debate about just how effective the U.S. economic embargo against Cuba has been in achieving its main goals. On the one hand, several scholars and analysts concluded that U.S. unilateral economic sanctions with respect to Cuba simply do not work (Sweig 2007; Knippers Black 2005; Weinmann 2004; Seiglie 2001; Peters 2000; Rothkopf 2000; Rich Kaplowitz 1998; Smith 1998). The most common argument is that sanctions have failed to promote significant changes in Cuba and hasten the end of the Castro regime while providing the latter with an easy scapegoat for its own shortcomings. Critics of Washington's isolationist and hostile stance toward Havana point out that U.S. policy is largely driven by domestic politics considerations, trapped in a sort of cold war nostalgia, and basically disconnected from the reality in Cuba. The embargo also imposes unjustifiable costs on American firms in terms of forfeited businesses with the island. Given this situation, a policy of engagement would more effectively serve U.S. interests in post-Soviet Cuba and increase U.S. chances to influence economic and political developments there.

On the other hand, supporters of U.S. policy toward Cuba justify the existing economic sanctions mostly by arguing that engagement with the island would be unlikely to induce the Castro government to implement meaningful democratic changes. While recognizing that the embargo by itself would not produce liberalization, they contend that the lifting of sanctions would facilitate the continuation of a defiant totalitarian regime, lead to greater repression and governmental control, and further reduce the possibilities for a genuine democratic transition in Cuba (Suchlicki 2000, 2007; Kaufman Purcell 2000; López 2000; Radu 1998). In essence, as Fisk (2001, 101) unequivocally put it, U.S. policy "is not driven by what has happened in Cuba; it is driven by what has not happened."

Limitations of Current Research on Economic Sanctions

The role and usefulness of economic sanctions as a coercive tool in international relations has been debated for decades. Although military instruments are often thought to be the only effective means for achieving ambitious foreign policy goals, since World War I sanctions have come to be viewed as the liberal alternative to war. The rationale behind their use is that they will inflict economic deprivation and provoke public anger. This in turn will unleash domestic political pressures on a target government and lead to changes in its behavior or its removal from power (Jonge Oudraat 2000, 105).

While the first major body of research on sanctions during the 1960s and 1970s reached a consensus that they were not as effective as military force, growing optimism on the utility of economic pressure began to emerge around the mid-1980s. A new wave of liberal scholarship became convinced that international organizations may constrain state behavior and significantly affect international outcomes (Martin 1992, 250-51). Neoliberals argue that cooperation among states is bound to increase in the modern world as higher levels of interdependence make the costs of defection more burdensome (Oye 1985, 14; Keohane 1983, 97). But potent economic sanctions are vital to ensuring a stable outcome because states might not cooperate with each other unless they expect to be punished for defecting and fear the resulting costs (Drezner 1999, 9; Axelrod and Keohane 1985, 236).

The aforementioned optimism among liberals has not gone unchallenged. Pape (1997, 106-107) found little valid social science research supporting claims that economic coercion can achieve major foreign policy goals and that multilateral cooperation can make sanctions an effective alternative to military force. He maintained that economic sanctions had succeeded in less than 5 percent of all cases since World War I and challenged a study by Hufbauer, Schott, and Elliot (1990) that showed a much higher success rate. Pape concluded that sanctions, despite the increasing multilateral cooperation of the early 1990s among superpowers, are unlikely to gain importance in the future mainly because the modern state is not fragile. According to him, target states are able to mitigate the impact of sanctions by shifting the burden to opponents and disenfranchised groups or through economic adjustments, while external pressures tend to increase the nationalist legitimacy of their rulers. Using bargaining theory and strategic interaction models, other scholars demonstrated that sanctions have little impact on dispute outcomes and argued that they can seldom be effective policy instruments because the coercer and the target play against rational opponents trying to promote their own goals (Morgan and Schwebach 1997, 46; Tsebelis 1990, 20; Wagner 1988, 481-83).

It is worth underscoring that economic sanctions can still be a reliable alternative to the use of force even if they rarely work as claimed by Pape. Rational decision making requires the comparative assessment of policy options not only in terms of favorable outcomes but also in terms of costs and benefits for both the coercer and the target and the complexity of the undertaking. In sum, it might be preferable for policymakers to use sanctions rather than military force even when they are less likely to accomplish certain goals as long as the cost differential between the two policy alternatives is big enough (Baldwin 1999/2000, 86). Nevertheless, there seems to be at least a general acceptance among scholars that economic coercion is often unable to serve far-reaching foreign policy goals and promote major positive changes in a target country.

Economic sanctions can be imposed either by one state acting alone or by all states (or most of them) upon which the target government relies for external support. Multilateral comprehensive sanctions are usually thought to have a greater potential impact than unilateral ones, but they are rarely imposed due to the difficulty of reaching consensus among countries on another state's behavior. In contrast, unilateral coercive economic measures have been used frequently, especially by the United States. These foreign policy tools against target countries include the withdrawal of economic, military, and technological assistance, the seizure of assets in U.S. jurisdictions, restrictions on trade, investment, and travel, and pressures on international financial institutions to deny loans, credits, or grants.

My research is interdisciplinary and draws on notions of international and domestic (U.S.) law, international relations, transnationalism, history, and economics. It is a case study of the implementation and effectiveness of U.S. unilateral economic sanctions against Cuba. Since the communist island is subject to one of the most comprehensive U.S. economic embargoes in history, this study has great implications for the research on the role and usefulness of sanctions as instruments of foreign policy. It also sheds light upon a specific aspect that has been generally neglected by scholars of international relations and by the literature on the Cuban embargo: the influence of transnational actors in the globalizing post–cold war world.

Globalization and greater economic openness make target countries more vulnerable to comprehensive and fully enforced multilateral sanctions. Today, this kind of foreign pressure is potentially more harmful than it was a few decades ago as the world's economies are growingly connected through international trade in goods and services, transnational capital flows (foreign direct and portfolio investment, loans, and aid), and cross-border remittances by migrant entrepreneurs (Van Bergeijk 1995,

448). However, the same transnational linkages that enhance the impact of multilateral coercion on a target country also make the latter less vulnerable to unilateral sanctions with little or no international cooperation. With the declining dominance in the world economy of the United States, most U.S. unilateral sanctions simply transfer business from U.S. firms to foreign competitors in the same market. Interestingly, Hufbauer, Schott, and Elliott revealed that in several episodes either provoked or derived from East-West rivalry during the cold war, adversaries of the sender country (referred to as "black knights") assisted the target, thus eroding the chances of the sanctions' success. They predicted that, with the end of the cold war, "black knights may in the future be less likely to appear on the sanctions scene to rescue target countries" (Hufbauer et al. 1990, 96-97). But in the late 1990s, Schott (1998) warned: "Too often the economic impact of our (U.S.) sanctions is offset by alternative suppliers of goods and capitals whose governments agree with our goals but not the tactics to achieve them."

In other words, transnational actors such as multinational corporations and international migrants, often based in countries that share the same objectives of most U.S. sanctions, could be the black knights in today's global marketplace as their activities sustain huge flows of capital across national borders, including those of target nations. And in some cases, as the importance of Cuban-American remittances in the Cuban economy suggests, rescuers might be located in the same country that has placed economic coercion at the center of its foreign policy. Although the fundamental assumption of most research on sanctions is that they are an activity between states (Morgan and Bapat 2003, 65), transnational actors' practices and their economic impact on target nations should receive greater attention in an increasingly interconnected global economy.

While many scholars evaluate the utility of economic coercion by analyzing the behavior of the target government, this study focuses on transnational or non-state players such as multinational corporations, migrants, international travelers, indirect investors, and food exporters. A twofold question will be addressed. If transnational linkages sustain flows of capital and finance across borders, mainly in the form of foreign investment and remittances, is it possible that economic sanctions (especially unilateral ones) do not work because of activities carried out by overseas investors and migrants? And even more important, what is the role played by transnational actors located in the same country that has devised sanctions as an effective tool to achieve major foreign policy objectives?

This is exactly the area where my project, which is based upon extensive field research conducted in Cuba between 2000 and 2009, attempts to make its most important contribution. Although one of the reasons for the tightening of the embargo during the 1990s was to stimulate democratic reforms in Cuba, the prime objective of U.S. policy was to exert economic pressure on the Castro government (and eventually hasten its demise) by reducing the flow of hard currency to the island. I hypothesize that, in spite of stiffened sanctions, the United States has not only been unable to stifle the flow of foreign investment into Cuba but has actually contributed in a significant way to the recovery of the Cuban economy from the deep recession following the demise of the former Soviet Union. Furthermore, formal and informal activities by Cuban Americans, above all those who left Cuba in the 1980s and 1990s and retained strong bonds with relatives on the island, have been a major factor in mitigating the overall impact of U.S. sanctions against Cuba. The most vocal and influential groups within the Cuban-American community in favor of the embargo are instead composed to a great extent of older exiles who emigrated in the early 1960s or their children (Eckstein 2004, 330-33).

Hypotheses and Contributions of the Research

Two main hypotheses are tested in this study. The first one is that the Helms-Burton law largely failed to stem the flow of foreign investment delivered to Cuba and hinder the slow but steady recovery of the Cuban economy. There is no doubt that the Castro government faced growing difficulties in obtaining external financing for its main economic activities and probably lost some deals because of Helms-Burton's penalizing provisions against foreign firms that invest in or use U.S. expropriated properties. Nevertheless, it appears that the overall process of foreign investment in Cuba has not been halted as many foreign companies continue to run profitable businesses on the island and take advantage of the absence of U.S. competitors.

The second hypothesis of this study is that, despite the tightening of the embargo, the United States has played and keeps playing quite an important role in the Cuban economy in several different ways. More specifically, large amounts of hard currency were transferred into the Cuban economy through U.S. visitors (especially Cuban Americans) and remittances sent by Cuban exiles to relatives on the island. Smaller amounts were also channeled through U.S. telecommunications payments to Cuba and U.S. indirect investments. The fact that a significant share of hard currency reaching Cuba was in violation of U.S. regulations provides some evidence for the inability of the U.S. government to obtain compliance from its own citizens.

Based on available information on U.S. citizens' activities with respect to Cuba, this study attempts to demonstrate the following points.

1. Even with travel restrictions in place, legal and illegal visits to Cuba from the United States, primarily by individuals of Cuban descent, have increased dramatically since the early 1990s, consolidating U.S. citizens as one of the largest groups among foreign travelers to the island.

2. Remittances from abroad, mainly sent from the Cuban-American community in South Florida, were the single most important factor in stimulating the recovery of the Cuban economy after the collapse of the Soviet Union. In net terms, remittances were the top source of hard currency revenues for the Cuban government until the post-2004 booming of exports of professional services under special agreements with Venezuela.

3. The United States has played a key role in financing the development of Cuba's telecommunications sector since a large portion of the island's hard currency revenues from telephone services come from dollar charges applied to incoming calls (mostly Cuban-American calls) from U.S. territory.

4. American entities own equity interests of several foreign companies with major investment activities in Cuba.

5. Large amounts of U.S. agricultural sales to Cuba have turned the United States into the island's main source of imported food.

Overall, there is sufficient evidence to argue that U.S extraterritorial measures against Cuba's foreign business partners have had little success. Moreover, U.S.-based financial flows supplied the Castro government with sizable foreign exchange at a time when Havana was struggling so hard to find sources of external support. The aforementioned activities by transnational actors are emblematic examples of gaping holes in Washington's effort to economically isolate Cuba and provide a solid explanation of why the embargo has failed to achieve its main goal. My study, therefore, promises to make two significant contributions to the scholarship on economic sanctions.

First, it challenges the idea on the utility of unilateral economic coercion as an instrument of foreign policy and enriches the debate on whether sanctions are effective by analyzing the impact on the Cuban economy of activities carried out by transnational players. While some scholars have focused on the effects of the embargo on U.S. entities in terms of forfeited businesses with the Cuban government, very few have examined the possibility that foreign investors and U.S.-based transnational actors bear major responsibility for the failure of sanctions to achieve ambitious foreign policy goals with respect to Cuba. In the post–cold war context of economic globalization and transnational linkages, these actors deserve more attention from the academic community than they have received so far.

Second, this study provides conceptual tools that can be used not only to examine the U.S. embargo against Cuba but also other sanctions situations. Indeed, activities carried out by multinational corporations and other transnational actors (including individuals and entities of the coercer state) might have had a positive impact on the economies of various countries that, like Cuba, are subject to U.S. economic sanctions. In particular, foreign direct investment, remittances sent from exiles, and secondary or indirect investment operations may undermine the ability of sanctions to squeeze economically these target countries. Mainly as a result of increasing migration flows, recorded remittances have become the second largest source of external financing for developing countries after foreign direct investment (Ratha 2008). Money transfer and investment operations are also facilitated by the rapid growth of Internet and other electronic transactions. In short, the flow of hard currency reaching Cuba from abroad, especially from the United States, exhibits patterns that suggest a potential path for further research on the role and usefulness of economic sanctions.

The Organization of This Book

As previously observed, many scholars of international relations assess the effectiveness of sanctions by focusing on the economic adjustments introduced by the target country to cope with external pressure, neglecting the importance of growing transnational flows of capital and finance in the context of globalization. Chapter 1, therefore, examines the success rate of U.S. unilateral economic sanctions and explores the prevailing discourses on transnational linkages at both global and local levels in order to structure the proposed case study and identify theoretical assumptions relevant to its working hypotheses. Transnational practices by non-state actors such as multinational corporations and migrants will receive special attention since foreign investment and remittances have played a major role in keeping afloat the Cuban economy in the post–cold war era. Chapter 2 offers a review of the main developments in U.S.-Cuba relations from 1959 to the present time, with a focus on the history of U.S. economic sanctions with respect to Cuba that were first enacted in the early 1960s and then intensified during the 1990s with the Torricelli law and the Helms-Burton law. A major contention is that the strengthening of the embargo was linked to self-interested groups in the Cuban-American community seeking to serve their parochial interests and able to influence U.S. policymakers.

The remaining chapters of this book deal with transnational players whose activities have propped up the Cuban economy during the post–cold war era and helped the Castro government minimize the pressure of U.S. unilateral sanctions. Chapter 3 analyzes the evolution and results of foreign direct investment in Cuba to show the positive impact of foreign capital and know-how on the development of the Cuban economy. Chapter 4 describes the several different ways in which the Helms-Burton law affects prospective and existing foreign investors in Cuba. It also evaluates the impact of the legislation on Cuba's economic performance and the flow of foreign investment as well as its effectiveness in forcing overseas firms to pull out of the island. Chapter 5 tracks the flow of hard currency reaching Cuba from the United States in order to provide evidence of the importance for the Cuban economy of activities carried out by U.S. citizens and firms. More specifically, it analyzes the presence of U.S. visitors on the island, the flow of remittances from Cuban exiles, payments to the Cuban government by American carriers for telecommunications services, and U.S. investments in foreign companies that operate in the Cuban market. It also examines U.S. food sales to Havana and other recent developments. The concluding chapter summarizes the main findings of the study and provides some suggestions for a more effective U.S. policy toward Cuba.

Transnationalism in the Context of Economic Sanctions

Transnational linkages are broadly defined as movements of information, money, objects, and people across borders that are not controlled by organs of governments (Vertovec 2003, 642). The concept of "transnationalism" in the study of international relations came into prominent use in the early 1970s amid rapid growth of international organizations and particularly relations between nongovernmental bodies. Several scholars, mostly with a liberal background, began to question the prevailing state-centric view of international relations by analyzing the impact on interstate politics of transnational activities carried out by multinational businesses, revolutionary movements, nongovernment organizations (NGOs), trade unions, scientific networks, and the Catholic Church (Keohane and Nye 1971).

More recently, the growing interconnectedness of the world as a consequence of globalization and technological change has stimulated a proliferation of literature concerning various types of transnational practices by private individuals and groups, including tourists, migrants, students, NGOs, and corporations. Transnationalism is closely associated with globalization but its scope is generally narrower. The crucial difference between the two is that transnational activities, unlike global ones, refer to economic, political, and social processes that transcend nation-states yet remain linked to one or more national territories. International migration (which is embedded in globalization) is considered a transnational phe-nomenon because it involves the movement of people across national bor-ders. Similarly, transnational corporations (TNCs) carry out operations worldwide but retain an identifiable home base in one nation (Kearney 1995, 548).

The growing number of non-state participants in international activi-ties and the expansion of capital, cultures, and people across borders have provoked discourses on the crisis of the nation-state and the complex transnational linkages that bind societies together in today's interdepen-dent and shrinking world. As Guarnizo and Smith (1998, 3) observed, the nation-state is seen as weakened "from above" by multinational capital, global media, and supra-national political institutions, and "from below" by informal economic channels, ethnic nationalism, and grass-roots ac-tivism. However, while there is little doubt that transnational activities escape control and domination by the state, an analysis of power rela-tions and economic interactions in the context of sanctions must take into account an additional element. The movement of capital from above and from below sustained through transnational linkages might actually strengthen the target country by providing it with crucial financial where-withal to weather the impact of economic sanctions.

The Effectiveness of U.S. Unilateral Economic Sanctions

Since the end of the Second World War, the United States has been the dominant user of economic sanctions as a foreign policy tool. Besides joining some multilateral attempts and participating in sanctions taken by the United Nations Security Council, the United States frequently re-sorted to unilateral coercive measures against a broad range of countries. It applied a variety of restrictions on U.S. citizens' and entities' dealings with target governments, including the suspension of foreign aid or limi-tations on exports of narrow categories of goods and technologies (lim-ited sanctions), limitations on more broadly defined categories of trade or finance (moderate sanctions), and prohibitions of most trade and finan-cial flows (extensive sanctions). It also imposed or threatened sanctions against foreign companies or institutions that invest in or provide finan-cial supports to certain countries (Carter 2002). Yet, since the demise of the Soviet Union in the early 1990s there has been a significant decline of new cases of U.S. unilateral initiatives as broad coalitions under the umbrella of the United Nations began to play a bigger role in sanctions diplomacy (Hufbauer 1999).

The success or failure of economic sanctions obviously depends on their scope and the goals they are intended to achieve, the size of the target country, and its relationship with the sender (Elliott 1997). Nonetheless, there seems to be general acceptance that sanctions, mainly when they are unilateral, are often unable to achieve ambitious foreign policy objectives such as changing the behavior or governments of target countries (Drury 1998; Pape 1997; Hufbauer et al. 1990; Wagner 1988). The United States, above all, is no longer as dominant in the world economy as it was in the aftermath of the Second World War and at least until the early 1970s. In addition, the efficacy of economic coercion and the leverage of a single country are hindered by the effects of globalization. In an increasingly interdependent global economy, it is easier for target governments to minimize the impact of sanctions by tapping international trade and capital markets and finding alternative suppliers of goods and capital (Schott 1998).

To reliably assess the usefulness of sanctions, one must first conceptualize them and bear in mind the goals they set out to accomplish. According to Pape (1997, 93–94), "economic sanctions seek to lower the aggregate economic welfare of a target state by reducing international trade in order to coerce the target government to change its political behavior." Pape's view is that effective economic coercion should alter objectionable actions of a target country and force it to make concessions either directly, by placing a strong economic burden on the target government, or indirectly, by stirring popular pressure for change or eventually a popular revolt that topples that government. Thus, the aggregate gross national product or GNP loss of a target country over time is the most important indicator of the intensity of economic sanctions (Pape 1997, 94), and arguably a sign of their success.

Other scholars contend that the concept of sanctions should cover all aspects of "economic statecraft" rather than being limited to economic coercion aimed to change the policies of the target government. Baldwin (1985, 32) noted that the goals of the sender could be to alter the course of ongoing trade relations (trade dispute), engage in economic warfare to weaken the adversary's military capabilities, make a symbolic statement about its own identity and moral beliefs, show its disapproval of the target country's behavior, and satisfy domestic political interests. While acknowledging that policymakers have an incentive to publicly depict their goals as less ambitious than they really are in order to facilitate a claim of victory at a later time, Baldwin (1999/2000, 89) argued that sanctions might be deemed successful when they achieve one of the aforementioned policy objectives.

Overall, there is substantial evidence about the declining effectiveness of unilateral economic sanctions as a tool of statecraft and, more generally, about the limited utility of sanctions even when they are imposed multilaterally. The most cited and comprehensive database on the subject is that compiled by Hufbauer, Schott, Elliott, and Oegg (2008), who found sanctions to be at least partially successful in 34 percent of the 204 cases initiated between 1914 and 2000. More specifically, episodes involving modest objectives such as improvements in human rights and religious freedom, among others, succeeded in 51 percent of the cases. At the same time, efforts to destabilize a target government, impair a foreign adversary's military potential, and change a country's policies in a major way reached their objectives in about 30 percent of the cases (disruptions of military adventures only a meager 21 percent of the time), leading Hufbauer et al. (2008, 159) to conclude that "sanctions are of limited utility in achieving foreign policy goals that depend on compelling the target country to take actions it stoutly resists." It should be emphasized that a previous study by Hufbauer, Schott, and Elliott released at the end of the cold war (another one was published in 1985) had shown similar results, with sanctions being successful in about one-third of the 115 cases initiated between 1914 and 1990 (Hufbauer et al. 1990, 93). The success rate they found and the standards utilized to arrive at such figure have been disputed both as being too lenient (Pape 1997, 1998), and too strict (Van Bergeijk 1997; Baldwin 1985).

Table 1.1 provides data on success rates of economic sanctions at different periods of time during the twentieth century. Apart from a few attempts between 1914 and 1944, since the end of the Second World War the United States has acted as the only sanctioner against target countries

Table 1.1. Success Rates of Economic Sanctions by Period

	Total number	Number of successes	Success ratio (as % of total)
ALL CASES[a] (MULTILATERAL AND UNILATERAL)			
1914–2000	204	70	34
1914–44	16	7	44
1945–69	47	16	34
1970–89	75	23	31
1990–2000	66	24	36
U.S. CASES (MULTILATERAL)			
1914–2000	69	27	39
1914–44	5	3	60
1945–69	12	4	33
1970–89	13	5	38
1990–2000	39	15	38
U.S. CASES (UNILATERAL)			
1914–2000	71	20	28
1914–44	3	0	0
1945–69	16	10	62
1970–89	41	8	19
1990–2000	11	2	18

Source: Author's compilation from Hufbauer et al. 2008, 127.
Note: a. The United States was involved in about 69 percent of the cases, usually as the leading sanctioner and often alone.

on sixty-eight occasions, representing more than one-third of all cases of sanctions initiated since then. Washington's unilateral sanctions succeeded in ten, or 62 percent, of the sixteen cases launched between 1945 and 1969, but their success rate dropped to 19 percent during the 1970s and 1980s and only 18 percent during the 1990s. In contrast, cases where the United States joined a sanctions coalition or received substantial cooperation from third countries were successful 38 percent of the time between 1970 and 2000. Elliott (1997) observed: "If sanctions are to have any chance at all of producing favorable outcomes, they must be multilateral, they must be carefully formulated, and they must be vigorously enforced."

Comprehensive multilateral sanctions applied by a group of countries or by an international organization should be more likely to reach major policy goals than unilateral ones, as they inflict higher costs on the target government. In the post-1990 period, Washington did begin to act in a more cooperative and multilateral fashion. The crucial problem, especially for a dominant user of sanctions like the United States, is that multilateral agreements are difficult to achieve because they must reconcile the diverse security interests of potential coalition partners and often require diluting the sanctions imposed (Hufbauer 1999; Hufbauer et al. 1990, 96).

Since the early 1990s, the United Nations and the European Union have resorted to economic coercive measures with much more frequency than in previous decades. Yet, most United Nations actions are weakly enforced arms embargoes while several European sanctions involve relatively minor aid cutoffs (Elliott and Oegg 2002). As the fairly limited scope of these measures seems suitable for the achievement of modest policy objectives, the use of unilateral sanctions (even if they rarely work) might be in some cases the only option available to U.S. policymakers to pursue major foreign policy goals. And when U.S. goals are more modest, they could simply be pursued unilaterally from the outset since there is less need for international cooperation. After all, Hufbauer et al. (1990, 95) found that, in general, "the greater the number of countries needed to implement sanctions, the less likely it is that they will be effective."

The decline in new cases of U.S. unilateral actions in the post–cold war era is mainly due to the fact that, by 1989, the United States already had sanctions in place against a large number of target countries. During the 1990s, Washington launched high-profile cases against India and Pakistan (nuclear sanctions) and strengthened some existing sanctions programs, most notably those with respect to Cuba, Libya, Burma/Myanmar, Iran, and Sudan. Furthermore, U.S. efforts to combat terrorism and drug trafficking, promote human rights, reduce ethnic conflicts, and protect the environment led to a proliferation of "smart sanctions" targeting individuals and organizations rather than entire countries (Cortright and Lopez 2002). Crucially important, the drop of new unilateral initiatives is also the result of growing concerns among U.S policymakers and corporate leaders about the effectiveness of this kind of sanctions (and their costs for American businesses) in an increasingly interdependent world that facilitates transnational economic activities by non-state actors (Carter 2002).

Since global processes and micro-dynamics of migration are hypothesized to play a key role in the context of economic sanctions, the rest of this chapter presents an analysis of cross-border linkages based on the distinction between transnationalism "from above" and "from below."[1] In this two-level approach, activities initiated by transnational corporations with a global agenda belong to transnationalism from above. Local linkages between immigrants and their home-country counterparts, mostly centered on family ties, are considered as transnationalism from below. It must be noted that such a distinction focuses on who initiates and determines the direction of any cross-border action in order to capture the dynamics of economic and power relations in the transnational arena. The "above" and the "below" of transnational action should not be equated exclusively with global and local structures or agents since these categories are contextual and relational (Guarnizo and Smith 1998, 7, 29).

Transnationalism "from Above": Transnational Corporations (TNCs) and the Movement of Capital

Transnational corporations are defined as "all enterprises which control assets (factories, mines, sales offices and the like) in two or more countries" (UNCTAD 1995, xix–xx). There are currently at least three major categories of corporations that operate internationally: 1) relatively small TNCs with commercial activities only in a few countries; 2) medium-size enterprises that function in regional markets such as the Americas, Europe, or Asia; and 3) large TNCs, also known as global corporations, that operate on a worldwide basis and concentrate the greatest economic and political power. As a result of technological advances and increasingly liberal policy frameworks, TNCs have come to dominate the international economic system and, in some cases, they are more powerful than most states acting alone. By establishing universal systems of supply, production, marketing, investment, information transfer, and management, TNCs create the paths along which much of the world's transnational activities flow and pursue interests that are global rather than exclusively local or national (Sklair 2002; Vertovec and Cohen 1999). In short, the homogenizing and elitist forces of transnationalism from above undermine the economic, political, and cultural networks of more local units, including nation-states, ethnic groups, and grass-roots communities (Mahler 1998, 67).

Today, TNCs are capturing global markets with foreign direct investment (FDI) and creating global webs of production, commerce, culture, and finance virtually unopposed. They exercise substantial influence over the domestic and foreign policies of governments around the world, affect the economic prospects of many developing countries, and set the agenda of the World Trade Organization (Macleod and Lewis 2004, 77). Moreover, as they move across national boundaries and forge linkages between countries, TNCs encourage the intertwining of national economies, thus limiting the scope of government action and its controlling power (Suter 2004, 44). This particular aspect is very important in the context of economic sanctions since laws and regulations of the coercer state are specifically designed to halt business operations by TNCs in target countries and the resulting flow of capital. Transnational corporations' home bases are geographically concentrated in the industrialized countries of the north (mainly the United States, the European Union, and Japan), but their practices are assuming an ever more stateless quality. As noted by Karliner (1997, 6), "this combination of stateless corporations and corporate states . . . allows a large TNC to hide behind the protection of a national flag when convenient, and to eschew it when it's not."

Transnational corporations with enormous financial resources and capabilities have created considerable difficulties for other international actors like nation-states and labor unions. Although the behavior of a particular corporation (what we might call its "code of conduct") will depend on the way its management decides to use the available resources, several scholars documented how TNCs interfere in the domestic political affairs of sovereign nations (Kline 2003), tend to be labor abusive in their overseas investment destinations (Wang 2005), and frequently fail to uphold environmental standards and protect human rights in developing countries (Monshipouri et al. 2003; Cohan 2001). In order to raise public awareness of these harmful activities, the United Nations Global Compact of 2000 called upon TNCs to assume greater responsibilities toward those living in the countries in which they operate and abide by standards in the areas of human rights, labor, and the environment (Nien-he 2004, 643).

When imposing economic sanctions, however, the coercer state is mostly interested in finding ways and means for controlling the positive effects of TNCs on the target country's economy rather than ameliorating their damaging practices. Investment operations carried out by TNCs play a crucial role in the development of receiving economies as they contribute capital for the acquisition of modern technologies, increase theoretical and business knowledge for the integration into global marketing, distribution, and production networks, and stimulate greater international competitiveness of national firms. In other words, FDI is an important catalyst for economic growth in developing economies even though such a positive impact may vary across countries depending on the level of human capital, domestic investment, infrastructure, macroeconomic stability, and trade policies.

A key contention of this study is that states' attempts to control the activities of transnational corporations are doomed to failure for three main reasons. First, these firms have been growing very rapidly and exert a great deal of power in the globalized world economy. Through mergers and acquisitions, the leading TNCs are richer and more powerful than most of the nation-states that seek to regulate them. In 2000, the combined sales of the world's top two hundred corporations were far greater than a quarter of the world's economic activity. Of the one hundred largest economies in the world, fifty-one were TNCs and only forty-nine were countries (Anderson and Cavanagh 2000). Second, each TNC is headquartered in one country but operates across borders in a number of political jurisdictions. This inevitably creates enormous legal and political difficulties for the parties since the firm is only partially within the control of an individual state and must deal with different and often conflicting national requirements. Third, because of its hierarchical and highly integrated nature, a TNC has the capacity to shift its resources among jurisdictions in accordance with a central plan, which can easily escape national control (Bock 1979, 41). Modern corporations sell stocks and raise funds in international capital markets to help finance their expansion plans anywhere in the world, including in embargoed countries.

It should be emphasized that, among the world's major powers, the United States is not only the most frequent user of economic coercion against other nations but also the country with probably the lowest level of interdependence and cooperation between its government and corporations. Back in the late 1970s, Esterline (1979, 32) noted that the United States, unlike Japan, the European Community, China, and the Soviet Union, did not have a symbiotic relationship between government and private enterprises. The fundamental nature of U.S. policy on international investment was neither to promote nor discourage inward or outward investment through government intervention. While Esterline demonstrated that U.S.-based TNCs suffered disadvantages both abroad and at home because they operated in the absence of an American political-economic policy, his findings also suggested that the U.S. government's control over the activities of its own corporations was virtually nonexistent, or at least very limited.

The current situation seems to confirm that U.S.-based transnational enterprises continue to enjoy a high degree of autonomy in carrying out their operations. Despite numerous attempts to limit corporations' power and increase their accountability to the state, these TNCs maintain a strong grip on the domestic and foreign policies of their home country and, at the same time, use the accelerating process of globalization to gain independence from their government.[2] Admittedly, all major economic powers face great obstacles in regulating their corporations' business practices as a result of the ever more integrated international financial system and growing corporate mobility (Karliner 1997, 9–11). But this is particularly problematic for a country like the United States, which is the most open political system and the most committed to the promotion of trade liberalization, privatization of state enterprises, deregulation, foreign investment, and legal security for property rights. Indeed, the U.S. commitment to neoliberal economic policies seriously complicates its strategy to isolate target countries economically and undermine their governments through the burden of sanctions.

In a global economy driven by competition and the search for the best short-term return on investment, it is very difficult, if not impossible for the United States to dictate through the imposition of extraterritorial unilateral sanctions where foreign-based TNCs can or cannot invest worldwide. States have little chance of controlling the huge sums of capital that move electronically every minute from computer to computer, bank to bank, and country to country. In addition, transnational firms headquartered in foreign countries can devise effective strategies to circumvent U.S. restrictions by using offshore centers to disguise the parties behind certain operations or spinning off their business into a separate company to minimize legal risks. Unilateral sanctions, especially when imposed by an economic power like the United States, may dissuade some TNCs from investing in a target country, but they are unlikely to stem the overall foreign investment process in that country. The reality is that relatively low levels of overseas investments, or just a few major business deals, may still provide sufficient resources for target states to resist changes and guarantee the survival of their governments.

In 2001, more than half of the world's population in seventy-eight countries, for the most part developing ones, was subject to some forms of U.S. unilateral coercive economic measures (Carter 2002). According to the United Nations' General Assembly, the use of unilateral sanctions "adversely affects the economy and development efforts of developing countries and has a general negative impact on international economic cooperation and on worldwide efforts to move towards a non-discriminatory and open multilateral trading system" (United Nations 1998). Even so, FDI flows into developing countries have increased notably since the early 1990s. While U.S.-based corporations account for a substantial share of these capital flows, third-country companies might have helped dilute the impact of U.S. coercive measures on several target nations, especially those where U.S. direct investments are prohibited. Currently, the United States maintains comprehensive economic sanctions against Cuba, Iran, Sudan, and Burma/Myanmar. Sanctions against North Korea and the Federal Republic of Yugoslavia (Serbia and Montenegro) were significantly relaxed in late 2000, and those against Iraq and Libya were practically lifted in 2004.

The sustained liberalization of FDI regimes and trade was a major factor for the remarkable growth of TNC activities in developing markets. Worldwide, the number of countries that each year introduced regulatory changes aimed to create incentives for foreign investment and strengthen market functioning rose from just 43 in 1992 to 103 in 2004 (UNCTAD 2008, 13). As a result, net FDI flows to developing countries jumped from about $40 billion in 1990 to $238.4 billion in 2000 and, after a sharp decline following the terrorist attack on the United States on September 11, 2001, peaked at $500 billion in 2007. While developing countries attracted, on average, 17.5 percent of global FDI inflows in the second half of the 1980s, their share grew considerably during the 1990s and reached 36 percent in 2004 before dropping again in 2007 to about 27 percent. In 2007, Asia (mainly China) and Latin America were the leading recipients of foreign direct investment among developing regions. Africa also experienced a sizable increase in FDI even though its share of the total remained relatively low (UNCTAD 2008, 37).

Overall, it is commonly believed that foreign direct investment by TNCs plays a key role in improving the economic performance of recipient countries (Lipsey and Sjoholm 2005). Transnational corporations are seen as development agents able to provide assistance to developing nations through an arsenal of economic, technical, and other managerial resources. Many scholars have documented how the deployment of these assets accelerates recipient countries' growth by augmenting domestic savings and investment, helping the transfer of new technologies, increasing production, exports, and foreign exchange earnings, and fostering spillovers from TNCs to domestic firms through imitation, competition, and training (Kohpaiboon 2006; Li and Liu 2005; Baliamoune-Lutz 2004; Ram and Zhang 2002; Campos and Kinoshita 2002; Barro and Sala-i-Martin 1995; Grossman and Helpman 1991; Findlay 1978). Such findings and the massive transformation of the global economy under way have great implications for the research on economic sanctions. While the United States continues to use unilateral economic coercive measures as a way to curtail the resources (and change the behavior) of target governments, especially in developing countries, FDI flowing through transnational corporations has become the single most important source of foreign capital for these countries (Ramamurti 2004, 277).[3] As they dominate the realm of global capital flows, promote economic growth and reduce poverty worldwide, and tend to escape control from nation-states, TNCs could bear a major responsibility for the failure of economic sanctions to accomplish far-reaching foreign policy objectives.

Transnationalism "from Below": Migration, Family Ties, and Remittances

In contrast to transnationalism from above in which TNCs play a crucial role, transnationalism from below is largely the terrain of grass-roots collectivities (local households, kin networks, elite fractions, and other emergent local formations) that are marginal to the centers of power and rely almost entirely on social capital. The latter usually refers to the ability to secure resources by virtue of group membership and networks (Bourdieu 1986, 249). Thus, social capital is a resource available through transnational linkages, facilitating the realization of certain goals that would not be reachable in its absence. As Keck and Sikkink (1998) demonstrated, since the 1960s non-state actors such as advocacy groups, local social movements, foundations, churches, and unions have created "transnational advocacy networks" that have successfully influenced state behavior and policy outcomes in various issue-areas.

Migrants' transnational practices are also believed to reconfigure the existing power hierarchies by sustaining material resources that finance "good-will projects" in their country of origin and challenging multiple levels of structural control: local, regional, national, and global (Mahler 1998, 68). Along with the big players in the global economy, international migrants who comprise the bulk of transnational communities are making an ever greater impact by transferring huge amounts of money across borders in the form of remittances. The resulting capital flows help reduce poverty and may contribute to the economic expansion of recipient countries.

Since the early 1990s, the rapid growth of international migration has ushered in a new era of transnational studies, mostly interested in the continuing relations between migrants and their places of origin rather than their adaptation to receiving societies (Basch et al. 1994, 6). The rebirth of the notion of diaspora, in particular, stemmed from academics using it to describe practically any group of people who live outside their homeland but maintain social, economic, and political linkages across national borders (Vertovec and Cohen 1999, xvi). In response to the process of globalization, migrants are thought to create transnational communities that are "neither here nor there" but in both places simultaneously. As they sustain economic activities that are grounded on the differential advantages established by state boundaries, these communities operate, to a large degree, in a way very similar to that of large transnational corporations. The key difference is that they emerge at the grass-roots level and their activities, like the transfer of monetary remittances, are typically carried out through informal mechanisms (Portes 1997, 4). It is the combination of migrants' commitment to preserving economic ties with relatives abroad and the extensive use of informal channels that makes remittances extremely difficult to police when they are part of comprehensive sanctions aimed to curtail hard currency flows to a target country.

Migrants construct and maintain social networks that are rooted in place even if those networks transcend place. Several scholars have challenged the image of transnational migrants as de-territorialized, free-floating people who are socially, politically, economically, and culturally unbound. While spanning across national territories, these actors' practices are conceived within specific historical and geographical contexts and within the confines of social, economic, and political relations fomented by shared interests and values. Thus, the social fields in which migrants are embedded are critical to our understanding of the processes and effects of transnationalism from below (Levitt 2001, 6–7; Guarnizo and Smith 1998, 13).

Analyses of migrants' connections with homeland people and institutions have focused on family obligations and marriage patterns, remittances, political engagement, religious activities, regular visits, and so on. In order to assess the effectiveness of economic sanctions against a target government, this study gives special attention to remittance practices and their significance for the recipient country's economy. The practice by migrants sending money "home" to family members left behind is hardly new. But the volume of these money transfers has become so large that in some cases they may determine the economic fortunes of entire countries (Portes 2003).

It has been argued that the extent, intensity, velocity, and impact of transnational activities are enhanced by the advent of new space- and time-compressing technologies that facilitate rapid communication across national borders and long distances (Kivisto 2001; Portes et al. 1999; Held et al. 1999). Whatever the migrants' motivations for sustaining economic ties with their countries of origin, technological improvements are believed to explain a good part, if not all, of contemporary migrant transnationalism. Improved modes of transportation and new electronic money transfer services have boosted the frequency of family reunions and provided cost-efficient ways to send remittances to relatives abroad, thus shortening the distance between sending and receiving countries. Yet, these connections cannot be fully understood without analyzing the growing family and kinship ties (mostly as a result of recent trends in international migration) that constitute a powerful agency for cross-border transmission of capital, values, customs, and culture. After all, it is within the linkages established through family relations that most migrants engage in transnational activities (Goulbourne 2002, 160–61).

Even if migration and family-based economic transactions undermine the autonomy of states, the latter have found ways to influence the volume and density of such activities and reap substantial benefits from them. Some developing countries encouraged international migration because they hoped that money transfers from abroad would raise the welfare of their non-migrant residents and stimulate economic growth (Chandavarkar 1980). In embargo situations, the potential contribution of remittances at both the macro- and micro-levels provides an incentive for target states to stimulate these financial flows and so minimize the negative impact of economic sanctions on their economies.

The dramatic growth of international migration and monetary remittances has stimulated extensive multidisciplinary inquiry on migrants' long-distance economic relations with their homelands (Guarnizo 2003). Between 1990 and 2000, the number of migrants in the more developed regions (mainly Europe, Asia, and North America) increased by 23 million persons, or 28 percent. In 2000, around 175 million persons resided outside the country of their birth, and almost one of every 10 persons living in the more developed regions was a migrant from developing countries (United Nations 2002, 2). Whereas early scholars of migration believed that most migrants severed ties with their countries of origin as they assimilated into the country that received them, more recent studies showed that a large number of these individuals remain oriented toward the communities they came from (Crawford 2003; Levitt 1998; Gmelch 1992; Thomas-Hope 1985; Rubenstein 1982). Remittances have become a major source of foreign exchange earnings for many developing nations and a key addition to their gross domestic product. They are often one of the main reasons why individuals decide to leave their home country to search for job opportunities abroad and an important consequence of the overall migration process.

Migrants' relationships with their places of origin are forged and sustained by complex and enduring transnational social networks. Rather than a movement of individual players, international migration is considered to be a process leading to the formation of groups and communities that bring social units into contact across national boundaries.[4] From this perspective, migrating means enlarging one's living space and making a more or less permanent commitment to maintain familial, economic, political, or other kinds of relations that span borders. Migrants carry out activities, from visitation to sending remittances and making telephone calls, which are transnational in nature and tie them to two or more societies simultaneously (Glick Schiller et al. 1992, 1–2). In order to describe this constant contact between communities of origin and destination, scholars have used terms such as "transnational migration circuits" (Rouse 1992), "transnational social fields" (Basch et al. 1994), "binational societies" (Guarnizo 1994), and "transnational communities" (Portes 1996).

As noted before, social capital mostly built through family linkages is a powerful agency for the transmission of monetary remittances. The latter are not a casual effect of migration simply linked to the wishes of an individual but are an essential component of the family's plan behind migration (Stark 1991). Coordinated efforts and arrangements by all or most members of a family allow the whole group to enjoy more resources than it could obtain in the absence of cooperation. The general idea is that the main stimulus for migration is the prospect of receiving remittances rather than the wage differential between two places. Once they have successfully established themselves in other locations, migrants play the role of financial intermediaries and substitute for missing or imperfect markets (Gubert 2002, 268).

The importance of remittances as a private mechanism of income redistribution has given rise to a burgeoning literature on the motives for and purposes of these money transfers. For some scholars, pure altruism motivated by the need to support family consumption plays a key role in the decision to remit (Becker 1974; Funkhouser 1995). Remittances may also be triggered by selfish interests such as the aspiration to an inheritance or the desire to channel one's investments through the trustworthy family both as purchasing agent and for subsequent maintenance (Hoddinott 1994; Ahlburg and Brown 1998). Finally, they might be the result of a mix of altruism and self-interest (Lucas and Stark 1985) or represent the repayment of an informal and implicit loan resulting from the household paying for education and the cost to emigrate (Poirine 1997).

In short, migrants decide to remit money for a variety of reasons. Commitment to home rests upon complex emotional and social foundations and manifests itself in the migrant's willingness to financially assist those left behind, share the costs and benefits of migration, pay back a loan to relatives, invest in assets in the home area and ensure their careful maintenance, and maintain social relationships that facilitate an eventual return at some time in the future. Nevertheless, a common element of most remittance decisions, whether they are triggered by self-interested or altruistic motives, is that they occur in the context of family linkages that often span national borders. The family is at the heart of contractual arrangements, bequests, loans, and social norms like guilt, solidarity obligations, and loyalty. These resources constitute a social capital that reinforces international migrants' connections to relatives in the source country and sustains transnational monetary remittances.

The flow of remittances, which are typically in cash rather than goods, has increased dramatically worldwide since the early 1980s. Official statistics tend to focus on capital flows from developed to developing regions, neglecting domestic and intra-regional money transfers. Accurate quantitative assessments are complicated by the fact that a very large, unknown amount of money (unrecorded remittances could be larger than recorded ones) is usually transferred through informal mechanisms and to countries that do not provide related statistics. Even so, it is reported that global remittances to developing countries rose from $15 billion in 1980 to nearly $100 billion in 2004 (Carling 2005, 9). Since then, remittances have more than doubled to reach an estimated $251 billion in 2007. They are currently the second-largest financial flow to developing countries after foreign direct investment, more than twice the size of official development assistance.[5] In terms of specific regions, Latin America was the largest recipient of remittances in 2007 ($61 billion or about one-fourth of the total), followed by East Asia and the Pacific, Europe and Central Asia, South Asia, the Middle East and North Africa, and sub-Saharan Africa (Ratha et al. 2008). Figures for the African region are grossly underestimated due to the lack of comprehensive data for most of its countries. The United States is by far the leading source of remittances to developing nations, accounting for $42 billion or approximately 17 percent of total money transfers in 2007 (World Bank 2008, 60).

To sum up, the impact of remittances on economic development depends on a variety of factors, including the type of migrant workers who left home, the receiving country's regional economic position, and especially how remitted funds are used by their beneficiaries (Solimano 2003).[6] But even if remittances simply enhance the welfare of recipient households, with little or no impact on the general economy, they would still play a crucial role in the context of economic sanctions. In order to intensify pressure on the economy of a target country and induce its government to comply with the requests of the sanctioning state (or eventually remove this government from power), the mechanism of sanctions requires the generation of massive shortages and popular discontent in the target territory that inevitably affect the lives of the civilian population. Because they increase the consumption of recipient families and help alleviate poverty, thus easing civilian pain, remittances to a sanctioned country may reduce the likelihood that its citizens will rally against their government. Put simply, remittances might undercut the transmission mechanism of sanctions by which widespread social suffering is translated into demands for political and economic changes or into calls for the removal of authorities.

The Case of Cuba

Transnational hard currency flows such as foreign direct investment and remittances are particularly important in the case of communist Cuba, where the government controls a large share of the economy and thus greatly benefits from all capital inflows. Unilateral embargo restrictions imposed by the United States against Cuba are specifically designed to deny the island's government those resources. The U.S. Commission for Assistance to a Free Cuba (CAFC), created by President Bush in October 2003, stated in its second report on July 10, 2006: "In order to undermine the [Cuban] regime's succession strategy, it is critical that the U.S. Government maintain economic pressure on the regime to limit its ability to sustain itself and repress the Cuban people. Moreover, as we rapidly approach the transitional moment, the more economic pressure there is on the regime, the greater the likelihood there will be dramatic and successful change for the Cuban people" (CAFC 2006, 29–30).

Like in other cases of U.S. unilateral sanctions, the absence of U.S. direct investors in Cuba was filled by transnational corporations that were not based in the United States. Despite serious hurdles created by the extraterritorial provisions of the Helms-Burton law of 1996, Cuba was able to attract FDI in virtually all key economic sectors.[7] In order to avoid potential penalties under Helms-Burton, quite a few foreign investors have developed roundabout methods to operate in Cuba, using offshore companies registered in fiscal paradises in the Caribbean and Central America to keep anonymity, reduce personal liability, and obtain easier access to capital funding. Other corporations simply decided to create legally distinct entities that are associated exclusively with their Cuban assets or reorganize their activities on the island in such a way as to escape the reach of the U.S. legislation (Spadoni 2001, 31–32).

Some scholars claimed that foreign direct investment plays a very limited, if not negligible, role in the Cuban economy. Criticism mainly focuses on the cumulative amount of delivered FDI, which is significantly lower than in many other developing countries (Werlau 2001; Cruz 2003). However, the significance of foreign capital in Cuba cannot be measured from a simple quantitative comparison with other countries. Cuban authorities make no secret that they resorted to foreign investment in the early 1990s out of necessity, and essentially against their will. By their own admission, the government policy is not intended to create a market economy and develop a real and substantial private sector but is aimed at establishing a state economy that regulates foreign capital so that the benefits of investment go to the entire society. In addition, Cuba's business environment and its economic system are very different from those of most developing nations. Therefore, quantitative cross-country comparisons based on delivered FDI have a limited value (Spadoni 2002, 173). Foreign investment activities in Cuba have had a positive impact on the island's most important economic sectors and stimulated the competitiveness of Cuban products both domestically and internationally.

Although direct investments in Cuba are prohibited for U.S. firms under the embargo, the United States allows individuals and entities subject to U.S. law to hold publicly traded shares of foreign-based TNCs that engage in business dealings with the Castro government. In March 1994, because of efforts by the U.S.-Cuba Trade and Economic Council or USCTEC, based in New York, the U.S. Department of the Treasury issued an opinion according to which an American entity can make a secondary, non-controlling investment in a third-country company that has commercial activities in Cuba as long as the majority of the revenues of this company are not produced from operations within the island (USCTEC 1998). The obvious difficulty for the U.S. government in limiting such practices is that the Cuban operations of most TNCs represent only a small fraction of their global activities. Given the enormous economic interests at stake (non-controlling investments in leading TNCs may be worth billions of dollars), it would be extremely problematic for U.S. policymakers to prevent American entities from holding shares of these corporations just because of their ventures in Cuba. Still, these TNCs undermine the main purpose of the embargo by supplying Cuba with the financial and technological wherewithal it needs to stimulate the economy. Washington's global economic interests are clearly at odds with its policy goals toward specific target countries in the context of sanctions.

While activities by TNCs complicate the efforts of governments to control their own economies and the global flow of capital, we must avoid confusing intentionality with consequences, as when actors are designated "resistant" or "oppositional" because their practices produce results that conflict with the intention of states. Foreign firms that invest in Cuba might help the Castro government withstand the economic pressure of the U.S. embargo, but their goals toward Havana are not necessarily different from those of the U.S. government. Many TNCs that are taking advantage of existing business opportunities in Cuba also realize that the introduction of political changes and profound economic reforms on the island would be beneficial to them. The same distinction is valid for Cuban immigrants in the United States and the money they send to relatives who have remained in Cuba. Even if the Cuban government captures the vast majority of remittances through sales in state-run hard currency stores, the primary goal of Cuban Americans is to support family members, not the Castro regime.

To illustrate the point that the Cuban version of transnationalism is not unlike others, Fernández (2005, xvi) described remittance practices this way: "The fact that Cuban Americans send millions of dollars to family members and loved ones on the island (estimates range from $300 million to more than $1 billion annually) has recently received considerable attention and has been met with surprise. Yet remittances should not be seen as atypical or unusual; on the contrary, they are normal in the context of diasporas and poverty-stricken homelands." It is the context of economic sanctions, though, that sets the Cuban case apart from many others. Cuban migrants' transnational economic ties follow "normal" diasporic patterns that U.S. government restrictions have long tried to hinder or disrupt.

A large share of U.S.-based remittances to Cuba, at least until President Barack Obama allowed unlimited Cuban-American visits and money transfers to relatives in early September 2009, arrived on the island in the luggage of friends or entrusted agents rather than through electronic transactions. Although such practices were surely aimed to circumvent the cap on money transfers to Cuba established by U.S. embargo laws and regulations, they also revealed the migrants' commitment to support family members abroad, or what Portes (1998, 8) called "bounded solidarity," no matter how difficult it could be to accomplish that goal. Hence, to a large extent, it is social capital mainly built through family ties that sustains the transnational flow of remittances regardless of improved technology, not the other way around. As Eckstein (2004, 338) pointed out, the rapid growth of remittances to Cuba since the early 1990s has hinged more on the strengthening of cross-border bonding and trust than on technological breakthroughs in wire transfer services.

Family remittances to Cuba have increased dramatically since Fidel Castro—amid a deep economic recession—legalized U.S. dollar holdings in September 1993 and allowed about thirty-five thousand Cubans to flee the island the following year, most of them resettling in the United States. What came to be known as the Balsero Crisis of 1994 ended with the United States agreeing to accept twenty thousand legal migrants a year from Cuba and vowing to expedite the admission process of an additional four thousand to six thousand people on a visa waiting list (Morley and McGillion 2002, 78). In May 1995, the Clinton administration also announced the new "wet foot/dry foot" policy allowing Cubans who reach U.S. shores to receive refugee status and remain in the country but sending back to Cuba those caught at sea. Nevertheless, in an attempt to stem cross-border family ties and remittances, Washington's immediate response to Castro's moves was to impose a ban on money transfers to Cuba and terminate the general license for travel by Cuban Americans.

In net terms, remittances from various waves of Cuban migrants are today one of the Castro government's top sources of hard currency revenues, perhaps surpassed only by exports of healthcare and other professional services. The vast majority of Cuban remitters are those who left the island after the Mariel Crisis of 1980, primarily for economic rather than political reasons (Masud-Piloto 1996).[8] The encouragement of out-migration (coupled with domestic economic adjustments) by sanctioned states may be used not only as an escape valve to release internal pressure on their governments but also as an effective way to boost foreign exchange earnings at particularly critical times and ease the burden of sanctions.

Altruism is undoubtedly a critical component in the Cuban migrants' decisions to remit money to relatives left behind. Transnational connections between Cuban exiles in the United States and their families on the island remained at relatively low levels for the first three decades after the Cuban Revolution of 1959, mainly as a result of institutional barriers imposed by the U.S. and Cuban governments and informal social pressures on Cubans in both countries to avoid cross-border bonding. However, when the deep recession of the early 1990s threatened the survival of the Cuban economy and many islanders tried to reach out to the Cuban diaspora, family visits and especially financial assistance from overseas relatives in the form of remittances witnessed a dramatic surge (Eckstein and Barberia 2002; Eckstein 2004). This could be seen as altruistic because migrants began to transfer substantial amounts of money to their families abroad when they needed it most. Remittances to Cuba may also be prompted by moral and financial obligations toward the family or by self-seeking motives such as the migrant's desire to raise his social status or prestige within the homeland context. Attempts to accumulate physical capital through purchasing agents or secure bequests in the country of origin play virtually no role as determinants for remittances to communist Cuba. Only a very small number of Cuban residents are permitted to hold private productive assets on the island and inheritance is extremely limited under Cuban law.

It must be stressed that both the U.S. and Cuban governments contributed to the deepening of family linkages and to bonding of potential economic worth between islanders and exiles during the 1990s. The

Castro government shifted its stance toward the diaspora and courted re-mittances by introducing reforms in its monetary policies, increasing the channels for converting or spending U.S. dollars, and allowing more exiles to visit relatives in Cuba. After 1998, the Clinton administration also en-couraged transnational connections by streamlining procedures for U.S.-based travel to Cuba, facilitating family reunions with the resumption of direct flights between the two countries, and easing limitations on money transfers to the island (Barberia 2002). Clinton's policy changes, in par-ticular, assumed great importance for subsequent U.S. attempts to stem the flow of remittances to Cuba through the creation of new cross-border barriers. Once formed, migrants' connections with relatives abroad often become self-sustaining, reflecting the establishment of formal and infor-mal networks of economic aid, duties, and information (Boyd 1989, 641). As Cuban exiles in the United States have widely demonstrated their abil-ity to circumvent U.S. sanctions, it is not surprising that large amounts of remittances continued to flow into Cuba after the Bush administration's decision in June 2004 to tighten restrictions on Cuban-American family visits and money transfers to the island.

The flow of remittances and their benefits to large segments of the ci-vilian population in terms of consumption are quite crucial in the case of communist Cuba, where the social welfare state is supposed to satisfy popular needs such as the supply of food and other consumer goods, ser-vices, jobs, and increased standards of education and health care. When the Castro government's supply of rationed goods to its citizens shrunk considerably in the early 1990s amid a profound economic slump, pur-chases of food products, clothing, medicines, and other items in state-owned dollar stores became the only relief from scarcity for many Cu-bans. Whereas Washington tried to capitalize on this precarious situation by strengthening the embargo against the island, the dramatic surge of remittances from the United States brought valuable hard currency into the hands of a large number of Cubans, and from there into the coffers of the Castro government. In practice, hard currency stores for Cubans would have little reason to exist without remittances since money trans-fers from abroad represent the main source of foreign exchange for the Cuban population. While remittances did not solve all of the problems of the island's economy and created inequalities that defy the revolution's egalitarian precepts (Blue 2005; Brundenius 2002),[9] they likely minimized the impact of U.S. sanctions and undermined their main goals by improving the living standards of many Cuban citizens, making them less prone to question their government and the inefficiencies of Cuba's socialist system.

Conclusion

Economic practices by transnational corporations and international migrants sustain hard currency flows across national borders that greatly complicate the attempts of coercer states to promote changes in a target country through the imposition of economic sanctions. Because of their structure, size, and supra-national decision-making powers, TNCs are major players in the global economy and tend to escape control from national governments. Stimulated by the free play of market forces, especially maximum profits and earnings, TNCs capture global markets with foreign direct investment and may adversely affect the purpose of sanctions by delivering capital and other resources to embargoed nations. At a more local level, transnational linkages mainly built through family ties sustain the flow of remittances from migrants to their homelands. These capital flows are centered on the family whether they are triggered by altruistic reasons such as the care of migrants for those left behind or by self-interested motivations like the migrants' desire to accumulate physical investments in their countries of origin. The positive effects of remittances on recipient families' consumption patterns, in particular, might play a crucial role in the context of economic sanctions by preventing social suffering from translating into a pressure for political and economic changes.

Having presented the theoretical concepts of the transnational literature that are relevant to the working hypotheses of this study, in the next chapter I shift to a review of the last five decades of tense U.S.-Cuba relations and the history of U.S. economic sanctions that have been the cornerstone of Washington's policy toward the island since the early 1960s. This will set the scene for the remaining chapters, which analyze transnational actors' practices with respect to Cuba.

Relations between Cuba and the United States, 1959–2009

For better or worse, the United States and Cuba had enjoyed a "special relationship" for at least a century and a half before the Cuban Revolution of 1959 led by Fidel Castro. During this period, the United States first tried many times unsuccessfully to purchase Cuba from Spain and then controlled developments on the island through military interventions and occupations, increased trade and investment, and extensive meddling in Cuban internal affairs.[1] However, most economic and political ties between the two countries were severed after Castro's victory over Fulgencio Batista.

On January 7, 1959, the Eisenhower administration recognized the new government of Fidel Castro, but relations rapidly deteriorated. By the early 1960s, it appeared impossible that Cuba and the United States could deal with each other in a normal and peaceful way. To be sure, it was neither Castro's record on human rights nor the lack of democracy in Cuba that worried Washington at that time. Castro's economic reforms were highly detrimental to American business interests on the island and represented the views of those Cubans who strongly rejected decades of U.S. imperialist schemes and paternalism. The Cuban government's efforts to export its revolution in the Western Hemisphere also troubled U.S. policymakers because they defied the basic assumptions of U.S. protection and dominance over the region embodied in the Monroe Doctrine.[2] Cuba's newly established ties with the Soviet Union at the height of the cold war further aggravated the bleak picture. Given this context, the United States quickly imposed an economic embargo against Cuba and engaged in countless covert operations to overthrow Castro throughout the 1960s. Since then, apart from timid attempts toward normalization during the 1970s, U.S.-Cuba relations have been characterized by tensions and hostilities that even the end of the cold war in the early 1990s failed to dissipate. What follows is a review of nearly fifty years of problematic relations between the two countries with special attention to the post–cold war period and the Helms-Burton law of 1996, the latest comprehensive package of U.S. economic sanctions against Cuba.

The 1960s: Origins of the U.S. Embargo against Cuba

One of the Cuban Revolution's main goals was to reduce economic dependency on the United States. As a result of expropriations and redistribution of land under the First Agrarian Reform of May 1959, nearly one hundred thousand small farmers were granted titles to the land they worked and many large farms were organized into state-controlled production cooperatives. The state assumed control over nearly 40 percent of the cultivated land whereas 59 percent remained with private farmers (Pérez-López 1995, 34–35). In February 1960, Cuba signed its first major trade agreement with the Soviet Union under which Cuban sugar was exchanged for Soviet oil, wheat, fertilizer, iron, machinery, and trade credits. Later that year, Castro initiated a wide program of nationalization involving many U.S. enterprises that ended private property in Cuba and led to the imposition of a partial U.S. economic embargo against the island (Pérez 2003, 243). Capitalism was virtually eradicated and foreign investment strongly rejected as a positive factor in economic development. Thanks to Soviet subsidies and preferential terms of trade, Cuba was now able to exclude Western capital and prevent foreign ownership.

Initially a reaction to Cuba's domestic reforms, U.S. economic sanctions were notably expanded during the Kennedy and Johnson administrations to raise the cost of Cuban adventurism in Latin America, raise the cost to the Soviet Union of maintaining its new relationship with the island, and reduce the latter's ability to find other capitalist trade and financial partners (Morley 1984, 28; Smith 1988, 47–49). But overthrowing the Cuban regime was Washington's ultimate goal from 1960 to at least early 1963, if not later (Morley 1987, 95). During this period, the U.S. Central Intelligence Agency (CIA) engaged in many assassination plots and covert operations to remove Castro from power. Most of these plans, which included the failed CIA-backed Bay of Pigs invasion of April 1961, were hatched less than a year after Castro seized power when the Eisenhower administration approved the use of exile groups, infiltration, sabotage, and clandestine maneuvers to seek his ouster. Even the Kennedy-Khrushchev agreement that put an end to the Cuban missile crisis of October 1962 did not mention a U.S. commitment to cease covert actions against the Cuban leader, which continued through the early presidency of Lyndon B. Johnson after Kennedy's assassination in November 1963 (Gleijeses 2002, 25).[3] Only around the mid-1960s, when Johnson ordered the CIA to abandon direct efforts to overthrow the Cuban government, did the economic and political isolation of Cuba (optimally to create economic destabilization and the regime's collapse) through the use of comprehensive sanctions clearly emerge as the overarching U.S. goal.

Between May 1959 and October 1960, the Cuban government expropriated seventy thousand acres of property owned by U.S. sugar firms, including thirty-five thousand acres of pasture and forests owned by the United Fruit Company. It also took over U.S. oil refineries after they refused to refine oil Cuba had acquired from the Soviet Union and U.S. properties in key sectors such as telephone, mining, banking, and electricity (Jatar-Hausmann 1999, 15). In response, the United States cancelled Cuba's portion of the annual U.S. sugar import quota in July 1960 and announced a ban on U.S. exports to Cuba (except for some food products and medical supplies) later in October. Furthermore, the embargo had become extraterritorial with regulations barring reexport to Cuba of any commodities or technical data that originated in the United States (Rich Kaplowitz 1998, 40). On January 3, 1961, the Eisenhower administration officially broke diplomatic relations with the Castro government.

On September 4, 1961, just a few months after the famous speech of Fidel Castro in which he defined for the first time the revolution as socialist and declared himself a "Marxist-Leninist," the United States promulgated the Foreign Assistance Act (FAA). The FAA granted the U.S. president the authority to impose economic sanctions against Cuba and deny all U.S. foreign assistance to the island. On February 7, 1962, the FAA was expanded and the Kennedy administration announced a total embargo of U.S. trade with Cuba. It should be noted that in the early 1960s the embargo was not simply a unilateral measure on the part of the United States but a more general Latin American attempt to contain the communist threat. In 1964, Washington persuaded all members of the Organization of American States (OAS), with the sole exception of Mexico, to break diplomatic and trade relations with Cuba (Brenner 1988, 13).

The legal foundations of the U.S. economic embargo with respect to Cuba are laid down in the Cuban Assets Control Regulations (CACR) promulgated in 1963 pursuant to the Trading with the Enemy Act (TWEA) of 1917. The TWEA, signed in the context of the U.S. entry into World War I, allowed the U.S. president to prohibit, limit, or regulate financial and commercial transactions with hostile countries in time of war. It was amended in 1933 to grant the president the authority to exercise the powers of the act during periods of national emergency. The main reason behind this amendment was to deny hard currency resources to sanctioned countries and their nationals and preserve their assets for possible vesting and use in the future settlement of American claims against them. The CACR of 1963 froze all Cuban assets in the United States and prohibited all unlicensed financial, commercial, and travel transactions by Americans with Cuba or its citizens. The Office of Foreign Assets Control (OFAC), established by the U.S. Department of State in 1962, was assigned responsibility for issuing, interpreting, and applying economic sanctions regulations. With the CACR, the U.S. government aimed to isolate Cuba, protect Cubans from having their assets in the United States confiscated by Cuban authorities, preserve Cuban assets for future disposition, and deny Cuba access to dollar earnings and financial facilities (Travieso-Díaz 1993).

On May 5, 1966, the U.S. Congress expanded the embargo by enacting the Food for Peace Act. The act outlawed food shipments to any country that sold or shipped strategic or non-strategic goods to Cuba except for specific circumstances in which the president could allow shipments of medical supplies and non-strategic goods. The Food for Peace Act was signed by President Johnson in November 1966, although he expressed some concern for certain provisions precluding food aid to countries that traded with Cuba and North Vietnam.

Well into the 1970s, the United States conditioned the reestablishment of normal relations with Cuba on the end of Castro's efforts to spread the revolution in Latin America and the end of his military ties with the Soviet Union. Washington's fears of a military threat from Cuban and Soviet expansion in the region materialized with the Cuban missile crisis and deepened in the 1970s when the island's army became engaged in Angola and Ethiopia. Nevertheless, there were no formal conditions regarding Cuba's internal system or demands that it move toward democracy and embrace a market economy.

The 1970s: Efforts toward Normalization

Despite its harsh anti-Castro rhetoric, the presidency of Richard Nixon (1969–74) produced no new major policy initiatives on Cuba even though some congressional support for an opening to the Cuban government picked up steam after Nixon began to ease trade and travel restrictions with China in 1971 (Haney and Vanderbush 2005, 24). In the mid-1970s, a more favorable international climate and some changes in the political scenario of the Western Hemisphere promoted the active resumption of economic ties between several Latin American countries and Cuba and undermined the overall support of the OAS for the U.S. embargo. Castro's decision to reach out to establish diplomatic relations with the same governments he had previously vowed to overthrow was a consequence of his failed attempts to export armed struggle in the region and growing pressures from the Soviet Union to adopt tactics less likely to provoke a confrontation between Moscow and Washington. On July 29, 1975, the OAS dropped its sanctions against Cuba in recognition of Castro's less aggressive policies in the hemisphere. In reality, given that many Latin American countries would have reestablished normal relations with the Cuban government anyway and emptied multilateral sanctions, the OAS action was urged by the United States (which voted with the majority) as part of a secret effort to negotiate normal relations with the island (Gleijeses 2002, 225).

Contacts with Cuba had begun in the last two months of the Nixon administration. In June 1974, the U.S. secretary of state, Henry Kissinger, transmitted a message to Fidel Castro stating that he was interested in conducting informal talks aimed at moving toward normal bilateral ties. Throughout 1975 Kissinger, now serving under President Gerald Ford, authorized his aides to undertake a number of unofficial meetings with Cuban officials to explore the possibilities for a fundamental change in U.S.-Cuba relations. As a State Department report of March 1975 noted, the White House wanted to move quickly toward normalization to remove Cuba from the domestic and inter-American agendas before Congress and the OAS stripped Washington of its bargaining clout (Kornbluh and Leogrande 2009). It was with that goal in mind that the Ford administration favored the OAS resolution in July and allowed subsidiaries of U.S. companies to expand commerce with Cuba through amendments to the CACR. Overseas subsidiaries of more than one hundred large firms based in the United States could now apply for a specific license to trade with the island from third countries. This kind of commerce increased constantly during the 1980s and reached its highest level at more than $770 million in 1991, just before the enactment of the Torricelli law (Aguilar Trujillo 1998). However, talks between Washington and Havana for a relaxation of tensions were drastically suspended in November 1975 when Cuba, in partnership with Soviet forces, deployed combat troops in the civil war in Angola. On December 20, 1975, Gerald Ford announced in a public speech that the Cuban involvement in Angola would preclude any chance of restoring full diplomatic relations with Cuba in the near future.

Talks resumed during the first year of the Carter administration. Between March and May 1977, Jimmy Carter lifted the travel ban and allowed charter flights to Cuba,[4] removed restrictions on U.S. citizens spending dollars on the island, signed agreements with the Cuban government on fishing rights and maritime boundaries, and quietly suspended surveillance flights over Cuba. The United States and Cuba opened interest sections (quasi-embassies) in each other's capitals in September and informally agreed to negotiate at the same time the issue of compensation for expropriated U.S. properties and the lifting of the embargo (Smith 1998, 535).[5]

Carter's measures were potentially a major crack in the embargo because they facilitated U.S. tourism in Cuba. After years of neglect, the Castro government had timidly begun to promote international tourism since the mid-1970s. About 4,000 hotel rooms were built for that purpose between 1975 and 1981. Yet, the island still catered mostly to visitors from socialist countries during this period and U.S. tourism never took off. Cuba had just 128,600 international arrivals in 1980 (Quintana et al. 2004, 100), almost one-twentieth of its current levels. In February 1982, with arrivals from non-socialist countries somewhat on the rise, Cuban authorities enacted Decree-Law 50, whose main goal was to attract foreign investment in the tourism industry and stimulate its development. Two months later, President Ronald Reagan reinstated the ban on travel to Cuba.

New congressional initiatives and business interests also spurred the impetus for change in U.S. policy toward Cuba that emerged after Carter came to office. Several U.S. policymakers and entrepreneurs visited the island in 1977–78 and various proposals for a partial lifting of the embargo were debated in Congress. A growing sentiment toward normalization was nurtured by the failure of sanctions to undermine the Cuban government and by the loss of business opportunities for U.S. firms stemming from existing trade restrictions with Cuba. The Cuban economy had improved markedly since the early 1970s despite a sudden drop in sugar prices around mid-decade (Pérez-Stable 1999, 130). Meanwhile, the U.S. economic crisis of 1974–75 had prompted a number of U.S. firms to seek new markets and favor a reestablishment of trade ties with Cuba. But they were unable to form a unified force and engage in substantial lobbying to advance their interests (Rich Kaplowitz 1998, 100–101). In contrast, citrus and sugar firms in South Florida that feared growing competition from Cuban producers and especially U.S. corporations whose properties in Cuba had been expropriated in the early 1960s lobbied heavily against the lifting of the embargo (Morales Dominguez and Prevost 2008, 85). With no real pressure from anti-sanctions business groups and strengthened by Cuba's new military activities in Africa, conservative members of Congress successfully blocked all attempts to further ease the embargo.

In early 1978, scarcely three months after the opening of interest sections, the Carter administration abandoned its conciliatory stance on Cuba and normalization efforts came to a halt as the Cuban government began sending military troops to Africa again. Fidel Castro's involvement with the Soviet Union in the conflict between Somalia and Ethiopia put an abrupt end to negotiations that were still at a very preliminary stage and led the U.S. government to add two more conditions for progress toward normalization: the removal of Cuban troops from Africa, which echoed President Ford's public speech of 1975, and Cuba's greater respect for human rights (Smith 1998, 535). The process of rapprochement was frozen and then reversed in the 1980s with the election of Ronald Reagan and the new wave of revolutionary socialism backed by Soviet and Cuban troops in Central America, the Caribbean, and Africa (Zimbalist 1995, 26).

The 1980s: Intensification of Sanctions and the Birth of the Cuban American National Foundation (CANF)

Ronald Reagan reinstated the traditional hard-line approach toward the Castro government. He intended to pursue the containment strategy with respect to Cuba much more vigorously than many of his predecessors and revive the goal of rolling back communism. Besides putting forward the same conditions for normalization laid out by the former president Jimmy Carter, the Reagan administration clearly aimed at countering and undermining the joint Soviet-Cuban military operations throughout the third world, especially in the Western Hemisphere (Erisman 1995, 132).

In line with a tougher position toward Cuba, U.S. economic sanctions were renewed and intensified during the 1980s. On April 19, 1982, the Reagan administration reestablished the travel ban prohibiting U.S. citizens (with the exception of officials, relatives visiting family, and certain professionals) from spending money in Cuba despite the fact that U.S. courts had upheld the constitutional right to travel. That same year, Washington warned U.S. subsidiaries in third countries not to exceed the limits allowed by the U.S. government. On August 22, 1986, the U.S. Treasury Department announced new restrictive measures that prohibited U.S. businesses from dealing with a list of foreign firms operating in the United States, Panama, and Jamaica, which were considered as "Cuban fronts intended to break the U.S. embargo" (Leyva de Varona 1994, 9). They also included lower limits on cash and gifts sent by Cuban Americans to relatives on the island and tighter regulations on companies that shipped humanitarian care packages to Cuba.

It should be emphasized that during the 1980s the Cuban-American community began to play an increasing role in framing the U.S. foreign policy debate over Cuba, a role that would become even more important in the next decade. In March 1981, a group of first-generation Cuban-American businessmen under the leadership of Jorge Mas Canosa founded the Cuban American National Foundation (CANF) in Miami, modeled on the powerful Israeli lobby run primarily by the American-Israeli Political Action Committee (AIPAC). While Mas Canosa once claimed that the foundation was the idea of a few friends acting on their own, the Reagan administration essentially stimulated the creation of CANF to gain support for its tough stance against Castro and other policies toward Latin America (Haney and Vanderbush 2005, 35).

The Cuban American National Foundation quickly set up a lobbying unit (the Free Cuba PAC) to penetrate the most influential circles of power in Washington and emerged as a key financial contributor to candidates for federal office who staunchly opposed any engagement with Cuba. It also raised funds for its activities by accessing government contracts awarded by the National Endowment for Democracy (NED), a non-profit entity formed by Reagan in 1983 to advance democracy abroad. Although congressional restrictions prohibited the use of NED funds for "lobbying or propaganda which is directed at influencing public policy decisions of the Government of the United States," CANF received grants to create and finance a front organization, the European Coalition for Human Rights in Cuba, based in Spain (Nichols 1988; Stone 1993; Franklin 1997, 295–96). Between 1983 and 1988, CANF obtained NED grants totaling $390,000 and its Free Cuba PAC made $385,400 in contributions to various candidates, among them Jesse Helms, a Republican senator from North Carolina (and a fierce anti-Castro stalwart), George H. W. Bush for his presidential bid of 1988, and, of course, Reagan for his reelection campaign of 1984 (Nichols 1988).[6] In 1985, as a reward for CANF's undeviating support, Reagan granted a concession to the Miami-based Radio Martí station controlled by Mas Canosa to start broadcasting into Cuba in an attempt to break Castro's monopoly on news inside the island.

The influence of CANF's hefty PAC contributions over Washington's Cuba policy during the Reagan years and afterward is widely acknowledged (Eckstein 1994, 210; 2009, 127–32; Haney and Vanderbush 2005, 72; Rich Kaplowitz 1998, 134). Another great achievement of CANF was to mobilize its Cuban constituency to support candidates favorable to its cause. Hoping for a possible return to Cuba under a different government, many Cuban émigrés in the United States had been slow to apply for U.S. citizenship (and thus acquire the right to vote) before 1980. The election of Ronald Reagan that year represented an important shift in the role of Cuban Americans because it fostered their growing participation in the U.S. electoral system as part of a strategy to further the exiles' traditional anti-Castro agenda. The emergence of sizable Cuban-American voting blocs in New Jersey and especially Florida in the second half of the 1980s fueled so-called low politics aimed to assure election. Both Republican and Democratic candidates for Congress and the presidency grew aware that supporting a hard-line against Cuba increased their chances of winning. In 1989, Ileana Ros-Lehtinen became the first Cuban American elected to Congress, and several others were soon to follow. In short, Cuban exiles were no longer mere agents of U.S. policy toward Cuba but directors of that same policy to which their personal interests were linked (Pérez 2000).

By the late 1980s, there was practically no natural domestic constituency in the United States favoring the resumption of normal relations with Cuba. The impetus in Congress for the Cuban Democracy Act (CDA), instead, started around that time. On July 20, 1989, Senator Connie Mack (R-Fla.) introduced an amendment to make it unlawful for U.S. subsidiaries located in third countries to trade with Cuba. Mack submitted the same proposal each year until the CDA with his amendment attached was passed in September 1992. Jorge Mas Canosa, soon after the enactment of the law, admitted that "without Senator Mack opening the way for three years with the Mack Amendment, the Cuban Democracy Act would have had a more difficult time becoming law" (Franklin 1997, 255). Not surprisingly, Mack had received large campaign contributions from CANF (Stone 1993).

The Early 1990s: Missed Opportunities for Rapprochement

By the early 1990s, the strong response of the United States to Cuban and Soviet ventures in the third world, the intensification of economic sanctions against the island, and most of all the collapse of the Soviet Union had produced significant changes in the areas of greatest concern to the United States. First, Cuba's military presence in Africa and Latin America practically came to an end. Second, a U.S. State Department's report of April 1989 recognized that the Castro government had "taken steps to demonstrate an improved human rights record."[7] Third, after the fall of the Soviet Union in late 1989 and the end of its special relationship with Havana, the massive amount of aid that had allowed Cuba to weather the U.S. embargo began to dry up. Without Soviet aid and without the external markets for its main products, Cuba suffered a deep economic recession and was forced to strengthen relations with capitalist countries and introduce limited market reforms. Its government was no longer able to finance revolutionary movements across the globe. Socialism had collapsed almost everywhere in Eastern Europe and the cold war was over. Apart from the eventuality of another mass migration across the Florida Straits and the potential use of Cuban territory to smuggle drugs into the United States, Cuba ceased to represent a threat to U.S. security interests (Leogrande 2007, 290; Peters 2000).

In short, three of the four conditions put forward by the United States (the end of Cuba's active support of revolutionary forces in Africa and Latin America and the end of its close ties with the Soviet Union) for resuming a constructive dialogue with Cuba toward normalization had been met. On the fourth issue, the area of human rights, the Castro government had at least given a few timid but encouraging signals. Therefore, the circumstances seemed to allow a possible relaxation of U.S. economic sanctions with respect to Cuba and the beginning of friendlier relations between the two countries. In addition, one might expect that the changing environment of the post–cold war era and reduced international tensions would usher in new commercial ties with countries, including Cuba, that were once entangled with the larger U.S.-Soviet confrontation (Roy 2000, 18). But things turned out quite different.

In the early 1990s, supporters of the embargo in Washington and within the Cuban-American community benefited from a number of factors. At that time, the fall of the Soviet Union and the problems still unresolved in Central America topped the Bush administration's list of concerns. Cuba was not high on that list (Fisk 2001, 94). It was also far down on the list of priorities of the early Clinton administration, which was immediately confronted with more pressing issues like the deteriorating political and human rights situation in Haiti and the need to halt the flow of Haitian refugees to U.S. shores. With the political vacuum left by the executive branch, the U.S. Congress, which was particularly susceptible to the influence of Cuban-American lobbying pressures, stepped up efforts to toughen the policy on Cuba (Pérez 2003, 274). Furthermore, the United States tried to capitalize on Cuba's economic dilemma and frustrated economic adjustments. Up to 1989, the impact of the embargo on Cuba's foreign trade was relatively minor because only 15 percent of that trade was conducted outside the socialist market. After 1991, the embargo placed conditions on more than 90 percent of Cuba's trade (Schwab 1999, 71–72). It appears obvious that U.S. policymakers were given an unparalleled opportunity to finally get the most of economic sanctions that had failed for thirty years to undermine the government of Fidel Castro. Instead of triggering improved relations between Washington and Havana, the situation of emergency of the Cuban economy led the United States to strengthen its sanctions against the island.

Along with an alleged commitment to promote democracy in Cuba, the United States retained the old cold-war strategic thinking that heightened economic warfare would accelerate the demise of the Castro government. But U.S. beliefs, rather than being learned from history, were mostly the result of domestic political considerations. Unwilling to defy an increasingly important Cuban-American constituency in Florida and New Jersey and its champions in Congress, both Bush and Clinton pursued a Cuba policy that, by admission of some of their advisors, was "anachronistic, even absurd" (Morley and McGillion 2002, 6). Domestic politics deserve special attention as they weighted heavily on the U.S. approach toward Cuba in the post–cold war era and prevented the White House from developing a more pragmatic stance that resembled the one adopted toward other unfriendly countries, including North Korea.[8] Even more significant, Washington repeatedly tightened its sanctions program against Cuba despite ample evidence that sanctions, albeit somewhat damaging to the target country, were by no means crippling the Cuban economy and fostering political changes on the island.

Pragmatism also made sense from a pure strategic standpoint if we consider the oft-heard charge that Cuban leaders actually would not want the embargo to be lifted because it is a useful scapegoat for failed economic policies and the continuation of socialism. According to Mesa-Lago (2004, 34–35), the strengthening of sanctions during the Reagan and Bush presidencies gave Fidel Castro an excuse to increase control as a defense against U.S. imperialism and capitalist influence. In the post-Soviet period, the Torricelli and Helms-Burton laws allowed Cuba to blame economic woes on Washington and mount a successful propaganda offensive in Europe and Latin America against the embargo (Roy 2000, 173–74; Domínguez 1993, 103–104). In short, the United States overlooked a number of good reasons for seeking engagement with Cuba in the early 1990s and ended up isolating itself rather than the Castro government.

The Torricelli Law

In 1991, under the Bush administration, the Treasury Department denied licenses for trade with Cuba to a number of U.S. subsidiaries in third countries and foreign firms trading products containing U.S. components. It also announced tighter restrictions on travel to Cuba and reduced the amount of money U.S. citizens could remit to family members on the island. Yet, Bush disregarded a request by Cuban-American state legislators from Florida's Miami-Dade County to condition U.S. aid to the Soviet Union on the latter's commitment to oust Fidel Castro (Franklin 1997, 279–80). In September 1992, in the heat of the presidential campaign, the Democrat-controlled Congress approved the Cuban Democracy Act or CDA (better known as the Torricelli law). The Cuban American National Foundation, frustrated as Congress was by what it perceived as presidential inattention toward Cuba, played a crucial role in the passage of the bill.

In February 1992, based on a draft proposal put to him by CANF's director, Jorge Mas Canosa, Robert Torricelli (D–N.J.) introduced the legislation into the House to further tighten the trade embargo while simultaneously promoting greater interaction at a people-to-people level between Americans and Cubans. Robert Graham (D-Fla.) and Connie Mack (R-Fla.) later submitted a virtually identical proposal into the Senate. Bush initially opposed the CDA by claiming that it would create problems internationally for the United States while having little impact on the Cuban economy. However, Mas Canosa skillfully turned his attention to other White House aspirants and soon found a supporter of the law in Bill Clinton, the Democratic presidential candidate.

In the spring of 1992, Mas Canosa first met Clinton in Tampa to explore the possibility of his endorsement for the CDA and then invited him to attend a CANF-sponsored fundraising banquet in Miami's Little Havana. On April 23, 1992, Governor Clinton announced to hundreds of cheering Cuban Americans: "I have read the Torricelli bill and I like it." He obviously seized the moment by adding that the Bush administration had "missed a big opportunity to put the hammer down on Fidel Castro and Cuba." Clinton's participation in the fundraiser in Little Havana and another one the same day in Coral Gables brought in $275,000 to his campaign, which was grasping for contributions in the aftermath of the New Hampshire primary (Franklin 1993).

Fearing to lose a traditional Republican advantage among Cuban-American voters in South Florida and forced to reassert his anti-Castro credentials, Bush almost immediately changed his mind and announced his support for the CDA on May 6, 1992. In a presidential election year, domestic politics considerations trumped all other issues when it came to U.S. policy on Cuba (Morley and McGillion 2002, 50). In late October, an independent Florida pollster featured in the *New York Times* observed: "In a close general election in which Cuban-Americans turn out more heavily than anyone else, they can give a Republican candidate a net gain of up to six percentage points."[9]

Despite his initial objections, Bush signed the CDA a few weeks before the general elections of November 1992. Congress had seized the initiative on how the United States should deal with Fidel Castro, and both presidential candidates had signed onto CANF's agenda of forcing a regime change on the island. The influence exerted by domestic politics, especially the electoral context linked to the partisan bidding for Cuban-

American votes in the pivotal state of Florida, was the "mobilizing incident" and the key for the passage of the CDA (Domínguez 1997, 61). By signing the legislation, Bush sent a very sharp message about his order of priorities: the national interest took a back seat to the interests of the hard-line exile community in Miami and, of course, the president's own domestic political advantage.

Conceived as an effective instrument for exerting pressure on the Cuban economy and offering positive inducements to democratic reforms in Cuba, the Torricelli law of October 23, 1992, established a two-track policy to reach out to the Cuban people while strengthening the embargo against the Castro regime. Here are the main provisions of the law.

- It prohibited foreign subsidiaries of U.S. firms from engaging in any transaction with Cuba.
- It prohibited any vessel from entering a U.S. port for a period of 180 days if that vessel had handled freight to or from a Cuban port.
- It maintained strict limits on remittances to Cuba by individuals subject to U.S. law.
- It permitted humanitarian donations, including medicines and medical supplies, after on-site verification.
- It authorized the president to prohibit U.S. economic and military assistance, military sales, or debt forgiveness to any country that provides assistance to Cuba.
- It authorized telecommunications and mail services (the latter with certain limitations) between the United States and Cuba and allowed payments to the Cuban government for telephone services.

The Torricelli law undeniably had an impact on the Cuban economy, in particular the provision that intended to halt Cuban imports from U.S. subsidiaries that were used to compensate for the shortfall in imports from the defunct Soviet Union. Whereas in 1992 the Cuban trade with U.S. subsidiaries was about $760 million, by 1994 such trade had plummeted to less than $10 million. The growing process of merger and acquisition of firms taking place on a global scale (in which the United States was the most active player) also amplified the reach of the law (Aguilar

Table 2.1. United Nations Votes on Resolutions against the U.S. Embargo on Cuba, 1992–2008

Year	In Favor	Against	Abstentions
1992	59	3	71
1993	88	4	57
1994	101	2	48
1995	117	3	38
1996	137	3	25
1997	143	3	17
1998	157	2	12
1999	155	2	8
2000	167	3	4
2001	167	3	3
2002	173	3	4
2003	179	3	2
2004	179	4	1
2005	182	4	1
2006	183	4	1
2007	184	4	1
2008	185	3	2

Source: United Nations (http://www.un.org/documents/resga.htm).

Trujillo 1998). Finally, the combined effects of U.S. sanctions, the end of preferential trade agreements with the Soviet Union, and unfavorable weather conditions pushed Cuban sugar production to a low of 4.2 million tons in 1993 from an average of 7.5 million tons a year between 1987 and 1991. The island was now able to earn hard currency sufficient to pay for little more than its necessary food and fuel imports. Cuban imports dropped from more than 8 billion pesos in 1989 to around 2 billion pesos in 1992 and fell by another 24 percent in 1993. By that year, Cuba was deeply embedded in an economic crisis threatening the survival of its government (Cole 1998, 4).

Thanks to economic adjustments introduced between 1993 and 1994 and a vigorous promotion of inward foreign direct investment and international tourism, the Cuban economy slowly began to recover around the mid-1990s. While successful in aggravating the economic crisis of the communist island, the Torricelli law ultimately failed to hasten the demise of the Castro government. The legislation also galvanized the international community against Washington's Cuba policy. Table 2.1 shows the

United Nations vote on resolutions calling for an end to the U.S. embargo against Cuba that were proposed each year between 1992 and 2008.

Prior to the passage of the Torricelli law, Cuba had never been able to obtain a resolution condemning the U.S. embargo on the floor of the United Nations General Assembly. In November 1992, as a consequence of widespread international concern over the extraterritorial character of the U.S. legislation, the General Assembly condemned the embargo by a vote of 59 to 3, with 71 countries abstaining. Since then, the vote has been more lopsided with every passing year. In 1995, a total of 117 countries expressed disapproval of U.S. policy. The United States was left with Israel and Uzbekistan as its lonely partners in voting against the resolution.[10] By 1998, the governments condemning the embargo were 157, with only 12 abstentions. Instead of gaining international support for its stance on Cuba, the United States became more isolated. In Roy's (2000, 102–103) words, "Washington had lost a public relations war." The number of countries opposing U.S. sanctions against Cuba reached 167 in 2000 and peaked at 185 in 2008.

The Helms-Burton Law

The United States enacted an even harsher package of measures against Cuba in 1996. The story of the Cuban Liberty and Democratic Solidarity Act (better known as the Helms-Burton law) is quite similar to that of the Torricelli law. Approval of the bill coincided with the Republican presidential primary elections in Florida in 1996 and preceded the general elections in November of that year. The conservative faction of the Cuban-American community lobbied heavily for a tougher approach toward Cuba. Nicholas Gutierrez, a Cuban-American lawyer for prominent Cuban exiles whose property was seized by the Castro government, made no secret that "nobody lobbied the bill as methodically and in as well-funded a fashion as CANF" (Kiger 1998, 52).

The only real difference was Jesse Helms's new role within the U.S. Congress (Domínguez 1997, 62). The conservative Republican senator from North Carolina had been installed as the chairman of the Senate Foreign Relations Committee after his party's electoral victory in the congressional elections of November 1994. The Republican takeover of Congress allowed Representative Dan Burton from Indiana to follow in the footsteps of Robert Torricelli by replacing him as the chairman of the House Subcommittee on Western Hemisphere Affairs and using that platform to gain influence on Cuba policy (Kiger 1998, 45). The new law, originally presented by Helms to the Senate in February 1995, was later introduced by Burton into the House of Representatives. Increasingly critical of President Clinton's commitment to the maintenance of the status quo vis-à-vis Cuba, Congress pressed ahead for yet another round of sanctions against the island. This time U.S. legislators sought to build a two-track approach by expanding the target of possible sanctions to foreign companies knowingly "trafficking" in U.S. properties expropriated by the Castro government without compensation in the early 1960s (Fisk 2001, 95).

Unresolved issues on property claims had been largely neglected for a long time, at least as a possible reason for new punitive measures against Cuba. The severe decline of the Cuban economy in the early 1990s nurtured fears among some U.S. congressmen that the Castro government would seek to cure its capital crunch by selling U.S. expropriated properties. The increasing number of foreign companies investing in Cuba after 1993 simply confirmed these fears and gave U.S. lawmakers a further pretext for tightening the embargo. The issue of human rights violations was raised as an important reason for their action, but the real goal of the Helms-Burton law was to bring about the collapse of the Castro regime by keeping foreign firms away from Cuba, thus denying the Cuban government much needed capital (Arreola 1998, 357). The law, engineered by hard-liners in Congress and leading figures in the Cuban-American community,[11] had nothing to do with resolving the original U.S. claims.

When the Helms-Burton law was first introduced into Congress in early 1995, President Clinton and Secretary of State Warren Christopher opposed it. The president, in particular, worried that the law limited his authority to conduct foreign affairs and feared retaliatory measures by major trade allies of the United States such as Canada, Mexico, and the European Union whose companies were trading with and investing in Cuba. Clinton noted in April 1995: "I support the Cuban Democracy Act, which passed in 1992 and which we have implemented faithfully. I think we should continue to operate under it. I know of no reason why we need further action" (Morley and McGillion 2002, 85). Given the international opposition and the reticence of the State Department, the future for Helms-Burton seemed gloomy in late 1995 and early 1996. The legislation had also lost the center stage because of the federal budget battle between Congress and the president.

Since September 1995, the Clinton administration had been making quiet attempts to stir opposition to the legislation in the U.S. business community as a way to offset the political leverage of conservative Cuban-American groups (Kiger 1998, 54). But the tide turned drastically on February 24, 1996, when two small planes that belonged to the Cuban exile group Brothers to the Rescue were shot down by Cuban forces over the Straits of Florida. This tragic event proved to be the key to the passage of Helms-Burton, mainly because of its proximity to important election dates. Unable to secure the enactment of the law until then, supporters in Congress and within the Cuban-American community capitalized on the outrage over the shoot down. The latter transformed the whole congressional debate and convinced Clinton that he needed "political cover" in Florida (Bardach 2002, 131). Clinton tried to negotiate a milder version of the bill with its proponents in Congress and with prominent Cuban exiles but was ultimately compelled to accept the initial version nearly unchanged. He even agreed to codify all existing embargo restrictions into law.

In early March 1996, Congress rapidly approved Helms-Burton by vast majorities in both chambers. Clinton was forced, as was Bush four years earlier, to set aside the national interest and prioritize domestic political concerns in order to avoid a major electoral setback in the presidential elections of November 1996. He ended up changing his initial position and signing the law on March 12, 1996, just seventeen days after the shoot down. Yet Clinton, unlike Bush, won his reelection bid by carrying Florida with a remarkable 34 percent of the predominantly Republican Cuban-American vote (Rothkopf 2000, 118).[12] To a large degree, Clinton's capitulation on Helms-Burton was the price he had to pay for that victory.

The final text of the Helms-Burton law is composed of thirty-three sections grouped into four titles. The law intends to assert the property rights of U.S. nationals affected by the extensive process of nationalization undertaken by Fidel Castro after January 1959. It also presents itself as an effective measure for fostering political change in Cuba and assisting the Cuban people in regaining democratic institutions (Groombridge 2001).

Title I codifies all embargo restrictions (including the Torricelli law) in effect as of March 1, 1996. In an attempt to multilateralize the embargo, it states the U.S. opposition to Cuban participation in international financial organizations and threatens sanctions against countries that provide anything that could be defined as "economic assistance" to Cuba (even in the form of favorable terms of trade). Title II lays down a series of conditions that would have to be met before Washington's reengagement with any future Cuban government. A key condition is that both Fidel and Raúl Castro cannot be part of that government. Apparently, the law eliminated the possibility of a U.S. "calibrated response" to changes in Cuba by preventing the president from responding positively to anything but the fall of the Castro regime (Leogrande 1997, 215). This is the first time that the objective of getting rid of the Castros has been explicitly stated as American policy. Other conditions are a democratically elected government, the release of all political prisoners, progress in moving toward a market economy, progress in returning properties confiscated by the Castro regime to U.S. citizens, including properties of those who were Cuban citizens at the time of the expropriation, and the end of Cuba's efforts to jam Radio and TV Martí.

While the first two titles of Helms-Burton seem to be designed primarily for Cuban consumption, both in the U.S. exile community and in Cuba, Titles III and IV are the aspects of the law aimed at Cuba's commercial partners. Title III allows U.S. citizens whose property was expropriated without compensation by the Cuban government, including those who were not citizens when the expropriation occurred, to sue in U.S. courts foreign firms or individuals that "traffic" in that property. Title IV authorizes the U.S. government to deny entry into the United States to senior executives of foreign companies that are accused of trafficking in properties subject to U.S. claims.

Apart from allowing a presidential waiver of Title III and discretion over the enforcement of Title IV (two prerogatives that the president effectively asserted as we will see in chapter 4), the Helms-Burton law transferred a great deal of control over the Cuba policy of the United States from the executive branch to Congress. Prior to the enactment of the law, the embargo was mostly based on executive orders that could be ended by the president. Substantial progress toward normal relations with Cuba would now require the repeal of Helms-Burton. As Leogrande (1998: 81) noted, "Helms-Burton left the President virtually no discretion whatsoever in formulating policy toward Cuba, and the President accepted it." In reality, the latter would still find ways to leave his mark.

Clinton, Bush, and the Primacy of Domestic Politics

Once he avoided political fallout in an election year, Clinton spent his second term in office trying to mend ties with Cuba. Between March 1998 and January 1999, he allowed the resumption of U.S. direct flights to the island, relaxed restrictions on family travel and remittances and, as part of his *people-to-people* contacts policy, loosened rules on certain categories of U.S. travelers, including academics, athletes, scientists, and religious groups. While avoiding calls for a fundamental review of U.S. policy toward Cuba, Clinton's approach was very much in tune with his overall foreign policy, which emphasized peaceful engagement and the use of soft power tactics as a way to achieve desired international outcomes through cooptation rather than coercion (Zebich-Knos 2005, 33).

Clinton asserted the executive prerogative to ease rules on travel and remittances to Cuba by using his limited licensing power to modify sanctions codified under the Helms-Burton law. Yet, his actions spearheaded strong rejections from several congressmen (mainly hard-line Cuban Americans) who claimed that the president's initiatives were not authorized by law. Helms-Burton conditioned the reinstitution of family remittances on Cuba's promotion of unfettered business operations and that of family travel on Cuba's release of political prisoners and the recognition of fundamental freedoms like the right of association.[13] Moreover, it was not clear if the authorization of direct flights fell under the president's authority. As for the simplification of licensing procedures for various categories of U.S. travelers, the president was at least allowed by Helms-Burton to grant exceptions on a case-by-case basis (Haney and Vanderbush 2005, 115–18). At any rate, Clinton had demonstrated that the executive branch was still able to shape some significant aspects of the Cuba policy even with a codified embargo. In the meantime, congressional moves on Cuba had become highly susceptible to pressures from certain groups within the U.S. agribusiness community that were eager to reestablish trade relations with the island.

In October 2000, Clinton signed the Trade Sanctions Reform and Export Enhancement Act (TSRA), a historic congressional legislation allowing U.S. companies to sell medicines and food products to Cuba. It was the most significant rollback of U.S. economic sanctions against the island in nearly forty years. Approved overwhelmingly by both chambers as part of a larger spending measure on agriculture, the bill was mainly the result of lobbying efforts by politically powerful agricultural groups eyeing a potentially lucrative market in Cuba and members of Congress from farm states trying to secure new trade deals for their constituents amid falling food prices. Activities by other U.S. trade and lobbying organizations, a growing sentiment about the ineffectiveness of the economic embargo, and the declining power of the Cuban American National Foundation after Mas Canosa's death in November 1997 also facilitated the relaxation of some commercial restrictions on Cuba. In the late 1980s, Philip Brenner wrote: "It has often been said, and it remains true, that there is virtually no natural domestic constituency for a normalization of relations with Cuba" (Brenner 1988, 73). A decade later, that constituency had finally emerged.

Business-driven pragmatism in U.S. dealings with the Castro government and domestic opposition to the embargo gained strength in the second half of the 1990s. In 1997, some four hundred U.S. corporations created USA Engage, a corporate coalition designed to lobby Congress to eschew economic sanctions in favor of engagement and trade relations with Cuba. Major agricultural organizations soon joined the call for a change of Cuba policy along with the Americans for Humanitarian Trade with Cuba (AHTC), a broad coalition of civic and corporate entities put together by the United States Chamber of Commerce. Founded in January 1998 in the context of Cuba's economic recovery and its reinsertion into the international capitalist market, the AHTC was instrumental in leading the fight to allow food and medicine sales to the island (Morales Dominguez and Prevost 2008, 130).

Additional support for the lifting of sanctions came from church and academic groups as well as moderate Cuban Americans who advocated a dialogue with Cuba (Brenner et al. 2003, 73). Throughout the 1990s, regular flows of Cuban immigrants drawn to the United States mostly by economic opportunities and the aging of the original exiles produced a more heterogeneous Cuban-American community with different views on Cuba policy. In 2000, a poll by Florida International University (FIU) of Cuban-American residents in Miami-Dade County, Florida, revealed a substantial shift in political attitudes compared to previous surveys.[14] The FIU's poll showed that a growing share of Cuban Americans favored a dialogue with the Castro government, unrestricted travel to Cuba, and U.S. food sales to the island. But the majority of respondents still supported the continuation of the embargo.

Lastly, the passage of the TSRA in 2000 represented a change of strategic beliefs and policy preferences on Cuba. Many Republicans and Democrats in Congress began to realize that stiffer sanctions had largely failed to undermine the Castro regime while hurting U.S. firms in terms of forfeited business with the island. They successfully pushed for a relaxation of trade restrictions that would benefit U.S. producers and enhance American influence on Cuba, or so they claimed.

The waning influence of CANF was further reduced by a split within its ranks that occurred in 2001, when more than twenty hard-liners resigned from the group's executive board. But Cuban-American members of Congress and pro-embargo lobbyists retained substantial power in shaping U.S. policy toward Cuba. Besides the introduction of a clause in the agricultural bill of 2000 that required U.S. companies to sell food to the Cuban government on a cash basis, anti-Castro legislators and their allies in Congress codified into law existing restrictions on travel to Cuba out of fear that Clinton would eliminate the travel ban right before leaving office. Because the TSRA fixed travel rules in place, it appeared that Congress had finally seized all major executive prerogatives over Cuba policy (Pérez 2003, 274). Yet, President George W. Bush ignored the law by ending a popular license for educational trips to the island in 2003 and tightening restrictions on Cuban-American family visits the following year. Under the TSRA, the president has the discretionary authority to regulate these travel activities,[15] but it remains unclear whether he can terminate or alter codified licensing arrangements. If pro-embargo forces in Congress were correct in asserting that Clinton was prevented from easing travel rules without congressional support, then there is all the more reason to think that Bush's measures went well beyond what the law permitted.

The Cuban-American community turned out to be a major factor in the hotly contested presidential election of November 2000 in which George W. Bush carried Florida by only 537 votes and received 80 percent of the Cuban exile vote (Weinmann 2004, 23). Whether or not the Cuban vote was fully responsible for Bush's victory, Cuban Americans took credit for the outcome, found in the new president a staunch supporter of the embargo, and claimed an even greater say in the formulation of the country's policy on Cuba.

When President Bush took office in January 2001, hard-liners in the Cuban-American community and in Congress were confident that he would do anything within his power to keep sanctions against Cuba in place. Indeed, despite considerable congressional support for closer ties with Cuba, Bush's vow to veto any further easing of the embargo was so unyielding and threatening that the Cuban-American representative Lincoln Diaz-Balart once called it an "atom bomb."[16] It remained to be seen, however, how far Bush was willing to go in meeting Cuban-American demands for tougher sanctions against the Castro regime and keeping his promise to hasten democratic changes in Cuba. Among the president's potential options were stiffer rules on travel, remittances, and agricultural sales to the island, increased financial assistance to opposition groups in Cuba, stronger enforcement of Title IV of Helms-Burton and the end of the waiver of Title III, and a revision of the "wet foot/dry foot" policy of 1994 under which Cuban migrants who make it to the U.S. shore are allowed to stay in the United States whereas those intercepted at sea are sent back to Cuba (Haney and Vanderbush 2005, 133).

Almost until the end of Bush's first term in office, Washington's Cuba policy remained characterized more by continuity than change. To be sure, Bush did pay close attention to his Cuban exile constituency and put right-wing Cuban Americans on the front lines of his foreign policy team dealing with Latin America and, of course, Cuba. Mel Martínez, a first-generation Cuban American who left the island at the age of fifteen, was appointed secretary of housing and urban development (Leogrande 2005,

21). On May 20, 2002, Bush presented the Initiative for a Free Cuba,[17] stating that the United States would be willing to lift the embargo and pursue reengagement with Havana only if the latter were prepared to hold free and fair elections, respect human rights, release political prisoners, permit the creation of independent organizations, and adopt a market-oriented economic system based on the right to own and enjoy property. Moreover, Bush stepped up enforcement of the travel ban on Cuba and, in late March 2003, announced new rules that eliminated people-to-people educational exchanges unrelated to academic coursework.

Nevertheless, the aforementioned rules also eased restrictions on Cuban-American trips and remittances to Cuba and came about only one week after Fidel Castro launched a massive crackdown on the internal opposition that led to the arrest of seventy-five dissidents. Between 2001 and 2003, Title IV of Helms-Burton was never enforced, Title III continued to be waived, a promised thorough review of Cuban immigration policy was not carried out, and a proposed sizeable increase of U.S. funding for dissidents in Cuba largely failed to materialize. By the end of his third year in the White House, at least from the perspective of many influential leaders in the Cuban-American community, Bush had not matched his hard-line rhetoric against Castro with major policy efforts, while U.S. visitors, remittances, and food sales to the island were on the rise. In addition, the war on terror that began after September 11, 2001, and especially the U.S. military intervention in Iraq, made some exiles wonder why the United States could not do the same with a country like Cuba that was on the State Department's list of terrorist states.[18]

Outraged by the Cuban president's action and frustrated with the U.S. president's inaction, a group of Cuban-American members of the Florida legislature sent a letter to Bush in August 2003 warning him of the risk of losing the backing of the exile communmity if a tougher stance on Cuba were not taken. The letter, in a clear reference to Bush's chances of winning Florida in the next general election, cautioned that without "substantial progress" toward fulfilling Cuban-American demands "the historic and intense support from Cuban-American voters for Republican federal candidates, including yourself, will be jeopardized.[19] Even Jeb Bush, the president's younger brother who had been reelected as governor of Florida in November 2002 with about 84 percent of the Cuban-American vote, criticized the White House for its decision in July 2003 to repatriate a group of Cubans suspected of hijacking a boat to come to the United States.[20]

It was not until 2004, with the presidential campaign already in full swing, that Bush moved decisively to toughen the policy on Cuba. An early signal was his decision in February to empower the Department of Homeland Security to stem unauthorized departures of Cuban-bound boats from U.S. waters "due to the potential use of excessive force, including deadly force, against them by the Cuban military" and as a way to "deny resources to the repressive Cuban government."[21] On May 6, 2004, the Bush administration notified the Jamaican tourism company Super-Clubs that its executives would be barred from entry into the United States under Title IV of Helms-Burton because of the company's investments on a U.S. confiscated property in Cuba. SuperClubs cancelled two hotel management contracts on the island in June. After almost seven years since the last application of Title IV, Washington flexed its muscles against a resort chain from a small country with far less political clout than European Union companies with a large presence in the Cuban market. Regarding the latter, Bush limited his actions to the imposition of fines on some European firms for engaging in trade and financial transactions that allegedly violated U.S. sanctions. The only move against European entities that has had some notable impact on the Cuban economy was the $100 million fine imposed by the U.S. Federal Reserve on the Swiss bank UBS in May 2004.[22] But Switzerland is not a member of the European Union.

In May 2004, the Commission for Assistance to a Free Cuba, which had been formed by Bush in October 2003 under the chairmanship of Secretary of State Colin Powell and Mel Martínez, unveiled its recommendations to the president for devising ways to "help and ease Cuba's democratic transition."[23] On June 30, 2004, in quick response to those recommendations and with an eye to the upcoming election, Bush introduced more stringent restrictions on U.S. travel and remittances to the island aimed to increase economic pressure on the Castro regime and deprive it of much needed hard currency. The new measures limited family visits to Cuba by Cuban Americans to just one trip every three years, reduced the amount of money they could spend while there, and established that only immediate relatives were eligible to receive remittances and gift parcels. The White House also said it would intensify propaganda broadcasts and boost financial support of anti-Castro groups in Cuba.

Bush's decision to target Cuban Americans was a calculated bet. Although the new provisions stirred some anger among recently arrived Cuban immigrants, a poll of Miami-Dade County's Hispanic Republicans (mostly Cuban Americans) conducted in January 2004 and released to members of the Republican Hispanic Caucus found that 70 percent of respondents agreed or strongly agreed with the demand for tougher sanctions against Cuba put forward by Florida legislators in August 2003.[24] Bush's bet paid off. He won his reelection bid in November 2004 and carried Florida more comfortably than four years before with 78 percent of the Cuban-American vote versus 21 percent for the Democratic candidate, John Kerry.[25]

Overall, it is hard to deny the fact that U.S. policy toward Cuba in the post–cold war era has had much to do with domestic politics and little to do with promoting democracy in Cuba. Some scholars pointed out that other driving factors should be taken into consideration. These include congressional activism, special interests of the executive and bureaucratic elites, and external pressures (Brenner et al. 2002) as well as ideological issues linked to U.S. hegemonic plans (Morales Dominguez and Prevost 2008, 146). Yet, except in 2008, all major U.S. moves to intensify or relax sanctions against the Castro government occurred in presidential election years, when partisan bidding for Cuban-American votes (and money) in the politically pivotal state of Florida takes center stage.

Despite their initial opposition, George H. W. Bush and Bill Clinton strengthened the embargo by signing, respectively, the Cuban Democracy Act in October 1992 and the Helms-Burton law in March 1996. Bush changed his mind after Clinton, his Democratic opponent, traveled to Miami in April 1992 and announced his endorsement of the CDA. Clinton had a similar volte-face four years later following the shooting down by Cuban forces of two Cuban exile planes in February 1996. Under increasing pressure from U.S. farmer groups, Clinton cleared the way for the sale of U.S. food to Cuba in October 2000, but he was not up for reelection. In the meantime, the Democratic nominee, Al Gore, tried to hamper George W. Bush's quest for Cuban-American votes in Florida by vowing to resist any openings to the Castro regime, breaking party ranks over the case of Elián Gonzáles,[26] and tapping a strong embargo supporter like Joe Lieberman as his running mate. The controversy over Elián was nonetheless so damaging to the Democratic Party that Gore won only 14.9 percent of the Cuban vote in his failed bid for the presidency in 2000 (Pedraza 2007, 290). Finally, Bush's tightening of restrictions on Cuba in June 2004 came about only after Cuban-American leaders urged him to do so and warned that the traditional support for the Republican Party among Miami Cubans could be in peril. That year, even the Democratic contenders Howard Dean and John Kerry partially reversed their previously anti-embargo stance. The primacy of domestic politics in Washington's Cuba policy is indisputable.

Furthermore, the alleged democratic commitment of the United States toward Cuba often ended up rewarding Fidel Castro for its bad actions and punishing him for more positive ones. When the Cuban government halted its support for revolutionary forces in Africa and Latin America and its special relationship with the Soviet Union in the early 1990s, U.S. authorities strengthened the embargo with the CDA. When Castro introduced capitalist-style economic measures in 1993 and 1994 and began to send timid signals to the United States for an improvement of bilateral ties, especially on migration issues, the United States reinforced its sanctions with the Helms-Burton law. In contrast, when Cuba's economic reforms virtually came to a stop in the late 1990s, Washington lifted some restrictions on agricultural trade with Havana. In March 2003, following the imprisonment of several dissidents and the execution of three hijackers in Cuba, the White House relaxed rules on Cuban-American family visits and increased the amount of remittances that U.S. authorized travelers could carry to the island. And in late 2003, even though a congressional resolution in April had unanimously condemned the systematic violations of human rights by the Castro regime, both the Senate and the House voted overwhelmingly to lift the ban on travel to Cuba. A perverse logic, if there is one, seems to have dominated U.S. foreign policy toward Cuba in the post–cold war era.

During his second term, Bush stood firmly behind the economic embargo, continued to put forward the same unrealistic conditions for reengagement with Cuba laid out in 2002, and undertook a number of new anti-Castro initiatives. In March 2005, in an effort to curb growing sales of American food products to the island, the Bush administration established more rigorous payment procedures by requiring Cuba to make cash payments before U.S. goods leave the United States rather than before they arrive at Cuban ports. As a result, Cuban authorities diverted some purchases to other countries and U.S. food exports to Cuba suffered a decline in 2005–2006 before resuming strong growth in 2007–2008. Bush's new rules on cash payments for U.S. food exports to Cuba were strongly rejected by several congressmen. Between 2005 and 2008, various bills were introduced in one or both houses of Congress to facilitate trade with Cuba and travel to the island for the marketing and sales of agricultural goods. All initiatives ultimately failed because the White House regularly threatened to veto any law that would weaken the sanctions on Cuba (Sullivan 2007, 18).

Bush's attempts to squeeze economically the Castro regime included renewed pressures on foreign banks to shun dollar transactions with Havana, a crackdown on U.S.-based religious organizations that allegedly abused their travel privileges to Cuba, and the launch of a controversial program in the summer of 2006 giving Cuban doctors stationed abroad the opportunity to apply for political asylum and move to the United States.[27] Mainly intended to disrupt the oil-for-doctors partnership that Cuba had formed with Venezuela, the program has done little to stem booming hard currency revenues to the Cuban government generated through exports of medical services.

On July 10, 2006, the Commission for Assistance to a Free Cuba, now headed by Secretary of State Condoleezza Rice and Commerce Secretary Carlos Gutiérrez, a Cuban American, disclosed a new set of recommendations "to hasten the end of the Castro dictatorship" ranging from tighter enforcement of existing sanctions to an offer of prioritized assistance to a "Cuban Transition Government" that would move rapidly on the road to democracy.[28] Yet the core of the plan, approved by President Bush, lied in its attempt to empower Cubans who want change by breaking the "regime's information blockade" through broadcasting and the Internet. The U.S. government committed itself to make available $80 million of taxpayers' money over a two-year period to intensify the Spanish-language transmissions in Cuba of its Miami-based TV Martí via satellite, expand third-country broadcasting into the island, and provide civil society groups with the necessary equipment to receive uncensored news from abroad. But a shocking turn of events was about to take place in Cuba.

In late July 2006, Fidel Castro announced that he had temporarily ceded power to his brother Raúl after undergoing a complicated intestinal operation. Although the interim Cuban leader initiated a national debate over potential economic reforms to the island's socialist system and went so far as to propose negotiations with Washington for a normalization of relations, the Bush administration rejected any softening of the embargo, reiterated its support for democratic changes and dissident groups in Cuba, and dismissed Raúl as "Fidel light."[29] Apart from missing yet another opportunity for devising some sort of rapprochement with its southern neighbor, the White House did not recognize that a policy of incremental sanctions had achieved no tangible success in speeding up a democratic transition in Cuba. The latter had actually been moving in the direction exactly opposite to the one envisioned by the United States. Between 2003 and 2006, Havana's authorities reverted some of the capitalist-style economic reforms they had implemented in the early 1990s to ensure the survival of a system then on the verge of collapse (Pérez-Stable 2007, 17). They also stepped up government control on the economy and exhibited greater intolerance of political dissent. Thus, from a U.S. standpoint, when Fidel Castro fell ill in 2006 Cuba was farther from democracy than it was a decade before.

As additional proof of the importance of domestic politics, Bush's stance on Cuban dissidents seemed to be carefully crafted to appeal to opposition figures in Cuba holding views closely aligned with the position of Cuban-American hard-liners. By focusing only on those dissidents who virtually reject all policies perpetuated by the Castro regime, the White House foolishly disregarded the will of many Cubans who favor a more moderate course of action by advocating economic changes within the existing socialist framework. In his remarks from the Rose Garden in October 2003, Bush condemned Castro's repression of internal dissent and praised the "brave" dissidents Oscar Elías Biscet and Marta Beatriz Roque for their struggle for freedom.[30] He made no mention of Osvaldo Payá, the leader of the pro-democracy Varela Project, who one week earlier had taken the dramatic step of delivering fourteen thousand signatures to Cuba's National Assembly, calling for democratic reforms within the island's system. Unlike Payá, both Biscet and Roque reject the Varela Project and support the U.S. embargo.

In November 2007, Bush awarded the Presidential Medal of Freedom to Biscet, calling his example "a rebuke to the tyrants and secret police of a regime whose day is passing."[31] Far from downplaying the plight of Biscet and other jailed opponents of the Cuban government, it is highly doubtful that Bush's rhetoric and increased financial support to anti-Castro groups aided the cause of reform in Cuba. Many Cuban dissidents, often portrayed as U.S.-backed "mercenaries" by the island's authorities, have described this policy approach as counterproductive and actually favor lifting the embargo. In short, Bush intensified his hostile policy against Cuba with measures and speeches ill-suited to stimulate democratic changes on the island but well received by hard-line segments of both the Cuban exile community and the Cuban opposition movement. As noted by the dissident economist Oscar Espinosa Chepe, "Change in Cuba will never be radical and happen overnight like President Bush said."[32]

The year 2008 produced no significant changes in U.S. policy toward Cuba. Raúl Castro was officially named Cuba's new president in late February and, between March and April, introduced a number of small but significant reforms aimed to address public complaints about Cuba's excessive regulations and prohibitions, increase efficiency and productivity, especially in the agricultural sector, and ultimately stimulate development and enhance living standards. Bush labeled the reforms "empty gestures" and even turned down a request by the Cuban dissidents Marta Beatriz Roque and Vladimiro Roca in early September 2008 to temporarily loosen travel and remittance restrictions to the island to help thousands of Cubans cope with heavy damages caused by the passage of two hurricanes.[33] Nevertheless, the election of Barack Obama as the new president of the United States in November 2008 raised hopes for the beginning of warmer relations between Washington and Havana and the lifting of the U.S. embargo against Cuba.

Obama and the Future of the Embargo

Throughout the presidential campaign, unlike his Republican opponent John McCain, Obama made clear that he favored lifting restrictions on

Cuban-American family visits and remittances and establishing a dialogue with the government of Raúl Castro. To be fair, Obama did not completely abandon the game of domestic electoral politics on the campaign trail. While in 2004 he said that he supported the end of the embargo that had "utterly failed in the effort to overthrow Castro," at a meeting in Miami in August 2007 he called for the preservation of such a tool as "an important inducement for change."[34] In any case, Obama's overall stance on Cuba was much more conciliatory than that of his Democratic predecessors and he still won an estimated 35 percent of the Cuban-American vote in the Cuban stronghold of Miami-Dade County, faring particularly well among younger voters who tend to favor rapprochement.[35] In 1996, to obtain a similar result, Clinton had to make a 180 degree turn on Helms-Burton and relinquish his power to lift most sanctions. But Obama's greatest achievement was to carry Florida comfortably with a historic majority of the Hispanic vote, which suggests that he would have won the state even with a much smaller share of the Cuban-American vote. He actually would have won the general election even without the Florida vote. This will give him latitude to pursue a policy shift on Cuba with little political capital spent.

Obama delivered on his campaign promise on April 13, 2009, by announcing that he would permit unlimited travel to Cuba by Cuban Americans and remove limits on the amount of money they can remit. Again, the president had decided to modify travel rules for certain U.S. citizens even though such prerogative was apparently granted to Congress with the codification of the travel ban under the TSRA. In an attempt "to help bridge the gap among divided Cuban families and promote the freer flow of information and humanitarian items to the Cuban people," the White House also said it would authorize U.S. telecommunications companies to enter into agreements with Cuban providers and expand the list of gifts Cuban Americans can send to relatives in Cuba.[36] Soon after Obama's announcement, U.S. diplomats initiated informal talks with officials at the Cuban Interest Section in Washington on prospects for a thaw between the United States and Cuba.[37] However, U.S. expectations that the Cuban government would reciprocate Obama's overtures with an easing of political restrictions on the island were almost immediately dashed. While stressing his willingness to discuss any topic with U.S. authorities, Raúl

Castro echoed Fidel Castro's words by claiming that it is up to the United States, not Cuba, to do more to foster better relations.[38] As talks continue, differences on the issue of conditionality will create serious obstacles for substantial progress toward normalization.

President Obama's new measures regarding Cuba, which took effect on September 3, 2009, have created impetus for the further relaxation of sanctions.[39] In order to smooth tensions with Cuba, Obama could rescind some limitations on people-to-people travel, facilitate U.S. agricultural trade with Havana, abolish the Commission for Assistance to a Free Cuba, and exclude reciprocity demands and politically charged themes from exploratory bilateral discussions in favor of less sensitive topics such as drug interdiction efforts, coast guard and port security collaboration, and environmental protection. But the true battle for the removal of the travel ban and the main provisions of the embargo embodied in the Helms-Burton law will happen in Congress.

On the one hand, a number of anti-embargo legislative initiatives introduced in Congress in 2007–2008 are being taken up again, this time without the looming threat of a presidential veto.[40] Current proposals include the removal of all sanctions and the travel ban, a special exemption for U.S. oil firms to drill for crude in Cuban waters, the expansion of educational travel, and the easing of restrictions on sales of agricultural products to Cuba. These efforts are aided by a Democratic-controlled Congress (although many of the bills have bipartisan support), an active business lobby, U.S. opinion polls showing considerable support for the repeal of sanctions, and the growing pro-normalization sentiment within the Cuban-American exile community. Yet, among the key challenges, those advocating change in U.S. policy toward Cuba must be able to coalesce the various business and citizen lobbies, maneuver the tortuous process in Congress required to ease sections of the embargo, and forge meaningful allegiances with the moderate elements of the Cuban-American community. As in the past, questionable actions of the Cuban government might also derail progress toward the betterment of U.S. relations with Cuba.

On the other hand, Cuban-American hard-liners and their allies in Congress will not go down without strenuous opposition to anti-embargo bills. On March 10, 2009, Congress eliminated Bush's stiffer cash-payment rules for U.S. food sales to Cuba and eased some restrictions on travel to the island for the purpose of selling agricultural products. The new provisions, attached to a budget bill proposed by the Obama administration, had faced strong resistance from the Democratic senators Bill Nelson of Florida and Bob Menéndez of New Jersey, who represent large Cuban-American communities. In a quest to secure the senators' votes and clear the passage of the bill, Treasury Secretary Timothy Geithner was forced to provide reassurance in writing that the White House would interpret the changes so narrowly as to leave them unenforced.[41] For those who want to keep economic sanctions against Cuba alive, however, a crucial challenge is to convince younger generations of Cuban Americans and newly arrived Cuban immigrants that isolation is a morally correct policy as well as an effective one. It might also be difficult to convince ordinary Americans that an activist, confrontational, and expensive (in terms of lost business) Cuban embargo is worth it at a time when the United States is coping with an economic recession and has just removed the more sinister North Korea from the list of states that sponsor terrorism.

In sum, all of the necessary conditions for a change of policy vis-à-vis Cuba are in place. In the United States, a Congress with larger Democratic majorities is in favor of easing sanctions, a vigorous business lobby wants to sell food, prospect for oil, and expand U.S.-based travel to the island, and public opinion supports rapprochement. In Cuba, Fidel Castro is mostly out of power, the economy is struggling but continues to receive much needed financial help from Venezuela, China, and other countries, a stable succession government has made public overtures to the United States, and citizens are calmly going along with their new circumstances while hoping for a better life. In the exile community, younger Cuban Americans and recent exiles have a more conciliatory approach than the older hard-liners who are, themselves, as old and infirmed as the Castro brothers. Moreover, pro-embargo exile politicians will have a harder time supporting unilateral sanctions against Cuba while Washington is seeking international cooperation to deal effectively with North Korea, the quintessential rogue state. Finally, in Latin America, Cuba is being woven back into the regional political and trade agenda with crucial help from several left-leaning governments.

Although the future of U.S.-Cuba relations remains unclear, one thing is certain. The Cuban Revolution has just celebrated its fifty-first anniversary and, despite recurrent problems, no sign of a breaking point is yet visible. A succession of power and the introduction of some timid reforms are taking place relatively smoothly and, more importantly, on Cuba's own terms and at its own pace. Since the whole point of the embargo in the post–cold war era, whether to hasten a democratic transition on the island, get rid of Fidel Castro, serve the parochial interests of the Cuban-American community, or for other reasons, was to deny hard currency resources to the Cuban government, this study turns attention to the practices of transnational actors that have propped up the Cuban economy during this period. Chapters 3 and 4 analyze the evolution and results of foreign investment in Cuba, the impact of the Helms-Burton law on potential and existing investors, and the most important cases of foreign companies affected by the U.S. legislation. Chapter 5 examines the activities carried out by U.S.-based individuals and entities that sustain hard currency flows into Cuba. It is widely acknowledged that U.S. economic sanctions against Havana have failed to achieve their main goals. The remaining chapters of this book will explain why.

Evolution and Results
of Foreign Investment in Cuba

Cuba's response to the deteriorating economic situation subsequent to the collapse of its former benefactor, the Soviet Union, was the implementation in September 1990 of an economic austerity program called the "special period in time of peace." The program consisted of a series of measures intended to conserve energy and raw materials, stimulate food production, expand markets for exports and imports, and accelerate the development of international tourism. But the main novelty was the opening of the island to foreign direct investment (FDI) in the search for the markets, technology, and financing that disappeared with the collapse of the socialist bloc.[1] While it cannot be argued that foreign investment plays a fundamental role in the Cuban economy, it is evident that foreign capital has helped Cuba to find new markets for its main exports, boost international tourism, raise production of oil and electricity, and increase domestic supplies to the tourism industry and the internal market in hard currency.

Following a cautious start during the worst years of the economic recession when a handful of hotel and oil exploration joint ventures were formed, foreign investment in Cuba gathered pace after 1993 as the economy began to show signs of a modest but constant recovery. Since then, and despite the passage of the Helms-Burton law in 1996, a sizable number of foreign firms have entered the Cuban market with investments in nearly all sectors of the island's economy. Yet, after more than a decade of uninterrupted growth, the number of joint ventures with overseas companies has fallen significantly since 2002, raising questions on just how wide the Castro government's welcome to foreign investment really is.

Although the level of interest for the Cuban market on the part of foreign investors has diminished, the recent decline of international economic associations (*asociaciones económicas con capital extranjero*, or AECEs)[2] is not due to the impact of Helms-Burton but rather to Cuba's increasing selectivity toward foreign investment and its unwillingness to create a more attractive business environment. In effect, the downward trend began several years after the enactment of the U.S. legislation and coincided with a process of re-centralization of the Cuban economy launched by Fidel Castro in 2003.

Cuban authorities have never concealed their intention to keep foreign ownership and capital in the communist island at a minimum level. They always said that foreign investment is a complementary measure to help strengthen and improve the country's state-run socialist system, not destroy it. While acceptance of new investments is based on strict consideration of what they can bring to Cuba in terms of capital, technology, and markets, the Cuban government has made it clear that it wants to keep overall state control of the economy. Furthermore, Cuba has done very little to address recurring complaints raised by overseas partners, which include excessive bureaucracy, project approval delays, payments problems, and a restrictive labor legislation. On the contrary, Fidel Castro's moves to introduce foreign exchange controls for state-run enterprises and other centralizing economic measures have lowered confidence among existing and potential investors about their ability to deal with bureaucratic hurdles and collect payments and arrears from the Cuban government. Raúl Castro, who assumed provisional power when his older brother fell ill in July 2006 and formally replaced him as the country's new president in February 2008, called for more foreign investment in Cuba in the summer of 2007,[3] but his words have yet to translate into meaningful changes to the overall FDI regime. The drop in the number of active AECEs in Cuba is therefore hardly surprising.

Any attempt to carry out a study of foreign investment in Cuba is hindered by the lack of thorough and reliable information on the activities of foreign firms and their contribution in terms of capital. Due to what Cubans call the "U.S. economic blockade" against the island, public disclosure of data on the presence of foreign capital in Cuba is basically limited to statistics on the evolution of international economic associations by year, by sector, and by country. This method of reporting the level of foreign investment in the country offers no idea of the value or strategic importance of the deals involved. Nonetheless, this chapter makes extensive use of not easily accessible official reports along with additional information collected from a variety of sources in order to provide a quite detailed analysis of foreign business activities in Cuba and their main economic effects.

The resulting picture is intended to complement the examination of the Helms-Burton law presented in chapter 4. There are certainly obstacles to foreign investment in any third-world country arising from excessive government involvement in the economy, aversion to certain market mechanisms, bureaucratic red tape, discriminatory practices, legal uncertainty, banking difficulties, and poor infrastructures. Cuba is no exception in this regard. Unlike many other developing countries, however, Cuba is subject to a comprehensive U.S. economic embargo whose extraterritorial provisions are supposed to make it harder for the island to obtain the level and kinds of foreign investment it wants and reap its benefits. In reality, the unilateral sanctions of the United States tend to be ineffective in preventing transnational corporations based outside the United States from entering a target country's market and taking advantage of the lack of U.S. competition. Furthermore, in a state-controlled economy like that of Cuba, it takes only a few major foreign investment operations to make a significant difference for the survival of a government with a non-market attitude that remains essentially uninterested in attracting large amounts of FDI. Thus, by demonstrating the positive impact of foreign investment on the Cuban economy, the analysis provided in this chapter also intends to show the limitations of U.S. attempts to effectively undermine the Castro government through the enactment of a law like Helms-Burton that, in a classical example of a secondary boycott, seeks its own implementation across national borders.

Foreign Direct Investment in Cuba

With the demise of the Soviet Union and the plunge of its economy in the early 1990s, Cuba's need to find alternative finances, technology, and markets grew more urgent. The Cuban government moved actively to seek new long-shunned foreign investment and the first handful of joint ventures were signed in the hotel industry and oil exploration under Decree-Law 50 of 1982. Regarding the latter, the limit of 49 percent for the foreign share of joint ventures and the low level of investment protection for overseas firms were certainly major dissuading factors for capital inflows. Cuban statutory guarantees fell considerably short of providing the level of investment protection foreign companies would demand. According to Article 24 of Decree-Law 50, if Cuba unilaterally terminated the activities of a joint venture, the Cuban National Bank simply guaranteed to foreign investors the ability to repatriate the proceeds of their share after liquidation. In addition, it was clear that the Cuban government intended to maintain the most important sectors of the economy in national hands (Confidential Report 1999, 10).

The opening to foreign investment and international tourism, matched by increasing interest but also growing complaints from foreign companies, led the government to draw up an updated and more attractive legislation in 1995. While repeating some of the basic aspects of Decree-Law 50, Law 77 of September 1995 set out specific guarantees for foreign firms by establishing full protection and security against expropriation and opened all sectors of the Cuban economy (except public health, education, and the armed forces) to foreign investment. It also abolished the limit of 49 percent of foreign shares for joint ventures and authorized for the first time the possibility of 100 percent wholly foreign-owned investments. Finally, in an attempt to speed up and streamline the authorization process of new agreements, the law required that approval or denial of an investment must be given within sixty days of the presentation of the formal request.

Cuba intensified the promotion of foreign investment after 1993. Through visits to foreign countries, participation in international investment events, and meetings with potential investors, Cuban officials became very active in publicizing the advantages of business activities on

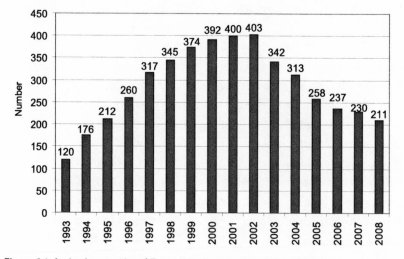

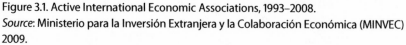

Figure 3.1. Active International Economic Associations, 1993–2008.
Source: Ministerio para la Inversión Extranjera y la Colaboración Económica (MINVEC) 2009.

the island (Pérez-López 1999). As a result, the number of international associations grew steadily and expanded to different sectors of the Cuban economy such as mining, construction, light and food industries, agriculture, and services. An important change of policy toward foreign investment occurred in 1998 when Cuban authorities declared their preference for AECEs that involved higher amounts of capital and loan financing. As a result of banking reforms and continued economic recovery, Vice President Carlos Lage announced that year the intention of the government to pursue a strategy of encouraging foreign investment in large development projects but limiting interest for smaller projects, unless they included the introduction of new technologies or new export markets. He added that Cuba's state-run banks were now in a position to provide small amounts of capital (USCTEC 1998).

As shown in figure 3.1, there were 211 active international economic associations in Cuba at the end of 2008, about 72 percent of them joint ventures (MINVEC 2009). The number of active AECEs, which had been increasing at an annual average rate of around 32 percent between 1993 and 1997, rose by just 5 percent per year between 1998 and 2002 (reaching a peak of 403 that year) and dropped by almost 50 percent between 2002 and 2008. Still, despite the lower number of associations, Cuban authorities argued that foreign investment is in a process of consolidation.

In February 2002, Marta Lomas, then the foreign investment minister, said, "While Cuba is often blamed for trying to detain foreign investment, what is happening in reality is the opposite. The country has been concentrating on businesses with results."[4] Early in 2007, she also said, "We are not interested in doing too many [joint ventures], we are only interested in those that have an impact on the economy."[5] Later that year, Lomas noted that the main economic indicators of AECEs had hit record levels in 2006 and that the declining number of joint ventures with overseas companies was part of a policy of "restructuring" (*reordenamiento*) of foreign investment aimed to boost Cuba's sales, revenues, and exports and establish "a more efficient control over resources."[6] In other words, Cuba remains interested in FDI proposals, but only in those that suit its development plans and come from major players.[7] Along with the aforementioned objectives, the Cuban government is seeking FDI projects that supplement state efforts to substitute imports of consumer goods, stimulate national production, and foster industrial and construction activities (Pérez Villanueva 2008).

Indeed, several foreign firms are engaging in profitable operations in the Cuban market and some have actually expanded their business interests on the island. It is true that foreign investors have had problems in recent years, further exacerbated by the global economic recession and the extensive damages of three hurricanes in 2008 that have taken a heavy toll on Cuba's finances and the overall Cuban economy. However, perhaps with the sole exception of the Canadian oil company Pebercan, none of the major investors has pulled out of Cuba. In January 2009, Pebercan revealed that its Cuban partner, the state-owned firm Cuba Petróleo, or CUPET, had prematurely revoked a sixteen-year-old oil production-sharing contract set to expire in 2018. Pebercan received a net lump sum payment of $140 million from CUPET and announced in late February that it would terminate all of its oil activities in Cuba.[8] Canada's Sherritt International, a third partner in the oil venture, received about $60 million of the lump sum. Neither Pebercan nor the Cuban government gave reasons for CUPET's move although public documents indicate that the latter was well behind its scheduled payments. In September 2008,

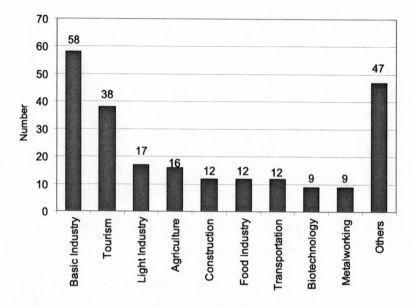

Figure 3.2. International Economic Associations by Sector in 2007.
Source: Ministerio para la Inversión Extranjera y la Colaboración Económica (MINVEC) 2008.

Pebercan reported that Cuba had been late in making its payments on many occasions, forcing the company to negotiate several debt-rescheduling agreements between 2002 and 2007.[9]

Sherritt International, Canada's largest investor in Cuba, with a diversified portfolio in oil, nickel, energy, tourism, and agriculture, experienced similar problems. In February 2009, the Canadian company signed a payment agreement with Cuban authorities to settle oil, gas, and power arrears of $162 million accumulated by Cuba at the end of 2008.[10] Yet, during 2008 Sherritt completed a brownfield expansion of its Pedro Soto Alba nickel plant at Moa Bay, in the Cuban province of Holguín, adding four thousand tons to the plant's annual production capacity, and drilled thirteen onshore oil wells using specialized directional drilling techniques. Further expansion plans in oil, nickel, and electricity production were temporarily put on hold in response to falling commodity prices and deteriorating market conditions.[11] Spain's Sol Meliá, the leader in Cuba's tourism sector, revealed that the island had been one of the most affected destinations in the Caribbean in 2002 as a result of the downturn in tourism after terrorist attacks on the United States on September 11, 2001. But the company added three new hotels with 1,709 rooms to its Cuba portfolio in 2006.[12] With only a few exceptions, not even those companies that have been targeted or sanctioned by the Helms-Burton law have divested themselves of their Cuban holdings. In short, 211 international economic associations remain active in Cuba and some must be making money.

As indicated in figure 3.2, at the end of 2007, the greatest share of economic associations with foreign capital was linked to basic industry (fifty-eight agreements), followed by tourism (thirty-eight), light industry (seventeen), agriculture (sixteen), construction (twelve), food industry (twelve), and transportation (twelve). From previous years, there was a decline of AECEs in nearly all major sectors of the Cuban economy. Official statistics also indicate that there were thirty-four AECEs in tourism, twenty-two in oil and petrochemicals, and twenty in the agri-food industry at the end of 2008. Currently, the Cuban government's foreign investment priorities include the promotion of new projects in tourism, mining, energy, oil, infrastructure, agriculture, and food packaging (MINVEC 2009).

Estimating the real value of foreign direct investment in Cuba to date is difficult, mainly because the Cuban government refuses to provide updated overall figures and, as Pérez-López (2007) pointed out, it has given inconsistent information on FDI stocks and flows over the years. The secrecy is justified by the government as a protective measure against the U.S. economic sanctions with respect to Cuba. Even the Havana-based embassies of major investing countries are unable to give complete figures because, according to them, investments in Cuba are often channeled through third countries or offshore financial centers, thus escaping registration by the real country of origin (Confidential Report 1999, 3–4).

Cuban experts calculate that, since the authorization of the first joint venture in 1988 until 2003, the total amount of committed FDI was about $6 billion, of which approximately half had been delivered.[13] Without including stock figures, the Cuban Ministry of Foreign Investment, or MINVEC, reported instead that 79 percent of pledged investment had been delivered by the end of 2005 (MINVEC 2006). As for FDI flows, the only official data are those included in Cuba's balance of payments, but

Table 3.1. Annual Foreign Direct Investment in Cuba, 1993–2003 ($U.S. Millions)

Year	1993	1994	1995	1996	1997	1998
Direct Investment	54.0	563.4	4.7	82.1	442.0	206.6

Year	1999	2000	2001	Total 1993–2001	2002[a]	2003[a]
Direct Investment	178.2	448.1	38.9	2,018.0	100.0	90.0

Sources: Oficina Nacional de Estadísticas (ONE) 2008a; Triana Cordoví 2003; "Deficit en Sector Externo," Economics Press Service, February 29, 2004.
Note: a. Unofficial estimates.

they have not been updated since 2001 (table 3.1). These statistics indicate that annual investment flows have fluctuated widely from $563 million in 1994 to just $4.7 million in 1995, and from over $400 million in 1997 and 2000 to only $38.9 million in 2001. Accumulated foreign direct investment was $2.018 billion between 1993 and 2001. Unofficial estimates from Cuban sources put the amount of FDI in 2002 and 2003 at $100 million and $90 million, respectively ($2.208 billion accumulated). These figures, if confirmed, represent a slight improvement from the poor result of 2001, but they are still considerably lower than the average annual flows during 1997–2000. Sectors with a significant presence of foreign capital are tourism, energy, oil, mining, construction, and telecommunications.[14] Albeit with reservations, two recent studies by Cuban-American scholars reported Marta Lomas as saying that foreign direct investment jumped to almost $1 billion in 2006,[15] which they attributed to Venezuela's growing role in the Cuban market (Mesa-Lago 2008, 14; Pérez-López 2007). Even though Venezuela's business activities in Cuba since 2004 have likely boosted FDI flows, Lomas was disclosing data on "direct income to the country" (ingresos directos al país) from international economic associations, which refers to dividends of the Cuban partners in AECEs plus revenues from workers' salaries, custom tariffs, taxes, and royalties.[16]

In terms of the number of foreign direct agreements (figure 3.3), countries of the European Union accounted for about half of the total in 2007. Spain was the first commercial partner for the island (sixty-three agreements signed), followed by Canada (thirty-seven), Venezuela (twenty-six), Italy (twenty-four), France (thirteen), and China (eleven).

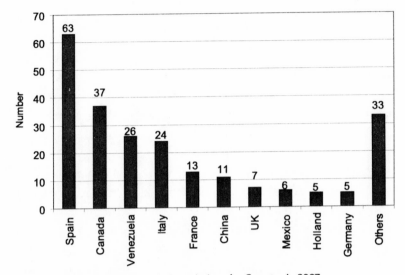

Figure 3.3. International Economic Associations by Country in 2007.
Source: Ministerio para la Inversión Extranjera y la Colaboración Económica (MINVEC) 2008.

Since 2003, there has been a reduction of joint ventures with almost all countries except China and Venezuela. In early 2006, Cuban sources revealed that 70 percent of all investment projects in stages of negotiations were with companies from China and especially Venezuela.[17] At the end of 2008, there were fifty-seven active AECEs with Spain, thirty-one with Venezuela, twenty-six with Canada, and twenty-three with Italy (MINVEC 2009).

Since 2004, the most important foreign investment operations in Cuba have targeted tourism and basic industry, above all nickel, oil, and energy. In the tourism sector, where partnerships with foreign companies are predominantly management contracts rather than joint ventures, Spanish chains such as Sol Meliá, Iberostar, Blau, and Barceló have incorporated several new hotels into their Cuban portfolio. China's Sinopec signed an agreement with Cuba's CUPET in early 2005 to jointly produce oil on the coast of the western province of Pinar del Río.[18] A sizable number of foreign firms from Spain, Canada, Norway, India, Malaysia, Vietnam, and Brazil, but not the United States because of the embargo, have acquired blocks in Cuba's waters of the Gulf of Mexico for potential offshore oil explorations. Brazil's Petrobras was the last foreign company to join the search for oil in Cuba's untapped offshore fields by signing a contract with CUPET in October 2008.[19] Canada's Sherritt International completed an upgrade of its energy power plant at Boca de Jaruco in the province of Havana, announced a major oil discovery in its Santa Cruz del Norte oil field, east of Havana, in late 2004 (the field was declared commercial in February 2006), and reached an agreement with Cuba in March 2005 for an expansion of its nickel plant in Moa aimed to increase annual output by sixteen thousand tons.[20]

But no other country has been more active than Venezuela. It should be noted that Cuba's partnership with Venezuela is in a category of its own and that unique rules and concessions apply to Venezuelan investments on the island. Initially centered on Venezuelan oil supplies in exchange for services provided by Cuban professionals (mainly doctors) as established by a cooperation agreement signed in October 2000, economic ties between the two countries received a major impulse from the creation of the Bolivarian Alternative for the Americas (ALBA) in December 2004. The latter was conceived not only as the cornerstone of a joint regional strategy to counter U.S.-backed neoliberal policies and free trade deals but also as an effective way to help Cuba minimize the negative effects of the U.S. embargo (Romero 2009). Under ALBA, which stimulated a dramatic expansion of the oil-for-doctors barter arrangement, the Cuban government made a commitment to grant tax exemptions on the profits of Venezuelan state investments (also private ones) and joint ventures in Cuba, remove any restrictions that could prevent 100 percent wholly-owned Venezuelan state investments, eliminate all tariffs and non-tariff barriers on imports from Venezuela, and give preferential treatment to airlines and ships of that country. For its part, Venezuela granted similar concessions to Cuba and agreed to finance the upgrading of the island's main infrastructures and a number of projects in the energy, agro-industrial, and service sectors.[21]

The vast majority of all new AECEs authorized by Cuba between 2005 and 2007 (twenty-four out of thirty-three) were formed with state companies from Venezuela (figure 3.4). In April 2005, besides various deals with Havana in the areas of construction and transportation, Caracas announced the creation of a joint venture with CUPET to revive an idled Soviet-era oil refinery in Cienfuegos. The refinery was inaugurated in

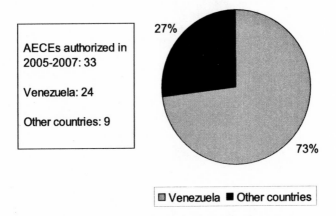

Figure 3.4. Authorized AECEs by Country, 2005–2007 (Cumulative).
Source: Ministerio para la Inversión Extranjera y la Colaboración Económica (MINVEC) 2006, 2008.

December 2007.[22] Earlier that year, Venezuela signed at least sixteen new joint ventures with Cuba in energy, oil, nickel, tourism, and infrastructure, with a committed capital in excess of $2 billion, and five joint ventures in agriculture to produce rice, dairy products, poultry, and leguminous plants. Venezuela also acquired blocks to hunt petroleum in Cuba's part of the Gulf of Mexico and even replaced China in a $500 million investment project to complete a mothballed nickel plant (Las Camariocas) in the eastern province of Holguín.[23] Venezuela's most recent investment plans in Cuba include an upgrade of the Cienfuegos refinery, the expansion of another oil refinery in Santiago de Cuba, the construction of an oil-fueled power plant in Holguín, the installation of an underwater fiber-optic telecommunications cable linking the two countries, and the creation of a joint venture fishing company.[24]

Another important FDI trend is that MINVEC has been promoting Cuban investments overseas in an effort to offset a diminishing flow of foreign capital invested in business activities on the island. In 1998, only 50 international associations operated abroad out of a total of 340 active AECEs (14.7 percent). By the end of 2002, there were 82 associations outside Cuba out of a total of 403 active ones (20.3 percent).[25]

In 2003, Cuba's investments abroad became even more important. Out of 360 active AECEs in mid-2003, 80 or about 22 percent were outside Cuba proper (figure 3.5). According to Havana's Centro de Promoción de

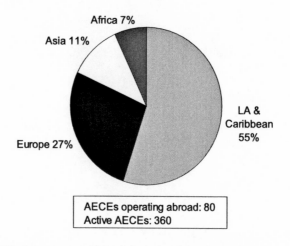

Figure 3.5. AECEs Operating Abroad by Geographical Area in 2003 (Percentage as of June 30).
Source: Centro de Promoción de Inversiones (CPI) 2003.

Inversiones (CPI), 55 percent of these associations (mostly joint ventures) operated in Latin America and the Caribbean, 27 percent in Europe, 11 percent in Asia, and 7 percent in Africa. The geographical distribution of AECEs is largely the result of Cuba's attempt to internationalize its enterprises and increase exports through a new global investment strategy that seeks "to establish companies in developing countries employing Cuban high technology, specialists, and know-how with native manpower."[26] The island specifically targeted neighboring markets in the Caribbean region. As observed by the CPI, Cuba maintains relations with all Caribbean countries and has established diplomatic missions in most of them "as an expression of the great interest the country gives to the strengthening of the relations with the Caribbean area" (CPI 2003).

Yet, more recent information shows that, with the exception of tourism activities in Mexico and China, Cuba's most important investment operations abroad have focused on biotechnology and pharmaceuticals joint venture projects in East Asia (China, Malaysia, and India), the Middle East (Iran), and Africa (Algeria and Namibia) (Pérez Villanueva 2006). Given the island's huge potential in these sectors,[27] the Castro government has begun to realize that investments overseas in knowledge-intensive industries and the penetration of new markets may generate good profits and provide alternative hard currency resources for the development of the Cuban economy. Washington's embargo does have an impact on Cuba's internationalization strategy not only because Cuban products cannot be exported to the United States but also because U.S.-based transnational corporations dominate the global pharmaceutical market and especially the higher-value first world markets. Even so, Havana's authorities are stepping up efforts to tap developing and emerging market countries where barriers to entry are relatively low and Cuban pharmaceutical and biotechnology products face less severe licensing and registration hurdles.

Cuba's Business Climate

Based on the number of joint enterprises and the available information on FDI flows, the results of foreign direct investment in Cuba in recent years have been disappointing. As previously observed, the total number of active international economic associations has declined by nearly 50 percent since 2002 as many joint ventures with foreign partners dissolved. The amount of foreign capital delivered to the country, at least until 2003, showed only a modest recovery from the sharp decline experienced two years earlier. Nevertheless, several new agreements with overseas companies were signed and some existing investors expanded their operations in the Cuban market. Moreover, official statistics on sales, exports, and profits of AECEs (discussed later in this chapter) suggest that the level of FDI activity in the country has grown.

A large number of AECEs, mainly formed in the first half of the 1990s, dissolved because of the termination of the regular contract between the Cuban state and the overseas investor. These are generally small- and midsize associations whose profits have been unsatisfactory, in part because of the lack of adequate financing. In fact, although changing priorities of the Cuban authorities toward foreign investment might have played a role in this development, it is not a secret that the Cuban partner in joint ventures is often unable to honor its payment commitments. Other AECEs dissolved because of the anticipated withdrawal of the foreign partner. The existing restrictions on the operations of enterprises, excessive bureaucratic practices, and failures to achieve the planned results seem to be

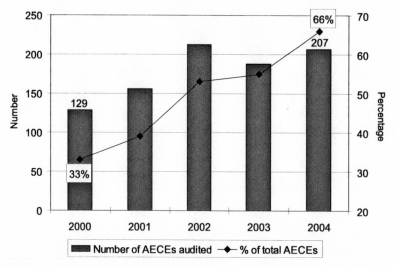

Figure 3.6. AECEs Audited, 2000–2004.
Source: Ministerio para la Inversión Extranjera y la Colaboración Económica (MINVEC) 2005.

the most common causes. Some Cuban scholars pointed out that Havana's deepening business ties with China and especially Venezuela were also a contributing factor (Pérez Villanueva 2006).

Considering the Castro government's increasing attention to the economic performance of businesses with foreign partners, it is conceivable that low levels of profits played a major role in the recent surge of the number of dissolved AECEs. As noted by a Cuban official, "We [Cuba] do not accept enterprises that operate with losses, except those joint ventures carrying out important social functions."[28] In the last few years, Havana's authorities have subjected not only each new joint venture proposal but also each existing joint venture to close scrutiny to verify whether satisfactory economic results and the state's original objectives for establishing the enterprise had been achieved. In 2001, Cuba created a special national commission (Comisión Nacional de Inspección a la Inversión Extranjera) specifically for this purpose (MINVEC 2002).

As shown in figure 3.6, the percentage of total AECEs that were audited by MINVEC's own audit committee, various territorial delegations, and the newly formed national commission doubled from 33 percent in 2000 to 66 percent in 2004, when the program of joint venture reviews involved

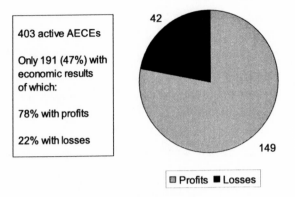

Figure 3.7. AECEs with Profits and Losses in 2002.
Source: Information provided by Ministerio para la Inversión Extranjera y la Colaboración Económica (MINVEC) June 2004.

more than two hundred enterprises. In particular, the Cuban government closely monitored the activities of joint ventures in sectors that have had a strong presence of foreign investment. In 2001, more than 50 percent of audits targeted AECEs in tourism, basic industry, and light industry, the sectors where the majority of dissolutions have occurred since 2002. It is reported that in 2005 Cuba's auditing agencies performed over three hundred inspections, more than the actual number of active AECEs (MINVEC 2006).

Information from Cuban official sources reveals the existence of many joint ventures with poor economic results and corroborates the thesis that the Castro government is indeed trying to consolidate foreign investment by getting rid of unprofitable businesses. As presented in figure 3.7, at the end of 2002 more than 50 percent of the 403 active AECEs in Cuba did not generate economic results in terms of profits and losses for several different reasons. For the most part, these associations were in the process of dissolution, waiting for additional documentation to begin operations, or performing an undefined social function. Additionally, of the 191 active associations (or 47 percent of the total) that generated economic results, 149 (78 percent) operated with profits and 42 (22 percent) with losses. In short, only 37 percent of total active AECEs yielded economic gains to Cuba in 2002 while about 10 percent ran at a loss. As the beginning of the process of dissolution for several AECEs was the result of shabby

performances, it is conceivable that the government took steps to eliminate unsuccessful enterprises. According to MINVEC, 75 percent of dissolved AECEs in 2005 either did not operate or had produced inefficient
results for more than a year, and failures to meet economic and social
targets had been the "fundamental" cause of dissolution (35 percent of
all cases) until then (MINVEC 2006). It should be emphasized that some
foreign firms are willing to operate with losses because the size of their
investment is relatively small and their main goal is to get a foothold in
the Cuban economy before the lifting of the U.S. embargo.

Cuban authorities blamed the "world economic crisis," the American
embargo, and the deteriorating relationship with the European Union for
the drop of FDI flows after September 11, 2001, although they specified
that such a decline mirrored a general tendency throughout Latin America and the Caribbean (MINVEC 2004). However, some foreign investors
argued that the situation was much worse in Cuba because of its business
climate. According to a European businessman, "They [Cubans] insist you
be partner with a state-run company, that you hire workers at high rates
through government-run labor agencies and then you run-up against the
bureaucracy and the U.S. embargo and threats to boot."[29] Canada's Pebercan noted in its information report of 2005 that investment operations in
Cuba "could also be affected to various extents by factors such as government regulation of production, price controls, export controls, income
tax, expropriation, environmental legislation, land improvements, water
use, local land claims, and security."[30]

In July 2002, the European Union embassies in Havana released a document that included business complaints and suggestions about Cuba's
foreign investment regime.[31] The document specified that it was essential
for European investors to have greater judicial security and a stable, trans-
parent, and reliable legal framework in order to avoid the discriminatory
application of business laws against overseas firms. In fact, a major source
of concern among foreign companies is that their partner on the Cuban
side will invariably be the Cuban state, which makes both laws and policies and interprets them according to its needs and interests. Additional
complaints included excessive utility costs due to the state monopoly on
services, delays in payments, a repeated need to renew visas and work
permits, and expensive dollar payments to a state employment agency

for the wages of Cuban workers (while the agency pays those workers in Cuban pesos).[32] Soon after the release of the document, Marta Lomas met separately with diplomats and businessmen from each European country to discuss their complaints. While offering assurance that Cuba would work harder to unravel its complicated bureaucracy, Lomas made it clear that the country was not considering changing the rules of the game and that foreign investors knew those rules when they arrived (Spadoni 2004, 126).

Rather than taking steps to make its business environment more flexible, Cuba moved in the opposite direction. Resolution 65, enacted in July 2003, marked the beginning of a process of re-centralization and de-dollarization of the Cuban economy. It substituted the use of the U.S. dollar for the convertible peso or CUC (a local currency that was pegged at par with the dollar since its introduction in 1994 but has no value outside the country) in the transactions of state enterprises and required them to obtain Central Bank authorization for all hard currency expenditures above $5,000. Such limit was later increased to $10,000. Although AECEs were exempted from these measures, several foreign investors complained about their ability to do business with and collect payments from state companies as the latter were now forced to hand over their dollars to the Central Bank and buy them back for imports, debt payments, and local purchases from joint ventures.[33] Moreover, Havana's government tightened controls over domestic and overseas accounts of Cuban entities and dollar accounts of foreigners (Mesa-Lago 2005, 26), reduced the number of Cuban agencies responsible for imports of a selected group of products (through the creation of purchasing committees or *comités de compras*), and established a fixed 10 percent markup price over the cost of production in the transactions between state firms (Triana Cordoví 2004).

More recently, Cuban authorities have begun to reassert central control over the tourism industry, Cuba's most dynamic economic sector during the 1990s and a key generator of hard currency. Unhappy about the loose spending and corruption that have limited profits, in late 2003 Cuban authorities fired several top executives from the island's largest tourism group, Cubanacan. Early in 2004, they replaced the tourism minister, Ibrahim Ferradaz, with Manuel Marrero Cruz, who at the time of his designation was heading the army-controlled Gaviota tourism group. Foreign media revealed that these moves were part of a plan to merge most, if not all, activities of four major state-owned corporations (Cubanacan, Gran Caribe, Horizontes Hoteles, and Isla Azul) that controlled 75 percent of the hotel rooms on the island.[34] The merging plan was reportedly completed in the second half of 2004 along with the centralization of retail stores, transportation, and car-rental services for tourists.[35]

In November 2004, the Castro government eliminated the commercial circulation of the U.S. dollar in Cuba in favor of the CUC and, a month later, ordered state enterprises to deposit all hard currency income (CUCs and other foreign currencies) into a single account at the Cuban Central Bank, then request bank permission to use the money. The Cuban convertible peso was revalued by 8 percent against all foreign currencies, including the U.S. dollar, in April 2005. There is no doubt that Cuba's shift toward a gradual but constant re-centralization of its economy and its increasingly regulated business environment caused serious concerns among existing and potential foreign investors.

In his speech of July 26, 2007 on the fifty-fourth anniversary of the beginning of the Cuban Revolution, Raúl Castro said he was prepared to stimulate foreign investment in Cuba "upon well-defined legal bases which preserve the role of the State and the predominance of socialist property." He added that doing so would allow the country to "recover domestic industrial production and begin producing new products that eliminate the need for imports or create new possibilities for export."[36] Indeed, MINVEC revealed that 27 percent of all projects in the negotiation stage at the end of 2007 were linked to import substitution initiatives in the areas of tourism, basic industry, construction, and agriculture. Furthermore, it stated that only 24 percent of total projects involved prioritized countries like Venezuela, China, and Brazil (MINVEC 2008), suggesting perhaps that Havana intends to revive and diversify business relations that have suffered because of Cuba's almost exclusive attention to Venezuela.

Facing a declining output of virtually all staple crops and unprecedented levels of food imports whose prices are soaring in the international market,[37] Cuban authorities have called for more foreign investment in agriculture. Marta Lomas stated in April 2008 that Cuba was seeking new economic associations with foreign firms in agriculture and livestock, especially for the production of rice.[38] One month later, however, the president of the National Association of Small Farmers (ANAP), Orlando Lugo Fonte, acknowledged that Cuba had consulted Chinese and Vietnamese experts on how to increase its domestic rice output, but he emphasized that the government had no immediate plans to promote FDI in the agricultural sector.[39] Several recent proposals from overseas companies to establish joint ventures on the island for the production of soybeans, grains, and cereals have yet to translate into actual deals. Raúl Castro's speech of July 26, 2008 made no mention of expanding foreign investment in agriculture and simply praised oil and petrochemical projects developed with Venezuela.[40]

Since Raúl Castro assumed power in July 2006, one of the few policy changes that directly involved foreign firms in Cuba has been Havana's decision in late 2007 to allow foreign firms to pay hard currency bonuses to their Cuban employees (generally a few hundred convertible pesos per month or dollars before November 2004) in addition to their regular peso salaries. Resolution 277 of December 13, 2007 established that foreign companies must keep records of these bonuses and Cuban employees must file annual income tax returns and pay taxes on that income (not on their regular peso salaries). Cuba's move, which legalizes widespread practices already taking place "under the table," was presented by Marta Lomas as a way to "normalize relations between foreign investors and Cuba" and thus improve the island's business environment.[41] Although many Cuban workers described it as just another government attempt to squeeze their revenues, the move was welcomed by most foreign businessmen not only because it makes their lives easier but also because it signals the acceptance on the part of the government that some Cubans can earn more than others. What very few foreign observers have noticed is that Resolution 277 applies only to branch and representative offices of overseas companies, embassies, and international organizations, not to joint ventures.[42] Joint ventures are still prohibited from paying unregulated hard currency bonuses to their workers, even though relatively small incentive payments in convertible pesos are commonly made (Travieso-

Díaz and Trumbull 2002, 195).[43] The Cuban workforce of joint ventures is also much larger than that of foreign companies falling under Resolution 277.

In early March 2009, as part of a wide cabinet reshuffle aimed at streamlining government administration and allegedly improving the socialist economic system, Raúl Castro merged the Ministry of Foreign Investment and the Ministry of Foreign Trade to form a new ministry headed by Rodrigo Malmierca.[44] Along with the selection of Malmierca, who was previously the permanent representative of Cuba to the United Nations, Castro appointed a number of trusted military officers to key cabinet positions, removed two of the most senior younger officials (Vice-President Carlos Lage and Foreign Minister Felipe Pérez Roque), and reinforced the involvement of the Cuban armed forces (Fuerzas Armadas Revolucionarias or FAR) in the economy. During the 1990s, when it was no longer engaged in military missions in Africa and Central America, a heavily downsized FAR took an unprecedented role in running the island's economy and gained a reputation for innovation and efficiency. It began by enhancing the performance of its own firms with the incorporation of certain market mechanisms and then exported its organizational model to civilian enterprises.[45] Today, the Cuban armed forces have a significant presence in many economic areas, including tourism, civil aviation, agriculture and cattle, import-export services, hard currency retail activities, real estate, and construction (Mora 2004, 6–13).

In search of more military-style efficiency, the Cuban government is promoting a major expansion of the process of business management known as *perfeccionamiento empresarial* (perfecting the state company system), first adopted by the armed forces in 1988.[46] This business model has no exact analogy either in capitalist economies or in socialist ones. It is based on the adoption of modern management and accounting practices, the promotion of greater decision-making autonomy for local managers, and the payment of wages more closely tied to productivity (Peters 2001a, 2). Decree-Law 252, signed by Raúl Castro in August 2007, ordered some 2,700 Cuban state firms to adopt *perfeccionamiento*, but less than one-third had been able to do it by the end of 2008 as the process hinges on further improvements in work organization, accounting, internal controls, costs, prices, and payment systems.[47]

It is clear that *perfeccionamiento* by itself will not solve efficiency problems and that a substantial restructuring of the Cuban financial system is needed. In a modest sign of decentralization, Cuba's new banking rules enacted in July 2009 eliminated the requirement for state enterprises to obtain Central Bank approval for hard currency expenditures in excess of $10,000, turned over management of such transactions to government ministries, and authorized the release of some funds in foreign business accounts that had been kept frozen since January 2009 due to mounting liquidity problems.[48] Foreign companies have expressed satisfaction with the banking changes since the latter make deal negotiations easier and streamline payment procedures. But the island's financial system remains overly centralized as the Central Bank still maintains a single account for hard currency deposits of state firms and exercises full control over the allotment of those resources.

In summary, the flow of foreign direct investment into Cuba is greatly inhibited by the island's rigorous evaluation procedures, its increasing selectiveness toward FDI projects, and its heavily regulated business environment. Although Cuban authorities have continued to encourage foreign companies to discuss the formation of joint ventures (and important agreements were recently signed with Venezuelan firms and a few other ones), many potential investors either withdraw during the process of negotiations because the terms offered by the Cuban partner are not sufficiently attractive or opt for lower levels of cooperation (EIU 2004). Overall, it can be expected that some major investors will continue to expand their operations in Cuba and receive substantial concessions from the Castro government given the latter's preference for well-established businesses and partners and for projects involving large amounts of foreign capital. It is also evident that Cuba wants to stimulate foreign investment without transgressing the limits beyond which the control of the fundamental wealth of the nation might be jeopardized (Pérez Villanueva 2004, 194). However, apart from projects with Venezuela, a significant long-term upward trend in the flow of FDI from European, Canadian, and other firms will occur only if Cuba promotes a gradual decentralization of its state-dominated economy by introducing profound internal reforms and taking steps to relax existing regulations on the activities of joint ventures and state enterprises.

Other Forms of Investment

Cuba's increased selectivity toward foreign direct investment and its preference for large projects have led to a substantial reduction of small- and
mid-size joint ventures on the island. Yet, at least until the launch in
mid-2003 of a re-centralization process, smaller businesses had been actively promoted through different mechanisms such as cooperative production agreements, which were regulated by Cuba's Executive Committee of the Council of Ministers on December 6, 2000 (Agreement N.3827).
As with joint ventures, the government said the objectives of these agreements are to obtain capital, new technology, and know-how, substitute
imports, and gain access to markets. Furthermore, in addition to the sizable number of management contracts in the tourism sector (promoted
since the opening to foreign investment in the early 1990s), Cuban authorities have encouraged administration contracts with foreign partners
in industrial sectors. This demonstrates that the search for technology and
markets is accompanied by a growing awareness of the value of management expertise.

Cooperative production was conceived as an effective way to solve
three major complaints raised by foreign investors in Cuba: the length
of negotiations, excessive bureaucracy, and high labor costs. Initially, the
approval of a cooperative production agreement was much simpler and
faster (between one and three months) than that of an international economic association, and the documentation required was less rigorous.[49]
While the latter must be authorized by the Executive Committee of the
Council of Ministers or by a government commission designated for that
purpose, the former was simply approved by the ministry of the Cuban
entity. But in 2005 Cuban authorities ruled that cooperative agreements
must be approved by the central government like AECEs. They also established that foreign companies involved in these kinds of investments
could no longer perform import and export activities independently from
the Cuban government.

Cooperative production agreements can take many forms. For instance, instead of purchasing equity, a foreign investor can provide capital
and sell on credit raw material, technology, and know-how to its Cuban
partner in exchange for a fixed sum per product produced (royalty), or

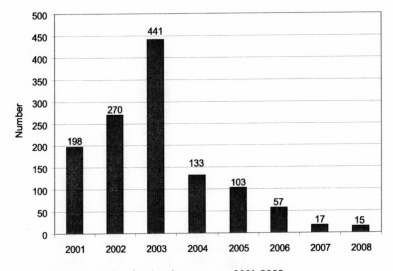

Figure 3.8. Cooperative Production Agreements, 2001–2008.
Source: Ministerio para la Inversión Extranjera y la Colaboración Económica (MINVEC) 2009 and previous years.

buy the finished product outright for export. These agreements are not too different from international economic association contracts regulated by Law 77. The main novelty of a cooperative production contract is that the state employment agency does not receive hard currency payments for the workers' labor, and the foreign partner pays no taxes because the enterprise remains 100 percent Cuban. With foreign companies able to avoid paying for labor in dollars, business operations contemplated by these agreements have been characterized by some investors as a sort of "maquila" in the style of U.S. assembly plants on the Mexican border.[50] Albeit uncommon, a foreign firm can engage in both a cooperative production contract and an administration contract, thus having the control of an enterprise and a share of its revenues.

In some cases, a cooperative production might represent the first step toward the creation of an international economic association. This is a way for the Cuban government to test the seriousness of a foreign company and its capacity to provide new markets and technological assistance. It is also a necessary process to increase the efficiency of existing installations and facilities. As noted by Jesus Pérez Othón, Cuba's former minister of light industry, "Sometimes you have 90% of the equipment, but without that vital 10% you can't make a new product that will succeed in the world market."[51]

Following Agreement N.3827 of December 2000, in 2001 the Cuban Ministry of Foreign Investment passed Resolution N.37, which regulates the process of registration, control, and supervision of cooperative production agreements in Cuba. The number of these agreements increased from 198 in 2001 to 270 in 2002, and peaked at 441 at the end of 2003 (figure 3.8). In 2003, 171 cooperative production contracts were approved, thus demonstrating the willingness of small- and mid-size companies to take advantage of new modalities of doing business on the communist island. But Cuban official sources indicate that the number of these contracts with foreign firms has dropped dramatically since then. Only 15 cooperative production agreements remained in operation in Cuba at the close of 2008, a decline of about 96 percent from 2003 (MINVEC 2009). They were mostly linked to construction and basic industry, mainly with companies from Spain. For some foreign analysts, this development signals the Castro government's intention to drive out small investors that contribute little to the island's economy and corrupt local entrepreneurs by introducing such practices as commissions and kickbacks.[52]

Similar to the experience of AECEs, the beginning of the downward trend in the number of cooperative production contracts coincided with Fidel Castro's decision to reassert state control over the island's economy and promote what Minister Lomas called the "restructuring" of foreign investment in Cuba. However, unlike most dissolved AECEs, all cooperative productions that broke up after 2003 had been authorized just a few years earlier. In such a short period of time, it is unlikely that economic results played a major role in the dissolution of so many businesses. A little known fact might help explain what really happened. Statistics of the Ministry of Foreign Investment show that 277 or 62 percent of the 446 cooperative production agreements registered in Cuba at the end of March 2004 had yet to begin operations.[53] The most likely scenario is that the vast majority of the 308 agreements that dissolved in 2004 never went into effect, and the fate of the others was decided by then. In other words, the search for profitability and efficiency was an important factor in Cuba's decision to get rid of many joint ventures with foreign partners while keeping its doors open to this form of investment. The elimination

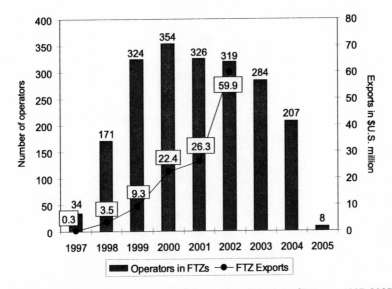

Figure 3.9. Free Trade Zones: Number of Operators and Value of Exports, 1997–2005. *Source*: Calculations of the author from Ministerio para la Inversión Extranjera y la Colaboración Económica (MINVEC) 2006 and previous years; Pérez Villanueva 2004, 192.

of almost all cooperative production agreements was the result of a fundamental policy change toward this particular business model that had less to do with an appraisal of economic performances.

Besides the massive removal of cooperative productions with overseas partners, foreign investment in Cuba's free trade zones (FTZs) was virtually halted by Cuban authorities in 2003. Decree-Law 165 of 1996 authorized the establishment of industrial parks and FTZs in Cuba and granted a number of tax and operational incentives to companies making investments in these areas. Between May and November 1997, three FTZs were inaugurated: Wajay and Berroa in Havana, and Mariel, located about thirty-six miles west of Havana on the northern coast.

The creation of free trade zones in Cuba aimed to foster the island's economic and social development by attracting foreign investment, stimulating and diversifying export activities (even though up to 25 percent of FTZ output could be sold domestically with prior approval of the Cuban government), generating new jobs, and developing new domestic industries through the assimilation of foreign technology and expertise. In effect, as shown in figure 3.9, the number of operators (local and foreign firms) in Cuba's free trade zones increased from 34 in 1997 to 354 in 2000. These companies were mostly engaged in commercial activities and, to a lesser extent, in services and manufacturing. But the number of operators has been declining since 2000 as Cuban authorities have stepped up control over businesses in FTZs. It is reported that Cuban officials investigated 111 operators in 2001 and revoked licenses to about 90 percent of them, mainly because of poor economic results, violations of established rules for the movement of goods, and delays in the recruitment of Cuban workers (MINVEC 2002). In 2003, no authorizations were granted for new activities in FTZs and 35 firms had their licenses revoked. By the end of that year, only 284 operators remained in Cuba's free trade zones (MINVEC 2004).

Cuba's experience with foreign investment in free trade zones has been unsuccessful. The total value of exports from FTZs grew from $300,000 in 1997 to almost $60 million in 2002, but the obtained results were far from meeting expectations (Pérez Villanueva 2004, 192). Additionally, Cuba was unable to attract major international companies in its FTZs, the amount of invested capital was relatively small and limited to low-technology sectors with little economic impact, and only a minor percentage of operators performed manufacturing activities (Marquetti Nodarse 2004). Some scholars argued that free trade zones failed because of Cuba's labor code, which prevents foreign firms from choosing their own workers and deprives workers of most of their salaries (Willmore 2000). It was therefore no surprise when the Castro government announced in 2004 that it would stop promoting the development of FTZs on the island and give existing operators a period of three years to find other business options in Cuba. By the end of 2005, only eight operators remained in Cuba's FTZs, and they were about to leave (MINVEC 2006).

Economic Results of FDI in Cuba

The main indicators of international economic associations have shown steady improvement since the opening to foreign investment in the early 1990s. Whatever the actual effects of the Helms-Burton law on the operations of foreign firms in Cuba and its power to deter or limit FDI flows to the island, the growing contribution of foreign investment to the overall

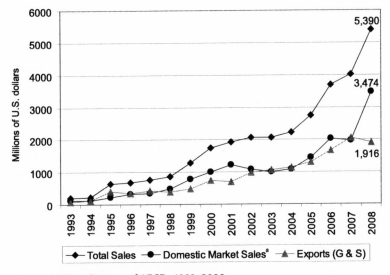

Figure 3.10. Main Indicators of AECEs, 1993–2008.
Source: Pérez Villanueva 2009.
Note: a. Calculations of the author.

performance of Cuba's key export sectors and other industries geared toward the domestic market clearly undermined the main goal of the U.S. legislation. This development also appears to confirm that Cuban authorities have been concentrating over the years on investments with positive economic results.

As shown in figure 3.10, total sales of international economic associations increased from $200 million in 1993 to about $5.4 billion in 2008. During the same period, exports of goods and services generated by AECEs rose from approximately $90 million to $1.9 billion, and domestic market sales from $113 million to nearly $3.5 billion. The Cuban Ministry of Foreign Investment also reports that direct income from international associations peaked at almost $1.1 billion in 2008 (MINVEC 2009). In June 2007, Minister Marta Lomas confirmed that even with fewer companies there was an increase in exports, domestic sales, and profits. She added that FDI operations in Cuba accounted for 8 percent of the country's GDP and had become more efficient over the years.[54]

In effect, Cuban official statistics suggest that both workers' productivity and the overall efficiency of international economic associations have improved. As displayed in figure 3.11, workers' productivity in AECEs

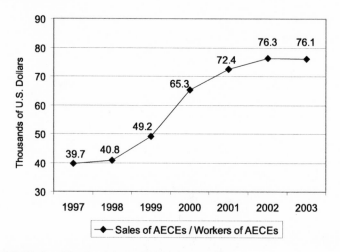

Figure 3.11. Workers' Productivity in AECEs, 1997–2003.
Source: Calculations of the author from Ministerio para la Inversión Extranjera y la Colaboración Económica (MINVEC) 2004 and Oficina Nacional de Estadísticas (ONE) 2004.

almost doubled between 1997 and 2003.[55] During this period, the number of workers increased by 42 percent from 19,200 to 27,200 whereas total sales of AECEs grew 270 percent from $762 million to about $2,070 million. It should be emphasized that 90 percent of all Cuban workers of joint ventures received small bonuses in hard currency at the end of 2002.[56] This shows the importance of incentive payments to stimulate productivity. Furthermore, MINVEC reports that the average annual growth of net profits of AECEs during 2001–2007 was 31.6 percent as compared to a 14.4 percent growth of total sales (table 3.2), which indicates a trend toward higher efficiency.

An analysis of FDI results in Cuba simply based on the number of active AECEs and the flow of foreign capital can be misleading. A small number of joint ventures have a large economic impact as many projects with foreign partners remain relatively small. A Cuban scholar revealed that seven mixed enterprises in the areas of nickel, tobacco, citrus, sugar, rum, tourism, and telecommunications accounted for more than 80 percent of total sales of AECEs in 2007 (Pérez Villanueva 2008). And only five major joint ventures, Moa Níquel S.A., Corporación Habanos, Havana Club Internacional, Compañía Azucarera Internacional, and ETECSA,

Table 3.2. Main Indicators of AECEs, 2001–2007 (Annual Average Growth)

Indicator	Growth
Total Sales	14.4%
Exports	19.9%
Net Profits	31.6%
Dividends	32.4%

Source: Ministerio para la Inversión Extranjera y la Colaboración Económica (MINVEC) 2008.

accounted for the vast majority of all exports of goods and services of AECEs that year.

Moa Níquel S.A., which was formed in 1994, is a joint venture between Cuba's Unión del Níquel and Canada's Sherritt International. Corporación Habanos is a cigar distribution joint venture signed in late 1999 and 50 percent owned by the Spanish-French conglomerate Altadis. Havana Club Internacional is a rum distribution joint venture of 1993 between Cuba Ron S.A. and the French company Pernod Ricard. Compañía Azucarera Internacional is a joint venture of 2001 between Cubazucar and an unknown foreign partner (allegedly the Paris-registered Pacol S.A., a firm connected to the British sugar trader ED and F Man) for the commercialization of Cuban sugar in the world market.[57] And ETECSA is a telecoms joint venture of 1994 in which the Italy-based Telecom Italia (through its subsidiary STET International) has a 27 percent interest. The majority of ETECSA's revenues come from dollar charges applied to incoming international calls, which are considered as exports of telecommunications services. In short, the increasing number of dissolutions of international economic associations will have little negative effect on the overall economic performance of FDI in Cuba as long as the big players continue to operate and invest in the communist island.

Cuba's reiterated claims that incoming foreign direct investment is not crucial (only complementary) to the economic development of the country appear questionable. For instance, as reported in figure 3.12, the share of export revenues generated through AECEs in Cuba's total value of exports of goods and services has increased significantly since the early 1990s. In 2002, AECEs accounted for more than 25 percent of the country's total dollar revenues from all sources. If we consider that

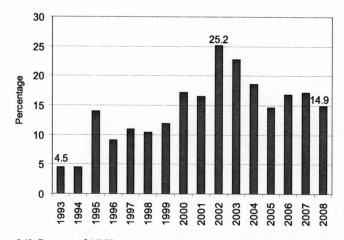

Figure 3.12. Exports of AECEs as Percentage of Cuba's Total Exports of Goods and Services, 1993–2008.
Source: Calculations of the author from Ministerio para la Inversión Extranjera y la Colaboración Económica (MINVEC) 2009 and previous years and Oficina Nacional de Estadísticas (ONE) 2008a, 2009.

FDI in Cuba between 1993 and 2002 represented just 8.2 percent of the gross fixed capital formation (Pérez Villanueva 2004, 173),[58] then the performance of enterprises with foreign participation appears remarkable. While exports of AECEs have continued to grow after 2002, their share in the country's total has dropped (14.9 percent in 2008) only because of Cuba's booming revenues from exports of medical and other professional services under special agreements with Venezuela.

It should also be stressed that export revenues generated by AECEs are derived to a great extent from products rather than services. The latter may include the sales of joint ventures in the tourism sector (where hard currency revenues are mostly linked to management contracts rather than AECEs) and international calls in telecommunications. Today, exports of goods are certainly less vital to the Cuban economy than they were during the 1980s, but they are still a precious source of hard currency for the country. In 2007, about 75 percent of export revenues of AECEs came from goods (MINVEC 2008), representing nearly 42 percent of Cuba's revenues from all merchandise exports.[59] The importance of FDI in Cuba's total earnings from goods is therefore undeniable.

Other indicators shed light on the role of FDI in the Cuban economy. By the end of 1997, joint ventures with foreign capital already accounted for the following shares of economic activity: 100 percent of oil exploration; 100 percent of metallic mining; 100 percent of the production of lubricants; 100 percent of the production of soap, perfumes, personal hygiene products, and industrial cleaners; 100 percent of telephone services (wire line and cellular); 100 percent of the export of rum; 70 percent of the production of citrus fruits, juices, and concentrates; 50 percent of the production of nickel; 50 percent of the production of cement; 10 percent of all rooms for international tourism and an additional 39 percent under administration contracts with foreign firms (Pérez Villanueva 1999, 119).

Since 1997, the importance of foreign investment has grown. In the oil sector, Cuban authorities announced that overseas companies had invested around $1.2 billion by 2004.[60] Foreign capital helped Cuba raise crude oil and natural gas production from 0.7 million tons in 1990 to 4.1 million tons in 2007. This is around half of the island's annual oil consumption (EIU 2008a). Two Canadian firms, Sherritt International (52 percent) and Pebercan (13 percent), produced approximately 65 percent of Cuba's total national oil output in 2007.[61] Crude oil extracted through exploration activities with foreign firms (along with the introduction of top-level technologies) has enabled the Cuban government to increase domestic production of electricity. For example, the Energas plant constructed with Sherritt in the province of Matanzas in 2000 uses the natural gas released during oil extraction for producing electricity and naphtha. Today, nearly 100 percent of the country's electricity is generated with domestic crude. The latter also fuels nickel activities and virtually the entire production of cement in Cuba (Torres Martínez and Torres Pérez 2006).

In the nickel sector, the impact of FDI over production has been significant. Total foreign investment in nickel amounted to over $400 million, increasing production from 26,900 tons in 1994 to 75,600 tons in 2007. Cuba's nickel output more than doubled between 1994 and 1998 as Sherritt International began to expand and modernize one of Cuba's three nickel-processing plants in the province of Holguín. The Pedro Soto Alba plant, operated by Sherritt, produced 31,392 tons of nickel in 2007 or 41 percent of the island's total production.[62] Nickel is today Cuba's most important

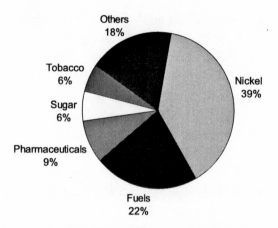

Figure 3.13. Cuba's Total Exports of Goods by Product in 2008 (Percentage Distribution).
Source: Estimates by Pérez Villanueva 2009 based on figures of Ministerio del Comercio Exterior (MINCEX).

export product, with revenues peaking at about $2 billion in 2007 before a sharp drop in 2008 due to falling nickel prices in the international market.

In tourism, there were 22,705 rooms under management contracts with 14 foreign hotel chains at the end of 2007, representing about 51 percent of the 44,800 available hotel rooms in Cuba. Rooms under joint ventures accounted for 12 percent of the total (Pérez Villanueva and Vidal Alejandro 2008). One company, Spain's Sol Meliá, manages nearly one-fourth of all of the hotel rooms on the island. Finally, foreign participation has a substantial influence over the production or marketing of Cuba's largest export products (in terms of gross hard currency revenues) such as sugar, nickel, tobacco, rum, fishing, and pharmaceuticals.[63] These goods accounted for more than 30 percent of Cuba's total hard currency revenues from all sources in 2004 and almost 25 percent in 2007 despite thriving exports of professional services.[64]

In 2008, as illustrated in figure 3.13, nickel was still Cuba's top hard currency earner among products, accounting for 39 percent of total revenues. Pharmaceuticals (9 percent), sugar (6 percent), and tobacco (6 percent) also had a significant presence. The main novelty was the emergence of fuel exports as the second largest source of foreign exchange income after nickel, generating approximately 22 percent (worth a little more than

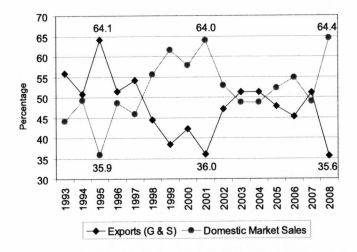

Figure 3.14. Exports of Goods and Services (G&S) and Domestic Market Sales of AECEs as Percentage of Total Sales of AECEs, 1993–2008. *Source*: Author's estimates from Ministerio para la Inversión Extranjera y la Colaboración Económica (MINVEC) 2009 and previous years.

$800 million) of Cuba's total revenues from exports of goods in 2008. This was primarily the result of the reopening in December 2007 of the Cienfuegos oil refinery, a joint venture between the state-run Petróleos de Venezuela S.A. (PDVSA) and Cuba Petróleo (CUPET). The refinery produces fuel oil, diesel, jet fuel, and gasoline for the domestic market and export to Caribbean and Central American countries. Although higher fuel prices in the international market helped boost Cuba's export revenues, data from the government's statistics office show that the Cienfuegos plant made a substantial contribution to national refining output in 2008 as the latter nearly doubled from 2007.[65] In any case, scholars and independent analysts have claimed for years that Havana resells on the open market a sizable share of the oil it acquires from Venezuela on preferential terms. This thesis is supported by the fact that Cuba receives far more oil from Venezuela than is domestically consumed, which allows the Castro government to reexport surpluses to accrue foreign exchange income (Corrales 2006).

Foreign investment has not only helped Cuba find new markets for its main products but has also increased the competitiveness of Cuban production and, therefore, the contribution of import substitution to overall economic expansion. If we analyze sales of international economic associations (figure 3.14), we can see that the share of exports dropped substantially in the second half of the 1990s as the domestic market gained importance. While in 1995 exports represented almost two-thirds of the sales of AECEs, in 2001 they had dropped to around 36 percent. In contrast, sales in the domestic market grew steadily during this period, accounting for 64 percent of total sales in 2001. Between 2002 and 2007, the share of exports somewhat recovered mainly as a result of higher revenues from nickel exports[66] and, to a lower extent, the creation of Compañía Azucarera Internacional in 2001 and its sugar activities. Nonetheless, domestic market sales still accounted for almost half of total sales of AECEs in 2007 and their share peaked at 64.4 percent in 2008. Of course, we are left without knowing the composition of these sales and their impact on import substitution. Even so, if AECEs sold in the domestic market goods and services worth more than $16 billion between 1993 and 2008, it is conceivable that such an impact has not been negligible.

By 2001, the use of domestic oil and gas to fuel electric power generation, cement, and nickel output had an import substitution effect greater than $450 million per year (Pérez Villanueva 2004, 183). Regarding only electric power, Vice President Carlos Lage noted in late 2007 that if Cuba had imported oil to generate the electricity annually produced with natural gas captured from domestic crude, then it would have cost the country between $400 and $500 million.[67] Moreover, the share of domestically produced goods provided to the tourism industry increased from 12 percent in 1990 to 72 percent in 2006. In the early 1990s, practically all products for hotels and restaurants had to be imported. The development of mixed enterprises in tourism has stimulated the formation of new joint ventures in other sectors (in particular food industry, agriculture, and services) to supply them at low cost.[68] Finally, the share of domestic goods sold to the network of hard currency stores on the island reached 53.1 percent in 2002 and was consistently over 40 percent in 2003–2007,[69] mainly because of foreign direct investment and, to a much lesser degree, cooperative production agreements in food processing and light manufacturing.

Conclusion

Although Cuban authorities argue that foreign investment in Cuba is consolidating, available figures on the number of international economic associations (mostly joint ventures) show disappointing results. Active AECEs dropped from 403 in 2002 to 211 at the end of 2008. If we include dissolved cooperative production agreements and firms in free trade zones that ceased to operate, Cuba lost more than nine hundred enterprises with foreign participation in just six years. While fluctuating over time, the amount of foreign direct investment delivered to the country remained depressed from 2000 until at least 2003. Since then, some existing investors have expanded their operations and new projects with overseas companies, for the most part from Venezuela, have likely pushed FDI flows upward. Yet, there is little chance that FDI from other countries will pick up considerably without market-liberalizing reforms and eased restrictions on the activities of joint ventures and state entities.

The current situation of foreign investment in Cuba is largely the result of Havana's increasing selectiveness toward FDI deals, its focus on major projects that involve large amounts of capital invested, and its almost exclusive attention to Venezuela. Cuba's heavily regulated business environment is an additional factor. Proposed investments are strictly examined in order to assess their contribution to the island's economy in terms of capital, technology, markets, and management expertise. Cuban authorities have also stepped up scrutiny of existing joint ventures in an attempt to eliminate unprofitable enterprises. Meanwhile, foreign investors keep complaining about unnecessary bureaucratic hurdles, discriminatory treatment, excessive costs, and payment delays. To further complicate things, Fidel Castro's moves toward economic re-centralization during 2003–2006 and his decision to establish foreign exchange controls for state-run enterprises lowered confidence among foreign companies about their ability to effectively operate on the island and collect payments from the Cuban government. Since assuming power in July 2006, and despite his early calls for more foreign investment, Raúl Castro has done very little to improve Cuba's business environment.

There are nonetheless positive aspects that should be emphasized. The main indicators of international economic associations have shown constant progress since the opening to foreign investment in the early 1990s, supporting Cuba's claims that the government has concentrated on businesses with good results. A major contention of this chapter is that FDI plays a significant role in the Cuban economy, certainly bigger than the Castro government is willing to admit. Moreover, even if the Helms-Burton law might have slowed the flow of FDI into the island, a sizable number of transnational corporations not based in the United States entered the Cuban market and weakened U.S. efforts in the post–cold war era to intensify economic pressure on Cuba and accelerate the fall of the Castro regime. Foreign investment helped Cuba find new markets for its main products, increased the competitiveness of Cuban production, and stimulated import substitution. Foreign participation is particularly strong in all of the industries that have experienced the highest growth over the past two decades, namely oil, electricity generation, nickel, telecommunications, and tourism. Overseas firms have a substantial influence over the production or marketing of Cuba's largest export sectors. Finally, joint ventures with foreign partners boosted domestic supply to the tourism industry and to the increasingly important internal market in hard currency.

The Impact of the Helms-Burton Law on Foreign Investment in Cuba

The previous chapter offered a comprehensive analysis of foreign investment in Cuba to shed light on the evolution of FDI and the main features of the island's business environment. It also demonstrated the decisive role of the Castro government in influencing FDI trends and the benefits for the Cuban economy of FDI projects with transnational corporations based outside the United States. These elements must be taken into account when assessing the failures and successes of the Helms-Burton law.

This chapter utilizes interviews with Cuban economists and foreign correspondents, official statistics and documents, and a number of secondary sources to illustrate how the United States has implemented Helms-Burton and evaluate the effectiveness of the legislation. Interviews with corporate leaders might have offered useful insights about the problems raised by Helms-Burton's penalizing provisions, but foreign investors in Cuba tend to be extremely wary and reluctant to share their experiences. The analysis gives special attention to the sizable number of existing foreign investors on the island that have been targeted by the U.S. law. After all, the U.S. government mostly targeted (with repeated threats and the imposition of sanctions in some cases) foreign companies with major business activities in Cuba in an attempt to produce a serious negative impact on the Cuban economy. It is therefore crucial to examine how U.S. pressures on these companies played out and, to the extent possible, isolate the factors that undermined the Cuban economy in the post–cold war era (discussed in chapter 3) from the specific impact of Helms-Burton. Figures on authorizations and dissolutions of joint ventures and the flow of FDI before and after the enactment of Helms-Burton are also discussed.

Some information on potential investors and their plans is provided even though it is extremely difficult to establish accurately how many foreign companies stayed out of Cuba and how much FDI was lost because of Helms-Burton. Furthermore, albeit for different reasons, both the U.S. and Cuban governments might have an incentive to overstate the impact of the law, the former to make the case that its policy is working and the latter to blame Washington for its economic failures. As for prospective investors who did not pursue their business plans in Cuba, they have little interest in publicizing the decision in order to avoid jeopardizing their future chances to resume those plans.

A Brief Analysis of Helms-Burton's Provisions

Titles III and IV of the Helms-Burton law of March 12, 1996 aim at discouraging FDI in Cuba through the threat of extraterritorial sanctions. Title III enables Americans, and Cubans who later became U.S. citizens, to bring lawsuits in U.S. courts against foreign firms and individuals who "traffic" in properties confiscated from them by the Castro government. Title IV empowers U.S. authorities to bar entry into the United States to senior officials of those firms and their immediate family members, such as spouses and any dependent children.

To make it more difficult for foreign companies to evade Helms-Burton's reach, the authors of the legislation consciously left a margin of uncertainty in the interpretation of trafficking. This is broadly defined and includes selling, leasing, managing, and purchasing expropriated properties. It also includes the use of trademarks or licenses claimed by U.S. firms. In short, "almost any commercial activity in Cuba can in principle be considered 'trafficking' and could be affected by the implementation of Helms-Burton" (Roy 2000, 64).

For the first two years after the enactment of the law, only claims that had been certified by the U.S. Foreign Claims Settlement Commission

Table 4.1. Ten Largest Certified U.S. Property Claims against Cuba ($U.S. Millions)

Company	Certified Claim (as of July 1972)
Cuban Electric Company	267.6
International Telephone and Telegraph Corp. (ITT)	130.7
North American Sugar Industries Inc.	97.4
Moa Bay Mining Company	88.3
United Fruit Sugar Company	85.1
West Indies Sugar Company	84.9
American Sugar Company	81.0
Standard Oil Company (now Exxon)	71.6
Francisco Sugar Company	52.6
Starwood Hotels and Resorts Worldwide[a]	51.1

Source: Foreign Claims Settlement Commission (FCSC), U.S. Department of Justice (http://www.usdoj.gov/fcsc/readingroom/ccp-listofclaims.pdf).
Note: a. Claim certified by FCSC in its Second Cuban Claims Program completed in August 2006.

(FCSC) could provide the basis for an action under Title III. Under the First Cuban Claims Program completed on July 6, 1972, the FCSC determined the validity and amounts of claims by U.S. nationals against Cuba and certified them to the secretary of state for use in future negotiations of a claims settlement agreement with a "friendly" government in Cuba. The FCSC recognized 5,911 property claims that were valued at approximately $1.8 billion at the time of registry and would be worth well over $6 billion today once accrued interest (6 percent per year) is added. Table 4.1 reports the ten largest U.S. claims and their approximate amounts.

Since 1998, uncertified claims can also serve as the basis for action. The claim must exceed $50,000 in 1996 dollars, excluding interests, costs, and attorney's fees. There are contrasting views regarding the potential impact of this specific provision. Kiger (1998, 57–58) argued that it would exclude all but seventy-five of the certified claimants and probably most claims by Cuban Americans. In contrast, a declaration by Warren Christopher, a former U.S. secretary of state, suggested a different scenario. Christopher stated in September 1995 that the implementation of Title III "would exponentially increase the number and value of U.S. property claims against Cuba from their current total of about $6 billion to as much as $100 billion" (Groombridge 2001, 4). If this is true, properties that were worth a few thousand dollars in the early 1960s might have easily surpassed the $50,000 value by 1996.[1] Therefore, the Helms-Burton law would actually expand the process of settlement of property claims.

Under Title III, a foreign company with investments in Cuba and the United States might be a victim of retaliation by U.S. claimants (backed by a court order) on its U.S. properties, which can be obtained legally as compensation (McKenna and Kirk 1998, 6). But the mere condition of trafficking in expropriated properties is by no means sufficient for the application of this kind of sanction. In order to be subjected to the jurisdiction of U.S. courts in case of a controversy based on Title III, a foreign firm must have "systematic and continuous" business links with the United States whose amplitude makes reasonable a process of reclamation. The provision is not applicable to foreign companies that simply trade with and obtain financing from the United States. Furthermore, Title III can be applied only in U.S. courts of the state where the foreign company has business activities. More specifically, if a foreign enterprise has investment activities in Miami, it is subject to the jurisdiction of Floridian courts and not to the jurisdiction of courts in other U.S. states (Krinsky 1996, 29).

We can fairly assume that claims against foreign firms with no U.S. exposure (mainly no assets in the United States) and requests of compensation for violation of Title III would likely be ignored by foreign investors. Without operations in the United States, a company is not obligated to defend an action. Another important issue is less clear. If the executives of that company do not appear before the U.S. court, can the subsequent default judgment be enforced in courts of other countries? In January 1997, Canada amended the Foreign Extraterritorial Measures Act (FEMA) of 1985 by establishing that any court judgment linked to the Helms-Burton legislation would not be recognized in Canada.[2] However, a Canadian lawyer had issued a warning a few months before: "With amendments to FEMA we could have a stronger case, but I am not going to give Canadians a guarantee that their assets would be protected" (Lacy 1996, 30).

Due to come into effect on August 1, 1996, Title III of the Helms-Burton law has never been implemented because Bill Clinton, George W. Bush, and Barack Obama used their discretionary power to waive it every six months. A clause included in the final draft of the legislation permits the president to delay the controversial Title III for national security reasons or to promote democracy in Cuba. Although the waiver can still be terminated in the future, past presidential actions raise the likelihood that the full force of Helms-Burton might not take effect any time soon during Obama's tenure in the White House.

Unlike Title III, Title IV cannot be suspended. The identification of "traffickers" and the application of sanctions are responsibilities of the U.S. Department of State. In principle, Title IV should not have a retroactive force because it focuses on trafficking activities initiated after March 12, 1996. Section 401(B)(2)(A)(i)(III) suggests that the exclusion from the United States would not be applicable if a firm in possession of a confiscated property avoids making any changes to the way it was conducting business activities in Cuba prior to the enactment of the Helms-Burton law. Improvements and investments in a confiscated property are permitted only if they are for routine maintenance (Lacy 1996, 29).

But how is it established that renovations, upgrades, or other constructions have been undertaken just for routine maintenance? The extreme vagueness of the provision makes it very difficult for foreign firms to avoid the reach of Title IV. If they do business on a confiscated U.S. property, they might be easily identified as traffickers. Just a few months after the passage of Helms-Burton, the U.S. Department of State sanctioned the executives of two foreign companies (another one was sanctioned in 1997) that were trafficking in expropriated properties in Cuba. Washington also pressured several other firms by sending them "warning" letters for potential violations of the U.S. legislation and threatening to deny their executives visa entry into the United States. In such a short period, it seems at least improbable that those foreign firms made enough changes to their activities in Cuba to justify the application of sanctions under Title IV.

The Effects of Helms-Burton on Potential and Existing Investors

The Helms-Burton law might have produced a number of adverse effects on foreign investment in Cuba. These effects can be summarized as follows:

- low profiles maintained by foreign firms operating in Cuba and frustrated investment plans;

- confusion among foreign investors, especially in the tourism sector, as a result of the broadly defined concept of trafficking;
- loss of considerable time and money in verifying origins of expropriated properties;
- disruption and delay of foreign financing for strategic sectors such as sugar and, to a lesser extent, tobacco;
- creation of off-the-shelf companies in the Caribbean and Central America to disguise business activities in Cuba;
- higher interest rates demanded by foreign lenders for providing credits to the island;
- increased negotiating power of foreign companies targeted by Helms-Burton;
- and a spinoff of Cuban interests by foreign firms to avoid running afoul of Title III of Helms-Burton.

The Helms-Burton law compels foreign firms to maintain low profiles in carrying out their business activities in Cuba. Basic industry (oil and mining), tourism, telecommunications, agriculture, and construction are the sectors where large (in terms of capital involved) expropriations took place, and where the pressure of the law should allegedly be stronger. Cuban and U.S. authorities have made similar claims that Helms-Burton has discouraged several potential foreign investors from pursuing their business plans on the island. Yet, the law seems to have been less effective in forcing major foreign firms operating in the Cuban market to withdraw from their investments.

Business activities in the tourism sector demonstrate how the broad definition of trafficking creates confusion among foreign investors. In May 1996, one scholar noted, "Canadian concerns in Cuba are mostly management contracts, except for some equity positions in Canadian hotels. So I would imagine that the risk is lower than if they had direct ownership. Nevertheless, there are some vexing property questions based on broad definitions of trafficking, as well as some of the U.S. exposure of Canadian hotel concerns" (Sagebien 1996, 43). Several European and Canadian firms operating in the Cuban tourism sector have been targeted by Helms-Burton not only for equity positions in confiscated properties but also for management activities.

Between 1996 and 1999, the U.S. State Department sent "warning letters" to Leisure Canada and Air Transat (Canada), Club Med (France), LTI (Germany), and Sol Meliá (Spain) advising them that their operations in Cuba might constitute "dealing in expropriated goods" and they could face penalties under Title IV of Helms-Burton. As recently as late 2005, some Spanish hotel chains based in Majorca received similar warnings because of their management and investment activities in Cuban hotels allegedly built on expropriated properties (United Nations 2006, 23). No formal sanctions have thus far been applied to any of these companies. It should also be noted that a possible lift of the waiver on Title III would grant Cuban Americans the right to claim their lands and industries. In this case, a much larger number of investment deals would fall under the reach of Helms-Burton, including the construction of new hotels. The lack of U.S. exposure of foreign investors in Cuba would then become crucial in escaping possible retaliations.

In order to avoid problems with Helms-Burton, prospective investors spend considerable time and money carrying out prior due diligence to verify that a project does not involve a confiscated property.[3] Official records are consulted both in Cuba and the United States. New investors often announce publicly that their projects are linked to "clean" assets. In 2001, a Cuban official recalled that foreign executives were persistent in their inquiries on expropriated properties soon after the enactment of Helms-Burton. But he claimed that things had changed and companies felt more secure in Cuba. By that time, according to him, potential investors focused on the U.S. legislation only after more important issues had been addressed.[4] It seems reasonable to believe that the Cuban perception of Helms-Burton's threat has evolved over time considering how rarely the law's penalizing provisions have been formally applied. A local consultant in Havana observed in 2001, "The first thing we do is to check the official record of the claims certified by the U.S. Foreign Settlement Commission. We do not check if the property was owned by some Cuban Americans because Title III has always been waived."[5]

The Helms-Burton law disrupted and delayed the flow of foreign financing into Cuba for strategic sectors such as sugar and, to a lower degree, tobacco (United Nations 1997, 13; SELA 1997). Many expropriations after the revolution of 1959 occurred in the sugar industry. Ten of the twenty-two highest claims belong to U.S. sugar companies and they are valued at slightly more than $500 million, or about 27 percent of the total amount ($1.8 billion) of certified claims (Alvarez and Peña Castellanos 2001, 113–14). Charges of trafficking were mostly brought against firms that financed or traded sugar originating in expropriated lands because direct foreign investment, at least until 2001, was permitted only in the sugar cane derivatives production and not in the raw sugar industry. The list of overseas banks, financial institutions, and companies that were targeted by Helms-Burton include the ING Bank (the Netherlands), ED and F Man (United Kingdom), Tabacalera and Banco Bilbao Vizcaya (Spain), and Redpath Sugar (Canada).

As a response to the U.S. legislation, some foreign firms (this is not the case of Redpath, which ceased to do business in Cuba) decided to reorganize their sugar and tobacco operations in Cuba. "Territorial financing" directed to specific provinces was abandoned for a more generic scheme of "national financing," in some cases through fiduciary mechanisms. In this way, it is more difficult to establish a connection between foreign credits and expropriated properties.[6] The Law of Reaffirmation of Cuban Dignity and Sovereignty (Law 80 of December 25, 1996) enables the creation of "fiduciary companies" or investment funds to hold disputed properties. According to Article 6, "The Government of the Republic of Cuba is empowered to apply or authorize the necessary formulas to protect foreign investors against the application of the Helms-Burton law, including the transfer of the foreign investor's interests to fiduciary enterprises, financial entities or investment funds." The creation, in August 1996, of the Cuban firm Compañía Fiduciaria S.A. appeared directed at solving some of the problems related to external financing. The company participates in operations that include financial solutions for investment contracts, administration of external funds channeled to specific activities, and deposits of guarantees. In 1997, Compañía Fiduciaria received its first $5.3 million for the acquisition of supplies necessary for the development of sugar production. At the end of 1999, the company had received $367.8 million from banks and financial entities.[7] Along with sugar production, these investments contributed to financing important economic sectors like textile, metal and machinery, and construction, among others.

In addition to the use of fiduciary mechanisms, a number of foreign banks developed circuitous routes using off-the-shelf companies in the Caribbean and Central America (Panama, Curaçao, and the Cayman Islands) to disguise their financial assistance to firms with outstanding U.S. claims. As acknowledged by Peter Scott, the chairman of the British investment fund Beta Gran Caribe Ltd., "It is easy enough to buy companies off-the-shelf in countries with closed ownership registers and create a trail of money transfers which is extremely difficult to track."[8] Even so, foreign banks with substantial interests in the United States have been less inclined to engage in procedures aimed at bypassing the U.S. legislation. For instance, Canada's Bank of Nova Scotia backed away from providing loans to Canadians wishing to invest in Cuba largely out of fear of running afoul of Helms-Burton and possibly jeopardizing its investments in the United States (McKenna and Kirk 1998, 6). It should be emphasized that not only banks but also many other foreign firms formed "shell" companies to conceal their real identities and business operations in Cuba.

The Helms-Burton law created a more uncertain and riskier business environment, resulting in foreign lenders providing credits to the island at higher rates. Even before March 1996, Cuba ranked among the most risky countries for investment due to its economic indicators (especially trade deficit), high foreign debt, government intervention in the economy, and the U.S. embargo (Pérez Villanueva 2001). But the passage of Helms-Burton drove interest rates for bank loans and other financing for investment projects to as high as 20 percent or more (Confidential Report 1999, 24). A Cuban official report submitted to the United Nations in September 1996 clearly stated, "It is estimated that in 1995 financing accounted, on average, for 13 per cent of the value of the loans, rising on occasion to 20 per cent, with the rate increasing as the blockade was tightened" (United Nations 1996, 19). The final cost of foreign credits is therefore particularly burdensome for Cuba, which was already obtaining short-term loans at high interest rates and had virtually no access to medium- and long-term financing from banks and financial institutions.

It is conceivable that Helms-Burton gave some foreign companies increased power in negotiating their projects with Cuban authorities. The acceptance of the risk of investing or expanding in Cuba might have been conditioned to important concessions in the contract. This seems to be the case of big firms that were targeted by the U.S. law, such as Canada's Sherritt International, Spain's Sol Meliá, and Israel's BM Group.[9]

Finally, some foreign investors with assets or operations in the United States decided to spin off their Cuban interests in order to prevent possible attacks under Title III of Helms-Burton. This strategy consists of creating a legally distinct and completely unrelated company, which is responsible for all of the benefits and potential risks associated with the Cuban assets. Since no cross-ownership exists between the original firm and the spun-off entity, an eventual lawsuit against the latter cannot lead to retaliation on the U.S. assets of the former (Lacy 1996, 30). One firm that opted for this strategy is Sherritt. A few months before the enactment of Helms-Burton, Sherritt spun off its Cuban operations by creating a new and legally separated company, Sherritt International Corporation. The company's executives are quite confident that Sherritt International is safe from Title III (Kiger 1998, 63–64). Yet, a case could be made against it as the two firms still maintain evident links (many executives and shareholders are the same).

The Application of Title IV

Soon after the enactment of the Helms-Burton legislation, and despite strong international opposition, the U.S. government pressed ahead with the implementation of Title IV of the law. In 1996, the U.S. State Department sent out letters to two foreign companies with investments in Cuba. Executives and senior officers of Canada's Sherritt International and Mexico's Grupo Domos were informed that they would be barred from entering the United States unless the companies divested themselves of their operations in Cuba within forty-five days, Sherritt in a nickel and cobalt ore processing plant and Domos in Cuba's telephone system. In November 1997, similar sanctions were applied against the executives of the BM Group, an Israeli-owned firm registered in Panama.

Sherritt International owns 50 percent of a nickel-cobalt mine at Moa Bay, in eastern Cuba, in a joint venture with the Cuban government. The U.S. sanctions against Sherritt were motivated by the fact that the company was making money off an American investment expropriated (without compensation) by the Cuban government. The United States said the mine had been "stolen" from the U.S. Moa Bay Mining Corporation, now known as Freeport-McMoRan Copper and Gold Inc., which is based in Phoenix.[10] Deploring the U.S. decision to deny entry visas to its executives, Sherritt reacted firmly by announcing the company's intention to strengthen its mining investment in Cuba and expand into real estate, sugar, electricity, and telecommunications.[11]

In the telecommunications sector, one of the most important agreements was the creation of the joint venture ETECSA in mid-1994 between the Cuban state-run telephone company EMTEL and the Corporación Interamericana de Telecomunicaciones (CITEL), in which the Monterrey-based Mexican company Grupo Domos held a 75 percent share and STET International, the international holding firm of Italy's Telecom Italia, a 25 percent share. With a total investment of more than $1.5 billion, CITEL acquired a 49 percent stake in EMTEL and received a concession of fifty-five years for the modernization of the sector (Pérez Villanueva 1999, 129). The application of Title IV against Domos originated from a claim of the U.S.-based ITT Corporation, which had owned the Cuban telephone company before the revolution.

The BM Group, in partnership with Cuba's Corporación Nacional de Cítricos, has citrus operations in the provinces of Matanzas and Isla de la Juventud that account for a substantial share of the island's total citrus exports. Sanctions against the Israeli company allegedly stemmed from several U.S. claims on a 96,000-acre plantation in Jaguey Grande, Matanzas.[12] But the U.S. government did not provide information either on the exact location of the expropriated properties or on the names of the claimants.

Whereas Sherritt International and the BM Group continued their business activities in Cuba in the face of U.S. pressure, Grupo Domos withdrew from its investment in 1997 by selling its stake in ETECSA to the Italian firm STET. Regarding Domos' decision, the Helms-Burton legislation seems to have played a minor role along with more important financial problems. It is reported that the Mexican company was never able to obtain the financing required under the investment agreement with ETECSA.[13]

Domos counted on a $350 million loan from the National Bank for Foreign Commerce controlled by Carlos Salinas, then the president of Mexico. The latter and a group of important Mexican firms strongly supported the telecommunications project. When Salinas left the presidency in August 1994, the bank raised the interest rates, thus forcing Domos to delay its payments to the Cuban government.[14] Management mistakes and the collapse of the Mexican peso in 1995 further exacerbated the situation. The application in 1996 of Title IV against executives of Grupo Domos simply gave the final blow to a company already vexed by untenable financial problems. Although Domos did not abandon its investment in response to Helms-Burton, the law did make it more difficult for the firm to acquire the necessary financing for its business activities in Cuba (Sagebien and Tsourtouras 1999, 7). In early 1997, at the time of its withdrawal, the company was months behind on its payments for ETECSA and was unable to obtain credit to honor the debt. Cuban exile groups and some U.S. officials celebrated Domos' withdrawal and cited it as a proof that Helms-Burton was an effective tool in weakening Castro and the Cuban economy.[15] However, in 2001 the Mexican firm was still performing minor activities in Cuba in an attempt to recover the capital invested or, perhaps, maintain a foothold in the island's economy for the time the embargo is lifted.

The strategy adopted by the Italian company STET International in filling Domos' place in Cuba's telephone system supports the thesis that financial problems were the major factor in Domos' withdrawal rather than the Helms-Burton law. In May 1997, STET received a letter from the U.S. State Department asking if it was using ITT equipment. A STET official in Rome said the Italian firm was not concerned by Helms-Burton because it had documents showing the equipment STET used was not seized from the former U.S. owner.[16] Even so, in addition to an initial investment of $300 million to purchase Domos' share, STET agreed with ITT on the payment of a compensation of about $30 million for the use of the confiscated property (Roy 2000, 113). If the Italian company was able to protect its investment in Cuba by reaching an agreement with ITT, the Mexican Domos could have probably done the same. Unfortunately, its precarious financial conditions did not allow this type of solution. The payment of compensation to the former U.S. owner is very important because it highlights a possible way for foreign investors to circumvent (or perhaps succumb to) the provisions of the Helms-Burton law.

Although Washington has continued to warn many foreign companies of potential violations of Helms-Burton, no formal sanctions under Title IV were applied between November 1997 and May 2004. In 2004, however, the Bush administration stepped up economic pressure on several foreign firms and banks doing business with Cuba as part of a broader attempt to further disrupt Cuba's limited access to international financing and hasten the end of Fidel Castro's rule over the island. In June 2004, the Jamaican tourism group SuperClubs pulled out of two hotel contracts in Cuba after receiving U.S. notice in early May that it had a forty-five-day grace period before the application of visa restrictions on its top executives for travel to the United States. Curiously, SuperClubs not only withdrew from the Breezes Costa Verde resort in the province of Holguín, a property confiscated from a prominent Cuban family (the Sánchez-Hill family) now living in the United States, but also from a separate Cuban venture not on the disputed property, the newly opened Grand Lido Varadero in the province of Matanzas. Some analysts claimed that the Castro government forced the Jamaican company out in punishment for its bowing to Washington's demands.[17] Confidential sources in Havana added that Cuba made the decision because many other foreign hotel chains were interested in running the Grand Lido Varadero.[18] The resort is now managed by Sol Meliá's brand Paradisus under the name of Princesa del Mar. SuperClubs still manages the Breezes Varadero and the Breezes Jibacoa in Santa Cruz del Norte, in the province of Havana.

The Bush administration's decision to single out a Jamaican firm for its operations in Cuba's tourism sector and not European firms with a more significant presence was no accident. In a presidential election year, Bush's tough stance on Cuba helped bolster support among hard-liners in the Cuban-American community. At the same time, the White House had to settle for sanctions against a firm of a small nation with little political weight while refraining from targeting European investors with greater support from their respective governments. Since the European Union had repeatedly warned the United States of tit-for-tat retaliatory actions, Bush could hardly afford a major dispute with its main trading partner over some European companies' business activities in Cuba.

Spain's Sol Meliá, in particular, was never sanctioned by the United States even though it has operations on the same Holguín property confiscated from the Sanchez-Hill family. As Zein Issa, SuperClub's vice president of marketing, put it, "We were caught in the middle of an international political struggle, and we were the victim."[19] While Daniel W. Fisk, the U.S. deputy assistant secretary, revealed in October 2004 that Washington was "actively investigating more than two dozen Helms-Burton Title IV visa sanction cases,"[20] the U.S. action against SuperClubs was the last application of Title IV to date.

Withdrawals from Investments in Cuba

Cases of withdrawals from existing investments or planned ones as a result of the Helms-Burton legislation are difficult to document because foreign companies prefer to avoid publicity. Moreover, an admission of the role of U.S. pressures in the decision to pull out from an investment or desist from pursuing a project might undermine the possibility for a foreign firm to resume business activities in Cuba at some future time.

Clear cases of companies that have ceased to do business in Cuba because of the U.S. law are those of Redpath Sugar of Canada and, at least temporarily, CEMEX of Mexico. CEMEX withdrew in 1996 from a cement production venture in Cuba after learning that it was going to receive a notification letter from the U.S. Department of State for violation of Title IV. The company did not renew a contract of administration for the plant Cementos Curazao N.V. in Mariel, which had been expropriated from the U.S. firm Lone Star Industries of Stamford, Connecticut.[21] While Cuban authorities never confirmed this version, it is believed that CEMEX decided to sacrifice its operations on the island to protect larger interests in the United States (Sagebien and Tsourtouras 1999, 7). Whatever the true story, it appears that CEMEX has returned to Cuba. Official sources indicate that Cementos Curazao is one of the six joint ventures with Mexican firms currently active in Cuba. The foreign partner in this mixed enterprise is almost certainly CEMEX.

In 1996, the Canadian sugar refiner Redpath also halted its operations in Cuba from apparent fear of Helms-Burton. The company was at that time a wholly owned subsidiary of the U.K.-based sugar producer Tate and Lyle PLC, which has extensive interests in the United States.[22] A key factor in the decision of Redpath was the company's desire to continue selling sugar to Canadian food processors that export to the United States. In a clear reference to Redpath, Cuban authorities reported in 2001 that Helms-Burton had provoked the termination of a sugar contract with a Canadian refiner, resulting in annual losses for the island of about $30 million since 1996.[23] Until its withdrawal, the Canadian company had been buying one hundred thousand tons of sugar a year from Cuba (Kiger 1998, 62).

In January 1998, the British Borneo Petroleum Syndicate pulled out of Cuba amid political pressure from the United States. Officials of the United States reported that Borneo was among three firms phoned by the U.S. State Department as part of a routine inquiry. In early March, the director of the oil exploration group denied that the company had been warned for a possible application of Title IV but concluded that "political reasons" had influenced its decision to leave Cuba.[24]

Regarding potential investors, available information from U.S. and Cuban sources shows that the inhibitive impact of Helms-Burton might have been substantial. But the vast majority of reported cases of frustrated investment plans took place within two years after Helms-Burton's passage, suggesting that the threat of sanctions declined considerably over time. In March 1998, Michael Ranneberger, then the director of the U.S. State Department's Office of Cuban Affairs, claimed that U.S. pressures had forced at least nineteen foreign firms either to pull out of Cuba or alter their investment plans and confirmed that "interest rates for projects in Cuba have been driven to as high as 22 percent."[25]

Since 1992, the Castro government has submitted annual reports to the United Nations describing thoroughly how the embargo has hindered Cuba's access to external financing and caused heavy losses in key economic sectors. According to Havana, between 1992 and 2000 Helms-Burton deterred a number of leading firms from investing in the island's mining sector, causing losses of about $130 million. The U.S. law also halted various projects in the tourism sector involving investments of more than $100 million and prevented some European oil companies from signing exploration risk contracts with Cuba between 1996 and 1998 (United Nations 2001). Despite their impressive attention to details, the Cuban reports reveal only a few minor cases of thwarted investment projects after the late 1990s.

By then, the inhibitive effect of Helms-Burton had lost its momentum primarily because of a strong response from the European Union that, as discussed later in this chapter, warned the United States of tit-for-tat retaliatory actions. While companies from the European Union were at that time the most active foreign investors in Cuba, Washington could hardly afford a major dispute with its main trading partner over some European transnational players and their activities on the island. Since 2004, Cuba has prioritized business deals with Venezuelan investors that are even less susceptible to U.S. pressures than European firms.

Reorganization and Relocation of Activities

Several firms reorganized their operations in Cuba in order to disguise their identities and avoid possible sanctions. For instance, before the enactment of Helms-Burton the British sugar trader ED and F Man occupied an office, clearly marked with a company sign, in Havana's Miramar district. After the law went into effect, the sign was taken down but ED and F Man continued its sugar operations in Cuba using a different identity, that of the firm Pacol S.A., based in Paris. Pacol's ownership remained unclear, but some of its personnel had previously worked for ED and F Man.[26]

Other companies took the necessary steps to conform their activities to the provisions of Helms-Burton (Werlau 1997, 57). This is the case of the Dutch banking group ING, the first foreign bank to open a representative office in Cuba in 1994. The bank had provided pre-harvest financing for sugar production in two Cuban provinces, Havana and Matanzas, during the 1995–96 season. In July 1996, citing Helms-Burton, the bank said that it would not be renewing its "territorial financing" although it would maintain its presence on the island. More specifically, ING backed out of cofinancing with the Spanish Banco Bilbao Vizcaya packages for the Cuban sugar industry worth nearly $60 million a year. The Dutch bank reportedly took this step as a protective measure to prevent possible U.S. sanctions after it was discovered that forty-five mills the group financed were claimed by Americans. A more generic scheme of "national financing" (or general loans to the sugar sector) was soon established through other European financial institutions, with ING acting as guarantor. The Spanish firm Tabacalera adopted a similar decision. From 1994 to 1996, Tabacalera had provided direct financing to the Cuban tobacco industry to boost tobacco production and cigar exports to Spain, Cuba's biggest single market. In 1997, the company changed the structure of its relationship with the Cuban industry to avoid the effects of Helms-Burton. Instead of directly financing the Cuban crop, Tabacalera now guaranteed funds coming from other Spanish financial institutions.[27]

In short, there is no doubt that the Helms-Burton law has had a negative effect on the flow of foreign financing for strategic sectors such as tobacco and sugar. By creating a riskier business environment for foreign lenders dealing with Cuba, the legislation forced the Castro government to accept credits from European and other investors at higher rates. Nevertheless, foreign firms and banks like ING and Tabacalera were able to reorganize their activities to avoid the reach of Helms-Burton and continue their operations in Cuba.

It was not until 2004 that the United States intensified its offensive against Havana's financial partners by imposing fines on a number of foreign banks dealing with Cuba. In May of that year, the U.S. Federal Reserve imposed a fine of $100 million on UBS, Switzerland's largest bank, for allegedly making transactions in U.S. dollars with Cuba in violation of U.S. law. Smaller fines were levied against the Italian group Banca Commerciale Italiana and the Spanish bank Santander for illegally transferring funds to the island.[28] Between 2006 and 2007, heightened scrutiny of banking transactions by the United States led several other financial institutions to reduce or completely cut business links with Cuba.[29] After about thirteen years of operations, ING finally closed its banking activities on the island in mid-2007. While executives of the Dutch company said this was "a purely business decision," the United States had blacklisted ING's banking joint venture in Cuba a year before, prohibiting U.S. entities from doing business with that firm.[30]

As a consequence of Helms-Burton, some foreign firms operating in expropriated properties decided to relocate their business. This is the case of Motores Internacionales del Caribe S.A. (MICSA), a Panamanian company selling Mitsubishi, Lada, and other vehicles in Cuba. Motores

Internacionales received a "warning" letter from the U.S. Department of State on January 23, 1997, saying that the company could be in violation of Helms-Burton. The firm was accused of profiting from the office it rented in Havana, a property of a Cuban-American family seized by the Castro government.[31] Executives of MICSA defended their position by claiming that the company had rented the building in 1993, three years before the enactment of the U.S. law. In their opinion, the firm had no responsibility because it could not have violated a law that did not exist.

In this regard, it is important to recall the provisions of Title IV. A foreign firm that had begun to operate on a confiscated property before the enactment of Helms-Burton may avoid sanctions if it refrains from undertaking renovations, upgrades, and constructions other than for routine maintenance. For MICSA, and for all of the other firms in a similar situation, it would have been very difficult to continue working on that property without running afoul of U.S. law. While minor activities such as painting the building to keep it in proper condition were clearly identified as part of routine maintenance, more important renovations like fixing the infrastructure or improving facilities could have easily been considered an expansion of interests, raising the likelihood of a violation of Title IV.[32]

In February 1997, just a few weeks after receiving the warning letter, Motores Internacionales announced that it was going to move to a larger location in Havana. The company claimed that it was changing its location because it was expanding and needed more office space, not because of the U.S. threat.[33] However, it is conceivable that MICSA moved to another property in order to avoid further problems and possible sanctions under Title IV of Helms-Burton. The head of the firm and his son were exempted from a potential travel ban because they held dual Panamanian and U.S. citizenships, but as many as eight members of the executive board faced the possibility of being denied entrance into the United States.[34]

Finally, some foreign firms decided to make the necessary arrangements before entering the Cuban market. The largest tour operator in the United Kingdom, Thomson Travel Group, allegedly communicated with the U.S. Department of State to make certain that its business activities did not violate Helms-Burton. It is also reported that a Canadian company specializing in hotel constructions, Leisure Canada, investigated 443 properties in Cuba in order to find a place with no links with U.S. claims.[35] In 1999, Leisure Canada launched a ten-year, $400 million venture to build eleven hotels in four locations around Cuba along with golf courses, spas, and entertainment complexes.[36]

The Case of Sol Meliá

A foreign company repeatedly threatened by Helms-Burton is the Spanish group Sol Meliá, the leader in the Cuban tourism sector and the twelfth largest hotel chain in the world.[37] In July 1996, U.S. authorities notified Sol Meliá that it was under inquiry for one of the hotels it manages and partially owns (equity interest) on the Cuban beach of Varadero, the Meliá Las Américas. Before 1959, the land on which the hotel was built belonged to the U.S. billionaire Irenee Dupont. Although the Dupont family never claimed the expropriated property, executives of Sol Meliá had to explain to U.S. officials that their business was not violating the provisions of Helms-Burton.[38] After a brief investigation, the United States informed the executives that there was not enough proof of an infringement of the law, thus freeing the Spanish firm from a possible application of Title IV. Sol Meliá said its inquiries had led it to conclude that it was beyond reach of the U.S. legislation, mainly because it had concentrated its investments on new properties (Haines 1997).

Since July 1996, Sol Meliá has significantly expanded its business interests in Cuba. It currently manages twenty-six hotels on the island with equity interests in four of them. While having been "cleared" by Washington three years before, in 1999 Sol Meliá's business in Cuba prompted one of the highest-profile scrutinies under Helms-Burton. This time, the controversy was mainly related to a plot of land in the province of Holguín on which the hotel Sol Río de Oro (only managed by Sol Meliá) was built. In 1959, the land belonged to the Cuban-American Sánchez-Hill family. The U.S. Department of State sent a second letter to Sol Meliá on July 30, 1999, notifying the company that a new Title IV investigation had begun. The letter called for an agreement between Sol Meliá and the former owner of the property in order to avoid possible sanctions. Washington also solicited details from the Spanish chain about two additional hotels in the province of Holguín (built on Sánchez-Hill's properties) and another one in Varadero.[39]

Once more, U.S. pressures against Sol Meliá did not produce any concrete result. The threat of sanctions under Title IV was temporarily withdrawn while an agreement between the Spanish company and the Cuban-American family was possibly attempted; no agreement, however, occurred.[40] Although Sol Meliá claimed many times that its involvement with Sanchez-Hill's properties predates the passage of the Helms-Burton law, it is believed to have offered a compensation of $1 million to the Cuban-American family. But the latter apparently demanded $10 million for the right to exploit twenty-eight acres of coastal land it once owned.[41]

Two factors played a major role in Sol Meliá's successful attempt to avoid sanctions. First, the Spanish government (backed by the European Union) strongly defended Sol Meliá's operations in Cuba. In November 1999, during a visit to the island, the Spanish prime minister José María Aznar publicly criticized the tightening of the U.S. embargo against Cuba. Asked about his choice of accommodation at the Meliá Habana hotel, Aznar replied that he intended to show support for the position of Spanish entrepreneurs and demonstrate that he was against Helms-Burton.[42]

Second, in the fall of 1996 the European Union decided to enact a blocking measure against Helms-Burton. The European Union's response involved the establishment of a "watch list" of U.S. companies and individuals filing lawsuits against European firms and considered placing visa and work restrictions on U.S. businessmen. Even more important, officials of the European Union repeatedly warned Washington that implementing Title IV against Sol Meliá and other European firms in Cuba would prompt a challenge to the extraterritorial character of Helms-Burton in the World Trade Organization (WTO).[43] To avoid a fight within the WTO, the United States and the European Union reached a preliminary agreement in 1997 and a more extended understanding on May 18, 1998. The European Union promised not to pursue retaliatory measures against the United States in the WTO and discourage investments in certain questionable properties. In exchange, U.S. authorities agreed to prolong the suspension of Title III, respect the current status of foreign investment in Cuba,[44] and pressure Congress for an amendment that would give the president the authority to waive Title IV (Roy 2000, 127, 152).

While Sol Meliá has maintained its operations in Cuba, several U.S. congressmen continued to push for the application of sanctions against the Spanish firm. In June 2000, Senator Jesse Helms sent a letter to Chris Patten, the European Union's foreign relations commissioner, in which he rejected the understanding of 1998 and reiterated his intention to seek punishment of Sol Meliá.[45] In November 2000, Helms asked the U.S. Department of State to formally determine that Sol Meliá was trafficking in Cuba and ban its top executives from entering the United States. Moreover, the Cuban-American representatives Lincoln Díaz Balart and Ileana Ros-Lehtinen tried to build support within the U.S. Congress for a more aggressive policy on Cuba. They asked President Bush to sanction Sol Meliá without further delay and remove the waiver on Title III of Helms-Burton. Overall, Title IV remains a potential threat for the Spanish firm, albeit an unlikely one. The risk for the United States of a major dispute with the European Union that would implode the mechanisms of the World Trade Organization makes Sol Meliá's position quite safe (Perl 2006, 13).

Helms-Burton: Failure or Success?

Cuban officials have provided contrasting assessments of the impact of Helms-Burton on foreign investment in Cuba. Since March 1996, and at least until 2001, they proudly insisted that economic associations with overseas firms and the flow of FDI continued to grow. At the same time, they claimed that the strengthening of the embargo had produced sizable damages to the Cuban economy. In particular, they acknowledged the external financing problems and the "inhibitive" effect of Helms-Burton on potential foreign investors. On the U.S. side, Senator Jesse Helms stated in March 1997 that Helms-Burton was having a devastating effect on the Cuban economy by forcing many foreign investors to abandon the island (Roy 2000, 161, 170).

In March 1999, Ibrahim Ferradaz, then the Cuban minister for foreign investment and economic cooperation, declared that Helms-Burton had been unable to stop the foreign investment process. He said that out of more than 360 joint ventures with foreign capital operating in Cuba at that time, more than 50 percent had been formed after the passage of the

U.S. law.[46] On February 2, 2001, his successor, Marta Lomas, maintained that foreign investment in Cuba was on the rise, as demonstrated by 392 active international economic associations at the end of 2000. She also claimed that 61 percent of those associations received approval after the Helms-Burton law came into being.[47]

Despite these declarations, in April 2000 the Cuban Ministry of Foreign Investment released the results of a study that attempted to quantify the damages of Helms-Burton to the island's economy. The study reported that the U.S. law had caused damages to Cuba totaling $208 million. It also presented six specific cases of projects affected by Helms-Burton and the correspondent amount of capital lost by Cuba. The names of the firms were omitted, but the cases are well known. Regarding the largest projects, Cuban authorities argued that U.S. pressures disrupted the export plan of a joint venture in the construction industry (clearly referring to the withdrawal of the Mexican cement company CEMEX), which resulted in a loss of sales of $138.1 million. Moreover, U.S. court decisions and the action by a foreign firm in the telecommunications sector (the Italian STET's payment of compensation to the former U.S. owner ITT for the use of confiscated properties) provoked damages of $37.6 million. Finally, the acquisition of a foreign firm in the transportation sector by a U.S. company (the Italian cruise line Costa Crociere, bought in 1997 by the U.S. Carnival Corporation) prevented the completion of a project estimated at $19 million (MINVEC 2000).

In short, Helms-Burton caused some notable losses for Cuba by hindering certain ongoing FDI projects, driving up interest rates on short-term loans, and producing a chilling effect on prospective investors, to a great extent shortly after the passage of the law. But how effective has the U.S. legislation been in forcing overseas firms already operating in Cuba to pull out of the island? This is indeed a fundamental issue. Helms-Burton would have had a tremendous negative impact on the Cuban economy if it had been able to spark an exodus of foreign investors or, more realistically, exercise enough pressure to persuade major foreign investors to exit the island.

Figure 4.1 presents data on authorized and dissolved international economic associations (AECEs) by year of dissolution. Between 1988 and

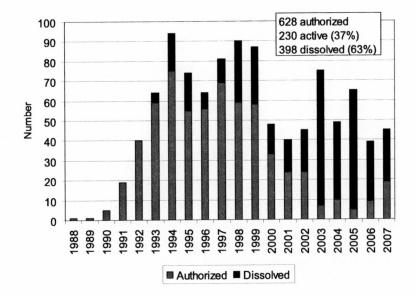

Figure 4.1. Authorized and Dissolved International Economic Associations by Year of Dissolution, 1988–2007.
Source: Calculations of the author from Ministerio para la Inversión Extranjera y la Colaboración Económica (MINVEC) 2008 and previous years.

2007, a total of 628 AECEs were formed in Cuba, most of them joint ventures; at the end of 2007, only 230 or 37 percent remained active, a sharp decline from the 403 reported in 2002. The number of dissolved AECEs was 398, approximately 63 percent of the total authorized. Almost 90 percent of dissolutions occurred after the enactment of the Helms-Burton legislation. Dissolutions were generally due to the termination of the regular contract between the Cuban state and the overseas investor. Less frequently, they were the result of an anticipated withdrawal of the foreign partner. However, except in a very few cases, there is no evidence that Helms-Burton played a key role in forcing existing investors to abandon Cuba or, eventually, to refuse the renewal of a contract. More important factors seem to have been the inability of the Cuban government to meet its payment obligations, its increasing selectiveness toward FDI projects and unwillingness to create a more attractive business environment, and the existing restrictions on the operations of state and foreign enterprises.

Between 1996 and 1997, when the United States stepped up enforcement of Title IV of the Helms-Burton law, 125 new AECEs were formed and only 20 dissolved.

The United States, through applied sanctions or "warning letters" for potential violations of Title IV, has tried to curb the flow of FDI delivered to Cuba and exercise economic pressure by targeting, for the most part, major firms with a significant presence in the island's market. Table 4.2 summarizes the impact of Helms-Burton on selected foreign firms operating in Cuba whose cases have already been discussed. Only the Canadian Redpath Sugar and the Mexican CEMEX clearly ceased to do business in Cuba because of the U.S. law and to save their investments in the United States. But CEMEX later resumed its operations. A less clear case is that of British Borneo Petroleum, which pulled out of Cuba in late 1997 because of unspecified "political reasons" along with poor results of its oil exploration activities. Grupo Domos withdrew from its investment in the Cuban telephone system but did not abandon the island, at least until 2001. Finally, the Jamaican group SuperClubs pulled out of two hotel contracts in June 2004 but still manages two hotels in Cuba. Although Washington's punitive action against SuperClubs might have discouraged new foreign investment in the Cuban tourism sector, official statistics show that hotel management contracts with overseas companies (mainly from Spain) increased from fifty-one in 2003 to sixty-three at the end of 2008 (Pérez Villanueva and Vidal Alejandro 2008; MINVEC 2009).

In all of the other cases presented in table 4.2, we can see that U.S. pressures on foreign investors in Cuba failed to prompt a general pull out. In order to avoid the effects of Helms-Burton, some overseas firms have taken specific steps such as the reorganization and relocation of their activities (ED and F Man, ING Bank, Tabacalera, MICSA), the spinoff of their operations (Sherritt International), and the payment of compensation to the former owner of the property (STET International). Other investors have simply continued to operate and expand in Cuba undeterred by sanctions or U.S. inquiries (BM Group, LTI, Sol Meliá). A Cuban official revealed in 2001 that "foreign companies carefully analyze the potential risks of their operations in Cuba and undertake the necessary preliminary arrangements to avoid running afoul of the Helms-Burton

Table 4.2. Impact of Helms-Burton on Selected Foreign Firms Operating in Cuba

Company	Country	Type of Operations in Cuba	Nature of Impact (Outcome)
BM Group	Israel	Joint venture in citrus sector	Application of Title IV (remained in Cuba)
British Borneo	U.K.	Oil explorations	Halted operations for "political reasons" and poor results (pulled out)
CEMEX	Mexico	Cement production venture in Mariel	Did not renew administration contract (pulled out but returned to Cuba)
ED and F Man	U.K.	Sugar trader	Reorganized operations to disguise its identity (remained in Cuba)
Grupo Domos	Mexico	Joint venture in telecommunications (ETECSA)	Application of Title IV (withdrew from investment but remained in Cuba)
ING Bank	Holland	Pre-harvest financing for sugar production in 2 provinces	Changed financing scheme (remained in Cuba until 2007)
LTI	Germany	Manages and markets 3 hotels in Cuba (under the brand name Maritim)	Received warning letter (remained in Cuba)
MICSA	Panama	Car seller (Mitsubishi)	Relocation of activities (remained in Cuba)
Redpath Sugar	Canada	Sugar refiner	Halted purchases of sugar from Cuba (pulled out)
Sherritt International	Canada	Nickel/cobalt ore processing plant	Spin off and application of Title IV (remained in Cuba)
STET International	Italy	Filled Domos's place in Cuba's telephone system	Payment of compensation for use of confiscated property (remained in Cuba)
Sol Meliá	Spain	Leader in Cuba's tourism sector	Repeatedly threatened by Title IV (remained in Cuba)
SuperClubs	Jamaica	Manages and markets 2 hotels in Cuba	Application of Title IV (withdrew from investment but remained in Cuba)
Tabacalera	Spain	Financing for tobacco production and cigar exports	Changed financing scheme (remained in Cuba)

legislation. But they feel quite safe once [they have] entered the Cuban market."[48]

Notwithstanding the limitations in gauging the deterring impact of Helms-Burton, official data from the Cuban Central Bank (see table 3.1) show an increase of foreign direct investment in Cuba after March 1996. An annual average of $262 million in FDI was delivered in 1996–97 and $278 million in 1998–2000, compared to an average of $207 million in 1993–95. Even if the alleged inaccuracy of these numbers must be considered, Cuba's claim that FDI flows have expanded after the enactment of Helms-Burton appears correct. The amount of FDI delivered to Cuba dropped notably between 2001 and 2003, but foreign firms have pledged substantial capital for new investment projects (or the upgrade of existing ones) since then. Venezuela's investment plans on the island are by far the largest. The capital involved in various projects with Venezuela is more than the total amount of FDI ($6 billion) committed by hundreds of foreign investors between 1988 and 2003.

Finally, the Bush administration's punitive actions against Cuba's financial partners that were launched in 2004 deserve a special mention. These actions forced a number of Canadian and European banks (including ING Bank, which closed its Cuban operations in July 2007) to reduce or cut off business dealings with Havana. As Washington stepped up pressures on banking institutions to curtail their relations with the Castro regime, one would expect a substantial drop in the flow of international credit to the island. Furthermore, Cuba has experienced serious liquidity problems and failed to meet debt repayment obligations several times since the early 1990s. Most recently, between August and December 2008, Cuba informed the governments of Japan, Germany, and France that it was unable to respect its debt payments as scheduled. In response, Japan temporarily suspended trade insurance for exports to Cuba and stopped accepting new applications from the island.[49]

The exposure of foreign banks in Cuba actually increased between 2003 and 2007 (see table 4.3). According to the Bank for International Settlements (BIS), claims of foreign banks on Cuba, which refer to financial assets such as loans, debt securities, and equities, rose by almost 20 percent (or about $430 million) during this period. Claims of European banks, mainly from France, Spain, and Germany, grew 15.9 percent and

Table 4.3. Claims of Foreign Banks on Cuba by Nationality of Reporting Banks, 2003–2008 (Year-end in Millions of U.S. Dollars)

Country	2003	2004	2005	2006	2007	2008
France	574	455	466	521	670	566
Spain	313	321	314	391	413	444
Germany	189	207	184	230	306	237
Italy	134	125	92	66	63	117
Netherlands	312	298	237	201	134	96
Austria	71	72	67	57	93	34
Japan	35	68	98	65	111	30
Belgium	3	17	13	8	24	28
Sweden	21	26	18	14	20	28
United Kingdom	30	33	31	27	20	9
Switzerland	69[c]	3	1	3	40	1
Canada	—	75	—	—	—	—
European Banks	1,555[b]	1,557	1,429	1,524	1,802	1,585
Total Foreign Claims[a]	2,216	2,245	2,211	2,266	2,648	2,034

Source: Bank for International Settlements (www.bis.org).

Notes: a. Claims refer to financial assets such as loans, debt securities, and equities.

b. March 2004.

c. September 2003.

accounted, on average, for 68 percent of all international credit to Cuba as reported by BIS. Financial institutions from the Netherlands, Italy, Canada, Switzerland, and the United Kingdom (all countries whose banks were targeted by U.S. actions) reduced their exposure in Cuba, but the resulting drop in foreign credit was more than offset by growing loans from other entities. Washington's unilateral moves against foreign banks dealing with Cuba have little chance of working as long as other countries are willing to supply Havana with desperately needed financial resources.

Claims of overseas banks on Cuba continued to increase until March 2008, suggesting that the impact of Bush's moves on Havana's ability to obtain external financing had remained minimal. In the first half of that year, the Cuban government also secured new credits from Brazil and Iran that came on top of sizable credit lines from China and Venezuela.[50] The BIS statistics, which do not include lending activities of banks from the aforementioned countries, indicate that total foreign claims on Cuba began to fall considerably only in the second half of 2008. The decline took place against the backdrop of Cuba's severe liquidity problems, which were mainly caused by a combination of low nickel prices, unprecedented food imports, and an estimated $10 billion worth of damage from hurricanes. Indeed, the biggest drops in banking exposure were those of financial entities from France, Germany, and Japan, whose governments were notified by Cuba that official debts needed to be renegotiated.

Overall, the Helms-Burton law has been unable to detain the flow of foreign capital delivered to Cuba and force major overseas investors to halt their operations on the island. It should be noted that Cuba's foreign partners in some of the most important joint ventures (in terms of export revenues) in the country have been targeted by or could be potential targets of Helms-Burton. Besides the cases of Sherritt International, STET International, and ED and F Man previously analyzed, the Spanish-French tobacco group Altadis was the target of a lawsuit filed by General Cigar Holdings Inc. of New York in November 2000. The lawsuit focused on Altadis's alleged jawboning of U.S. retailers to buy its non-Cuban products now if the retailers hoped to buy Cuban cigars after the lifting of the embargo. Yet, General Cigar also contended that Cuba's Corporación Habanos (partially owned by Altadis) is using its warehouse in Havana that was confiscated by the Castro government.[51] Similarly, the Cuban family Bacardi has accused the French firm Pernod Ricard of using its expropriated distillery in Santiago de Cuba to produce the rum Havana Club. Pernod Ricard denied the accusation by claiming it simply markets the rum, which is produced in two distilleries in Santa Clara and Santa Cruz built in the 1970s and 1980s.[52]

Given the importance of foreign investment for the Cuban economy as documented in chapter 3, it is not surprising that Helms-Burton also failed to undermine the process of economic recovery of the communist island (figure 4.2). The Castro government was able to achieve what it had hoped in the early 1990s: using FDI in selected economic activities to stimulate the development of the country while maintaining national state control wherever possible over investment, areas of business, and strategic sectors.

During the deep economic recession that started in 1990 and reached the lowest point in 1993, Cuba's GDP contracted by an annual average of about 10 percent. Since then, the economic performance of the country has been positive, although the growth rate fluctuated substantially from

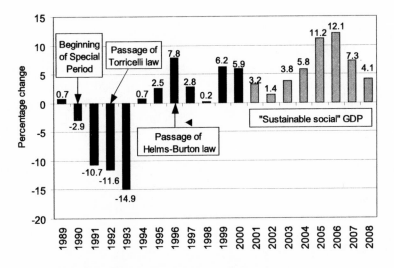

Figure 4.2. Cuba's GDP, 1989–2008 (Annual Growth Rates).
Source: Oficina Nacional de Estadísticas (ONE) 2009; Comisión Económica para América Latina y el Caribe (CEPAL) 2009.

year to year. The macroeconomic performance in 2005–2007 was remarkable. Albeit using a new calculation method that substantially inflates the value of its economy, Cuba reported a GDP growth of 11.2 percent in 2005, 12.1 percent in 2006, and 7.3 percent in 2007 (ECLAC 2008).[53] Even the CIA and the Economist Intelligence Unit, presumably using the conventional GDP formula, put the island's growth, respectively, at 9.5 percent in 2006 and 6.5 percent in 2007 (CIA 2007; EIU 2008b). Strong economic expansion was mainly triggered by exports of professional services under an oil-for-doctors barter deal with Venezuela and, to a lower extent, the dynamism of the internal demand due to increased public investment and private consumption. Soft credits from China and growing nickel revenues were additional stimulating factors.

The revival of the Cuban economy clearly remains incomplete and far from satisfying the needs of the country (Mesa-Lago 2008, 36). Nonetheless, the island did recuperate steadily from the devastating blow caused by the collapse of the Soviet Union and managed rather effectively the external pressure of Helms-Burton. It is still too early to determine whether

Cuba's liquidity troubles and deteriorating economic conditions that began in 2008 will force some existing foreign investors to abandon their projects and lead to another full-blown crisis. But if we move beyond conjunctural factors to trace the root causes of the economic malaise, it is safe to argue that Cuba suffers more from low productivity and efficiency, little export diversification, and other shortcomings of its market-averse policies than anything else. Even some scholars who favor the use of unilateral sanctions as a tool of foreign policy recognize that Cuba's economic performance "probably has more to do with the economic errors of Cuban socialism than with the Helms-Burton legislation" (Kaufman Purcell 2002, 16).

Conclusion

There is little doubt that Helms-Burton has complicated the business operations of foreign investors in Cuba and produced some negative effects on the Cuban economy. First, possible links with expropriated properties and the extreme vagueness of the concept of "trafficking" forced foreign companies to keep a low profile, resort to expensive legal assistance, disguise or reorganize their activities, and eventually renounce further expansion. Second, the higher risk introduced by the Helms-Burton law raised the cost of external financing for Cuba and convinced quite a few potential investors, mostly during 1996–98, to withhold their projects or look elsewhere for less problematic business environments. Third, it is conceivable that certain foreign firms with operations in the United States stayed out of Cuba because of the U.S. policy toward the island that was reinforced by Helms-Burton.[54]

However, the overall foreign investment process clearly has not been halted. Several foreign companies are engaging in profitable activities in Cuba, expanding their operations, and taking advantage of the lack of U.S. competition. In addition, U.S. pressures were largely ineffective against foreign firms with little or no U.S. exposure. Finally, those companies that verified that their projects do not involve confiscated properties moved forward with their investments (McKenna and Kirk 1998, 9). The flow of foreign direct investment into Cuba remains low if compared to other

Latin American countries, but this seems to be more a consequence of Havana's limited commitment to FDI rather than of Helms-Burton.

In summary, Helms-Burton has met with some success but missed its main targets. The law was moderately effective in dissuading a number of foreign companies from entering the Cuban market but largely failed to force existing investors to pull out of Cuba. It also failed to hinder Cuba's economic recovery in the post–cold war era and detain the flow of foreign capital delivered to the island. Besides foreign investment, substantial amounts of hard currency reaching Cuba from the United States, especially in the form of remittances, played a major role in reactivating the island's economy after the deep crisis of the early 1990s. The next chapter provides an analysis of U.S. financial flows in the Cuban economy in the context of tightened U.S. economic sanctions against the Castro government.

5
U.S. Financial Flows in the Cuban Economy

During the 1990s, the United States reinforced its decades-long economic embargo against Cuba with the enactment of the Torricelli law in 1992 and the Helms-Burton law in 1996. Although one of the stated goals of additional sanctions was to offer positive inducements to democratic reforms in Cuba, the key objective of U.S. policy was to intensify economic pressure on the Castro government (and eventually hasten its collapse) by curtailing the flow of hard currency to the island. A spokesman for the U.S. Treasury Department admitted in 2003 that sanctions against Cuba were mainly intended to "deprive the Castro regime of the financial wherewithal to continue to oppress its people."[1]

There has been considerable debate about just how effective Washington's unilateral sanctions against Havana have been in denying hard currency earnings to the Cuban government. In light of the available information, it can be argued that the United States has not only been unable to foster fundamental political reforms in Cuba, but actually has contributed significantly to the recovery of the island's economy from the deep recession of the early 1990s. Despite the tightening of the embargo, sizeable amounts of hard currency were channeled into the Cuban economy by means of U.S. visitors (mainly Cuban Americans), remittances sent by Cuban exiles to their families in Cuba, U.S. telecommunications payments, and American investors who hold shares of foreign companies doing business on the island. Moreover, U.S. agricultural exports to Cuba, much of it allocated by the Castro government through its rationing system with a small share sold in state-run hard currency stores, have catapulted the United States into becoming the top supplier of food to its communist neighbor.

This chapter begins with an analysis of international tourism in Cuba and the presence of U.S. visitors on the island. It continues with an examination of the significance for the Cuban economy of remittances sent from Cuban exiles and payments to Cuba by U.S. carriers for telecommunications services. Finally, it provides an assessment of U.S. investments in foreign-based transnational corporations that operate in the Cuban market and the latest developments in U.S. food sales to Havana. Overall, this chapter demonstrates that the United States has played and continues to play quite an important role in the Cuban economy and that a substantial portion of hard currency reaching Cuba is in violation of U.S. regulations. However, as briefly discussed at the end of the chapter, the role of U.S.-based transnational players in undermining sanctions put in place by their government has become less critical since 2004 due to the emergence of Venezuela as Cuba's main economic lifeline.

International Tourism and U.S.-Based Travel to Cuba

Since the late 1980s, Cuba has targeted tourism as a priority sector because of its ability to generate foreign exchange. Until the upsurge of exports of professional services that began after an accord with Venezuela in 2004, international tourism was, at least in gross terms, the single most important source of hard currency for the Cuban government. Cuba is again emerging as one of the Caribbean's most popular holiday destinations.[2] The tourism industry, which was relatively small prior to 1990, has grown at an astounding 10.7 percent annually (as measured by the average increase in the number of tourist arrivals) since the legalization of the dollar sector of the economy in 1993, with a small decline in the aftermath of the attacks of September 11, 2001 on the United States and another drop in 2006–2007.

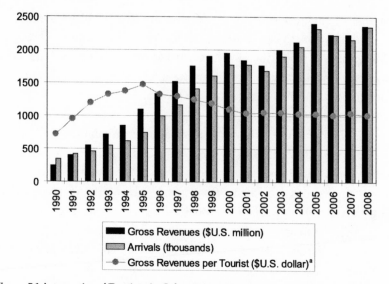

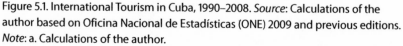

Figure 5.1. International Tourism in Cuba, 1990–2008. *Source*: Calculations of the author based on Oficina Nacional de Estadísticas (ONE) 2009 and previous editions. *Note*: a. Calculations of the author.

There has also been a notable improvement in the integration between local industries and the Cuban tourism sector. While in the early 1990s the overwhelming part of the inputs to the sector had to be imported, local corporations and especially joint ventures with foreign firms currently supply a wide range of products (72 percent of total inputs) such as mineral waters, soft drinks and alcoholic beverages, processed meat, omnibuses, air conditioners, telephones, and electronic equipment. It is estimated that 105,000 Cubans work directly in the island's tourism industry, with some additional 210,000 Cubans working in it indirectly (Quintana et al. 2004, 202).

Figure 5.1 reports data on gross revenues from international tourism, the number of tourist arrivals, and gross revenues per tourist from 1990 to 2008. According to official figures, arrivals rose from 340,000 in 1990 to over a million in 1996, and broke the 2 million mark for the first time in 2004. Similarly, gross revenues from tourism increased from $243 million in 1990 to about $2.1 billion in 2004, making the tourism industry, as Cuban officials often described it, the "engine" of the island's economy. Between 2005 and 2007, however, total arrivals and gross revenues shrank by 7.2 percent and 6.8 percent, respectively. Among various factors, recent monetary measures implemented by the Castro government bear major responsibility for this negative trend. In November 2004, Cuban authorities put an end to the circulation of the U.S. dollar on the island in favor of the convertible peso or CUC and slapped a 10 percent fee on dollar/CUC exchanges. Then, in April 2005, they revaluated the CUC by 8 percent against all international currencies. It goes without saying that the aforementioned currency moves have made Cuba a more expensive and thus less competitive tourism destination in the Caribbean region. On a positive note, tourist arrivals peaked at 2.35 million in 2008 (an increase of 9.1 percent from 2007) and gross revenues reached $2.36 billion (an increase of 5.5 percent).

Additional indicators show critical efficiency problems in Cuba's tourism industry. In terms of tourist expenditures, gross revenues per tourist per year grew from $750 in 1990 to $1,475 in 1995. Since then, annual gross revenues per tourist have decreased steadily to just $1,005 in 2008, about 32 percent below the level of 1995. The number of tourism rooms in Cuba rose from 12,900 in 1990 to approximately 48,000 at the end of 2008, but gross revenues per room plummeted more than 16 percent during 1999–2008. Overall, these problems suggest that the future contribution of tourism to economic growth could diminish greatly once the sector reaches its maturity.

Although they have changed many times since 1963, restrictions on travel from the United States to Cuba have been a key component of U.S. policy toward the Castro government for most of the last forty-six years. During the 1990s, President Clinton made several changes to travel regulations in response to actions by the Cuban government. As a reaction to the *balsero* crisis of 1994,[3] Clinton banned family visits to Cuba by Cuban Americans except in cases of "extreme humanitarian need." In 1996, after the shooting down of two U.S. planes flown by Cuban exiles, he suspended direct flights between the two countries (Robyn et al. 2002, 2). Yet, in 1999, as part of a policy aimed to promote people-to-people contacts, he streamlined travel procedures for students, athletes, artists, and other groups and individuals to visit Cuba. Clinton's policy, inaugurated in the wake of Pope John Paul II's trip to Cuba, also allowed resumption of charter flights from Miami to Havana as well as new direct flights from New

York and Los Angeles. These changes were mainly intended to facilitate family reunions between Cuban Americans and their relatives on the island (Eckstein and Barberia 2001, 12).

In order to travel to Cuba, individuals subject to U.S. law must be authorized by a general license (which requires no written authorization) or a specific license (which requires approval) from the Office of Foreign Assets Control (OFAC) of the Department of the Treasury. Currently, the list of individuals who can travel without specific documentation from the OFAC includes Cuban Americans on family trips, government officials, journalists who are regularly employed by a news organization, full-time academic researchers, employees of U.S. firms selling eligible agricultural goods and medical items to Cuba, and employees of U.S. telecommunications service providers. In contrast, a specific license is required for freelance journalists, members of religious and humanitarian organizations, university students, and amateur or semi-professional athletes participating in sports competitions.

In March 2003, the Bush administration introduced regulations on travel (and remittances) that allowed more Cuban Americans to visit family members in Cuba once a year under a general license (a specific license was nonetheless required for more than one visit per year) and forbade trips to the island that combined non-credit educational activities with people-to-people contacts. The latter had become a loophole for groups to travel to Cuba when the educational aspect was barely evident. The rules of 2003 eliminated the previously established requirement that Cuban-American visits could take place only in cases of a self-defined "humanitarian purpose," like a sick or dying relative, thus easing the conditions under which U.S. citizens of Cuban descent could travel to Cuba. On June 30, 2004, Bush implemented tougher measures aimed to stem the flow of hard currency reaching Cuba and hasten the end of the Castro government. In addition to further restrictions for U.S.-based educational travel to the island, these measures prohibited Cuban Americans from visiting relatives in Cuba more than once every three years (a specific license was required for every trip), limited their stay to fourteen days, and reduced the amount they could spend during their visits from $167 to $50 per day.

In early September 2009, fleshing out an announcement made almost five months before, the new U.S. president, Barack Obama, officially granted Cuban Americans unrestricted rights to visit family and send remittances to Cuba. Obama's measures, which represented a significant change in U.S. policy toward the island, also broadened the range of relatives that Cuban Americans can visit and removed limitations on the duration of their trips and related expenditure amounts. As with all other licensed U.S. travelers to Cuba, Cuban Americans are now allowed to spend up to $179 per day for lodging, meals, and ground transportation.[4]

Cuban official statistics include data on U.S. citizens of non-Cuban origin traveling to Cuba with a U.S. passport but do not report the actual number of Cuban Americans making trips to the island with a regular Cuban passport. Anyone who left Cuba after December 31, 1970, is still considered a Cuban citizen by Havana's authorities and required to travel with a Cuban passport. However, data provided by the Castro government to the United Nations World Tourism Organization (UNWTO) report the annual number of all Cuban residents abroad who visit the island as "other Caribbean arrivals." This special category can only refer to Cuban visitors because arrivals from each Caribbean country are reported separately in the UNWTO's tourism statistics. A publication of the United States International Trade Commission in 2007 used the same category to estimate Cuban-American trips to Cuba (USITC 2007, 3–14).

Based on interviews with Cuban experts, this study estimates that about 90 percent of such "other Caribbean arrivals" during 1990–98 represented Cuban Americans traveling to Cuba. But more recent works, perhaps taking into account the growing number of Cubans who are migrating to European and Latin American countries, claim that approximately 80 percent of all Cuban visitors are Cuban Americans (García Jiménez et al. 2006, 14). For the 1999–2008 period, this study therefore calculates annual Cuban-American arrivals as 80 percent of all Cuban residents abroad who visited Cuba that year. Such estimates seem reasonable (and possibly even conservative) if we consider that by the year 2000 about 85 percent of all Cuban residents abroad (including Cuban descendents) lived in the United States, mainly in Florida (Aja Díaz 2002, 12). In any case, whatever the exact number of Cuban-American annual visits to the island, one

Table 5.1. U.S.-Based Visitors to Cuba, 1990–1998

	1990	1991	1992	1993	1994	1995	1996	1997	1998
U.S. citizens not of Cuban descent	7,375	11,233	10,050	14,715	17,937	20,672	27,113	34,956	46,778
Cuban Americans[a]	2,600	4,600	14,600	19,400	33,500	39,300	58,300	71,700	94,900
Total	9,975	15,833	24,650	34,115	51,437	59,972	85,413	106,656	141,678
U.S. Rank[b]	7	7	6	6	5	4	4	4	4

Sources: Oficina Nacional de Estadísticas (ONE) 1996, 1998, 2000; Alvarez and Amat 1996; United Nations World Tourism Organization (UNWTO) 2003 and previous editions.

Notes: a. Estimates of the author. Annual Cuban-American arrivals are calculated as 90 percent of all Cuban residents abroad who visited Cuba that year.
b. The rank refers to the position of the United States among countries whose citizens visit Cuba.

thing is clear: if trips to Cuba by Cubans living abroad increase, Cuban-American trips most likely increase.

Table 5.1 reports data on U.S.-based visitors to Cuba for the years 1990–98, making a distinction between U.S. citizens of non-Cuban descent and Cuban Americans. Despite travel restrictions, the number of U.S.-based visitors to the island increased significantly during the 1990s. Trips by U.S. citizens of non-Cuban origin rose from about 7,000 in 1990 to more than 46,000 in 1998. Regarding Cuban Americans, the number of visitors grew from approximately 2,600 in 1990 to almost 40,000 in 1995. Between 1996 and 1998 (when Clinton banned direct travel), visits by Cuban Americans to Cuba almost doubled from 58,300 to 94,900.[5] In short, whereas in 1990 about 10,000 individuals subject to U.S. law traveled to Cuba, representing the seventh largest group among foreign travelers, in 1998 this number had jumped to more than 140,000. By 1995, the United States was already the fourth largest source of visitors to the island after Canada, Italy, and Spain.[6]

In recent years, the presence of the United States in the Cuban tourism market has become increasingly important. Table 5.2 presents data on international arrivals to Cuba from selected countries for the years 1999–2008. In 1999, an estimated 169,000 overseas visitors to Cuba came from the United States (about 107,000 were Cuban Americans), more than from any other country except Canada and Germany. Between 1999 and 2003, arrivals from the United States grew steadily, consolidating U.S.-based visitors as the second largest group among foreign travelers.[7] At the same time, tourists from some European countries such as Germany and Spain declined.

Approximately 126,000 Cuban Americans and 78,000 U.S. citizens of non-Cuban descent visited Cuba in 2002, representing 12 percent of total arrivals to the island. About 50,000 were tourists traveling via third countries with or without their government's authorization.[8] As recalled by a Canadian official some years ago, U.S. tourists "are quite visible among visitors arriving in Cuba on flights from Montreal, Toronto, Kingston, Nassau, and Mexico City" (USITC 2001, 3–25). In 2003, the number of Cuban-American trips to Cuba reached nearly 135,000, with an additional 84,529 trips by other U.S. citizens. For the purpose of Washington's policy toward Havana, it is worth emphasizing that U.S.-based visitors to Cuba

Table 5.2. International Visitors to Cuba by Origin, 1999–2008

	1999	2000	2001	2002	2003	2004	2005	2006	2007	2008
Canada	276,346	307,725	350,426	348,468	452,438	563,371	602,377	604,263	660,384	818,246
United States	169,145	186,598	190,089	203,646	219,129	150,156	156,333	163,608	194,821	223,404
U.S. citizens (ncd)[a]	62,345	76,898	78,789	77,646	84,529	49,856	37,233	36,808	40,521	41,904
Cuban Americans[b]	106,800	109,700	111,300	126,000	134,600	100,300	119,100	126,800	154,300	181,500
United Kingdom	85,829	90,972	94,794	103,741	120,866	161,189	199,399	211,075	208,122	193,932
Italy	160,843	175,667	159,423	147,750	177,627	178,570	169,317	144,249	134,289	126,042
Spain	146,978	153,197	140,125	138,609	127,666	146,236	194,103	185,531	133,149	121,166
Germany	182,159	203,403	171,851	152,662	157,721	143,644	124,527	114,292	103,054	100,964
France	123,607	132,089	138,765	129,907	144,548	119,868	107,518	103,469	92,304	90,731
Mexico	70,983	86,540	98,495	87,589	88,787	79,752	89,154	97,984	92,120	84,052
Others	386,891	437,795	430,573	373,790	416,900	505,786	676,606	596,096	533,978	589,803
Total	1,602,781	1,773,986	1,774,541	1,686,162	1,905,682	2,048,572	2,319,334	2,220,567	2,152,221	2,348,340
U.S. Rank[c]	3	3	2	2	2	4	5	4	3	2

Sources: Oficina Nacional de Estadísticas (ONE) 2009; United Nations World Tourism Organization (UNWTO) 2009; Data provided by the Cuban government to the UNWTO in July 2009.

Notes: a. Individuals not of Cuban descent (ncd).

b. Estimates of the author. Annual Cuban-American arrivals are calculated as 80 percent of all Cuban residents abroad who visited Cuba that year.

c. The rank refers to the position of the United States among countries whose citizens visit Cuba.

have become a valuable source of hard currency for the island's tourism industry. By 2001, even with sanctions in place, American travelers were believed to spend about $200 million a year in Cuba,[9] thus contributing to more than 10 percent of the Castro government's revenues from tourism activities.

In the aftermath of the Bush administration's restrictions on U.S.-based travel to Cuba implemented in June 2004, both the U.S. and Cuban governments said those restrictions were having a tremendous negative impact on trips taken to Cuba from the United States. The U.S. State Department revealed that, from July to December 2004, the number of reservations on charter flights to Cuba plummeted by more than half as compared to the same period in 2003. The decline was particularly marked during Christmas time, when a 75 percent drop in reservations took place.[10] Moreover, Washington said that the number of U.S. legal visitors to Cuba dropped by more than 60 percent between June 2004 and June 2005. Similarly, Cuban officials maintained that overall U.S. travel to the island decreased by 46 percent in 2004 as compared to 2003, especially Cuban-American arrivals (which had decreased by 50 percent). They also claimed that all visitors from the United States continued to decline, albeit slightly, in 2005 and 2006 (Sullivan 2008, 14).[11]

In reality, Cuban official statistics show a drastic plunge of trips taken to Cuba by Americans of non-Cuban descent after 2003 but suggest that Cuban-American trips suffered a less marked drop. In other words, the main targets of Bush's travel restrictions with respect to Cuba seem to have been the least affected by those measures. Only 36,800 U.S. citizens of non-Cuban origin traveled to the island in 2006 and little more than 40,000 per year in 2007–2008, still less than half than in 2003. Cuban-American arrivals shrank by approximately 25 percent in 2004 and have gradually recovered since then. They actually reached about 154,000 in 2007 and peaked at more than 180,000 in 2008. In March 2008 at a meeting in Havana of Cuban Residents Abroad, the Cuban foreign minister Felipe Pérez Roque confirmed: "In 2007, close to 193,000 Cubans, including from the United States, visited our country, which is a new historic record."[12] Pérez Roque's figure coincides precisely with the number of "other Caribbean arrivals" for the same year, which totaled 192,847. After dropping to fifth place in 2005, the United States was again the second largest source of foreign visitors to Cuba in 2008 after Canada.

Illegal trips sustained by family ties might have a lot to do with the stark difference between Cuban-American and other U.S. citizens' travel activities with respect to Cuba in the period after 2004. But illegal U.S.-based travel to the island is not something new. Many individuals from the United States have been visiting Cuba through third countries without U.S. travel permits for quite some time, technically violating U.S. sanctions prohibiting the spending of money for unlicensed purposes. Between 1994 and 2002, the number of individuals subject to U.S. law traveling to Cuba, but not authorized from the OFAC to do so, increased on average 19 percent to 21 percent, while legal visits rose by just 9 percent to 11 percent. For instance, it is reported that approximately twenty-two thousand U.S. citizens visited Cuba in 2000 without authorization from the OFAC (USCTEC 2003). Other estimates put the number of U.S.-based illegal visits to Cuba between forty thousand and fifty thousand per year, representing up to one-fourth of total U.S. travel to the island. Cuban authorities, eager to accept U.S. visitors paying in hard currency, do not stamp the passports of Americans, leaving no official trace of their presence.[13] An artist from Minneapolis said she was vacationing in Toronto, Canada, in 2002 when she spotted a sign publicizing a trip to Havana. She wasted no time booking a plane ticket and spent a week touring the island's capital. Another U.S. citizen from Dallas said he headed illegally for Cuba via Cancún, Mexico. He carried gifts for local people and depleted a cash budget of about $2,000 because embargo restrictions make credit cards issued in the United States unusable for transactions in Cuba.[14]

After President Bush took office in 2001, the OFAC began to crack down on those traveling to Cuba without permission. During the Clinton administration, the OFAC took steps to levy fines (the average fine is $5,500) on between 46 and 188 Americans a year. That figure jumped to 700 in 2001.[15] Yet, U.S. fines still affected fewer than 3 percent of the annual number of violators. Furthermore, Washington's authorities paid little attention to Cuban Americans since the latter were allowed to visit relatives on the island once a year without approval from their government. As U.S. Representative Jeff Flake (R-Ariz.) pointed out in early 2003: "U.S. authorities pay no attention to Cuban-Americans even as they harass and level fines against Americans who go to the island. While being allowed to travel for a self-defined humanitarian need, their relatives always seem to get sick around the same time, like Christmas and other major holidays."[16]

It was not until June 2004 that the Bush administration enacted stricter licensing regulations for Cuban-American trips and finally intensified enforcement actions against all U.S. travelers to Cuba. The key issue is that Cuban Americans were still better positioned than other U.S. citizens to circumvent travel restrictions. Americans of non-Cuban descent traveling to Cuba illegally through a third country get their U.S. passports stamped when they leave the third country for Cuba and then again when they return from Cuba to the third country but no stamp from Cuba itself. When the travelers arrive in the United States, attentive U.S. immigration officers can easily spot the missing link and figure out the country they visited. Cuban Americans can use their U.S. passports to enter and leave the United States and the third country, while using their Cuban passports for the rest of the journey. Ironically, it is the Castro government's requirement that they hold a valid Cuban passport when entering the island that has helped many Cuban Americans bypass U.S. travel rules.

A look at recent U.S. government data on specific licenses for travel to Cuba gives some insight into the magnitude of illegal trips to the island by Cuban Americans. The U.S. Office of Foreign Assets Control issued 19,766 licenses for family visits in 2004 (each individual received a separate license), 25,304 in 2005, and 40,308 in 2006 (USITC 2007, 3–4). During this period, estimated Cuban-American trips to the island were more than three times the number of annual licensed persons. It should be noted that each year the OFAC also issued more than 200 licenses for religious activities (multiple travelers may travel on one license) that apparently were utilized by many Cuban Americans to get around travel restrictions. In late March 2005, the U.S. Treasury Department launched an investigation of virtually all religious Cuba-travel licensees in the United States after some Florida-based religious groups were accused of abusing their licenses to promote family visits to Cuba.[17] As a result, the OFAC implemented more stringent rules for these organizations by restricting the number of people they could send to Cuba and the frequency of their trips.[18] No such limits previously existed.

In sum, George W. Bush's restrictions on travel to Cuba curtailed substantially trips to the island by Americans of non-Cuban descent but were unable to stem illegal travel by Cuban Americans who maintain close ties with relatives in their country of origin. Once formed, family connections tend to become self-sustaining despite new regulations that may interfere. Keeping Cuban families apart might have been a bigger challenge than U.S. authorities had envisioned. The other part of the story is that family ties stimulated bonding of considerable economic worth that undermined the main goal of U.S. economic sanctions against Cuba.

Remittances to Cuba

As a result of the deep economic recession that threatened Cuba's survival in the early 1990s, the Castro government decriminalized both the possession and the use of hard currency (especially U.S. dollars) in August 1993. It also legalized dollar-denominated remittances under its monetary reform program of 1994. Since then, family remittances mainly sent from Cuban Americans have become a vital source of supplemental income for many Cubans. Even more important for the purpose of this study, such practices significantly boosted the domestic dollar market in Cuba. As Jatar-Hausmann (1999, 68) observed, the legalization of the use of foreign currency encouraged more family remittances, and the high prices at state-owned dollar stores acted as a hidden sales tax on them, effectively allowing the Cuban government to obtain access to that money. In light of this development, some scholars contended that money sent from abroad was the single most important factor in reactivating the Cuban economy in the second half of the 1990s.

Pedro Monreal, an academic from the island, argued in the late 1990s that Cuba had become increasingly dependent on remittances and donations from abroad. He specified that, in strict terms, the Cuban economy could not be qualified as an economy depending fundamentally on remittances because other important activities such as tourism and mining had emerged. Nevertheless, he concluded that the importance of money sent from abroad was beyond question. In net terms, remittances were at that time (and remained at least until 2004) the biggest source of foreign exchange for the country, bigger than tourism and sugar (Monreal 1999, 50).

For years, many of those who analyze data on revenues from tourism (about $2.3 billion in 2008) have identified the tourism industry as the main generator of hard currency for the Cuban economy. But these are gross figures. In net terms, revenues are significantly lower. In March 2001, the Cuban vice president Carlos Lage estimated the cost per dollar of gross income from tourism activities at $0.76.[19] This indicator is very high and refers only to the direct cost in dollars, not the indirect cost incurred by the state in the tourism sector. Also consider that domestically produced goods for tourism have an imported (indirect) component in dollars, which implies that the cost per dollar of gross income would be even higher. Direct and indirect costs per dollar have been estimated at more than $0.80, which would mean for the country a net result of just $0.20 for every dollar of gross income from tourism activities.[20] This was confirmed by Marta Maíz, the Cuban vice minister of tourism, in May 2003. In an interview for the Cuban magazine *Bohemia*, Maíz said that in 2002 "income from tourism was $52.2 million less than in 2001, with a cost of USD 80 cents for every dollar captured by the country."[21] To make things worse, some Cuban economists estimated that, in 2003, the cost per dollar of gross income in the tourism sector increased from $0.80 to $0.83, which would mean a net result of just 17 percent of gross revenues.[22]

Before President Obama removed limits on family remittances to Cuba, Cuban Americans could send no more than $300 every three months to relatives on the island. Apart from a short-lived easing of restrictions introduced by the OFAC in March 2003 that lasted until mid-2004, a cap of $300 in remittances was also applied to licensed travelers to Cuba, who were required to produce the visa recipient's full name, date of birth, and the number and data of issuance of the visa or other travel authorizations issued. A licensed traveler was allowed to carry only funds that he or she was authorized to remit and could not carry remittances made by others. Since 1999, the U.S. government has authorized several companies in the United States to legally transfer money to the island by relying on individuals in Cuba who are contracted to deliver the funds. Within the limit of $300 per trimester, remitters in the United States (who must be at least eighteen years old) could send smaller amounts more than once in that period, paying a fee each time the money was transferred. In early 2009, the average total cost of remitting to Cuba through official operators was about 17 percent of the amount being sent, among the highest in Latin America (Orozco 2009, 6). Although Western Union is by far the most established business, there are currently over seventy U.S.-based firms holding licenses to operate as remittance forwarders to Cuba.

The OFAC's regulations of March 2003 allowed U.S. authorized travelers to Cuba to carry as much as $3,000 in household remittances, up from $300 every three months. The increased amount of remittances was intended to help up to ten households per traveler.[23] However, stricter rules on remittances implemented by the Bush administration on June 30, 2004, reestablished the cap of $300 dollars for licensed travelers and limited money transfers only to immediate relatives, excluding aunts, uncles, and cousins, all of whom were formerly on the list of cash recipients. Additionally, these measures banned U.S. citizens from including clothing and other such items in their gift parcel deliveries to Cuba. The parcels' contents were limited to food, medicines and medical supplies, and receive-only radio equipment.

Estimating the flow of remittances to Cuba is difficult given the lack of reliable information. Official counts (as reported by the Economic Commission for Latin America and the Caribbean, or ECLAC, only until 2001) make inferences from "net current transfers" in Cuba's balance of payments, which are mostly made up of remittances and, to a lesser extent, donations. But it is unclear how the Cuban government records remittances under net transfers. Some Cuban economists claimed that these figures simply include transactions thorough official mechanisms such as Western Union, Transcard,[24] and other services, excluding a variety of informal money transfers from abroad carried out through entrusted entrepreneurs (mules) as well as friends and relatives visiting the island.[25] Other economists argued that Cuban authorities use formal transfers only as a reference, to which they add estimates on the basis of sales in hard currency stores, exchanges of dollars/CUCs for pesos in money exchange houses (casas de cambio, or CADECA), and hoarding (money that people guard in the house for preservation or future use). Yet, they quickly

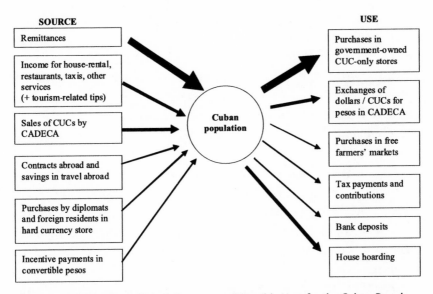

Figure 5.2. Main Sources of Hard Currency and Possible Uses for the Cuban Population. A thicker arrow indicates a larger amount of hard currency received and used by the Cuban population.
Source: Elaboration of the author from Aguilar Trujillo 2001, 100.

recognized that figures should be interpreted with caution. According to these economists, calculations exclude sales in tourist outlets (where Cubans also buy products) and make use of unreliable surveys to estimate the level of hoarding in Cuba.[26] Finally, some scholars contended that recorded figures under net transfers are calculated as the turnover of hard currency shops minus earnings accounted for by official payments in convertible pesos, mainly through incentive schemes (Barberia 2002, 13).

Whatever the method used by the Cuban government to record transactions under "net current transfers," it appears that official counts of remittances underestimate the amount of money sent from Cubans abroad to their families on the island. Although it is virtually impossible to provide accurate estimates of remittances to Cuba, the best way to proceed is to analyze the main sources of hard currency for the Cuban population and its possible uses as presented in figure 5.2. It should be noted that dollar stores no longer exist in Cuba as the U.S. dollar was taken out of circulation on November 8, 2004. Cuban citizens may continue to possess

U.S. dollars, but using the latter in commercial transactions or retail is now prohibited. Cubans must rely on the convertible peso or CUC for purchases of goods in hard currency (CUC-only) stores or purchases of regular pesos in money exchange houses. In this study, the convertible peso is referred to as hard money to distinguish it from the regular peso, which circulates in Cuba at a current rate of 24/25 pesos per CUC. Technically, the CUC is not a hard currency because its value is not recognized outside the island.

Experts believe that remittances benefit directly as many as 30 percent of Cuba's 11.2 million citizens even though that percentage nearly doubles when considering all Cubans who have some degree of access to hard currency. Remittances constitute, without any doubt, the most important source of hard currency for the population of the island.[27] Furthermore, apart from the option of using regular pesos to purchase CUCs in money exchange houses, many Cubans in the private sector can earn the equivalent of hundreds of dollars per month for services such as house rental, restaurants, and taxis. Several jobs in the tourism sector can also bring significant amounts of hard currency tips to Cuban workers such as cab drivers, waiters, bartenders, and other hotel employees. Finally, Cubans who work in joint ventures, embassies, foreign offices, and in certain key industries such as tourism, nickel, oil, and tobacco receive incentive payments in convertible pesos. In short, jobs that can earn hard currency salaries or tips from foreign businesses and tourists have become highly desirable in Cuba.

It is worth mentioning that Cubans with contracts abroad like musicians, technicians, and other professionals may obtain salaries in hard currency. The number of people enjoying these benefits has increased substantially since the deployment of Cuban doctors, teachers, and sports trainers to Venezuela and other countries was expanded in 2004. Nevertheless, the amount of money Cuban professionals abroad bring or send home to their families, which is essentially another form of remittances, still remains relatively low if compared with money transfers from Cuban migrants mostly based in the United States.

As to the potential use of hard currency, prior to November 2004 the large majority of Cubans used dollars to make purchases in government-owned dollar stores (mainly for food, personal hygiene products, and

Table 5.3. Estimates of Remittances to Cuba, 2001–2006 ($U.S. Millions)

	2001	2002	2003	2004	2005	2006
Sales in hard currency stores[a]	1,035	1,055	1,232	1,379	1,391	1,459
Dollar/CUC purchases by CADECA	100	100	96	135	120	70
Annual hoarded money	50	50	55	20	10	20
Total	1,185	1,205	1,383	1,534	1,521	1,549
From this amount subtract:						
Income for house rental, restaurants, taxis, other services[b]	180	180	200	210	221	150
Sales of CUCs by CADECA	65	68	80	90	150	100
Incentive payments in CUCs	20	20	25	27	50	94
Purchases by diplomats and foreign residents in hard currency stores	20	22	25	27	30	33
Total remittances	900	915	1,053	1,180	1,070	1,172

Sources: Oficina Nacional de Estadísticas (ONE) 2007 and previous editions; Spadoni 2003; "Déficit en Sector Externo," Economics Press Service, February 29, 2004; "La Encrucijada de la Economía Cubana, 2006–2007," Inter Press Service (IPS), Enfoque Especial, June 2007; Estimates of the author based on interviews with Cuban economists.
Notes: a. Dollar stores until November 2004, CUC-only stores since then.
b. Tourism-related tips not included.

clothes) or exchanged them for regular pesos in CADECA. At present, those Cubans who receive dollars or other currencies from abroad must exchange them for CUCs in order to carry out these transactions. Relatively small amounts of hard currency are utilized to make purchases in free farmers' markets, make tax payments and contributions, and open accounts in local banks. The level of hoarding may be quite significant, albeit it is difficult to reliably assess the extent of this practice.[28]

Using available information on sales in hard currency stores as the main reference, it is possible to estimate the level of remittances to Cuba. We must also take into account that sizable amounts of CUCs/dollars are either exchanged for regular pesos in CADECA or stored in Cuban homes. While remittances are the most important source of hard currency for the Cuban population, they are not the only one. Thus, in order to calculate the amount of money sent from Cubans abroad to their families on the island, we must consider other ways by which Cubans procure hard currency. Table 5.3 provides annual estimates of remittances to Cuba between 2001 and 2006. Figures for sales in hard currency stores are official data provided by the Cuban government while the other amounts are estimates from unofficial sources and interviews with Cuban economists.

As noted before, 2001 is the last year when the Economic Commission for Latin America and the Caribbean reported the value of remittances to Cuba based on "net current transfers." Total sales in dollar stores in 2001 were $1,035 million, with an additional $100 million of dollar purchases by CADECA and $50 million in annual hoarded money. From this amount, we must subtract the dollar income ($180 million) of Cubans who provide services such as house rental,[29] restaurants, and taxis. Tourism-related tips are not included as figures for these practices are not available. We must also deduct sales of CUCs by CADECA ($65 million), incentive payments in convertible pesos ($20 million), and purchases by diplomats and foreign residents in hard currency stores ($20 million).

As shown in table 5.3, total remittances to Cuba in 2001 were an estimated $900 million, substantially higher than the amount reported by sources like ECLAC that rely on the Cuban government's balance of payments data. If ECLAC's figures (just $730 million for 2001) are correct, then the level of transactions in dollar stores and CADECA plus annual hoarded money (a cumulative $1,185 million) imply that, in addition to remittances, Cubans obtained about $450 million in hard currency revenues in 2001. This is highly improbable. Admittedly, hard currency sources unrelated to remittances may not be negligible, but they can hardly make up for the difference between the amount of money transfers calculated by ECLAC and the cumulative sum of sales in dollar stores, transactions in exchange houses, and annual hoarded money. Cuban economists estimated that foreign exchange income from activities unrelated to remittances can, at best, represent about 25 percent of all hard currency revenues of the Cuban population.[30]

For 2001–2006, calculations of money transfers to Cuba using the method described above reveal that the annual share of people's foreign exchange income from activities other than remittances has consistently remained below 25 percent of total hard currency revenues except in 2005 (almost 30 percent). That year, the share was mainly inflated by increased sales of CUCs in CADECA after the Castro government more than doubled regular peso salaries and the pensions of millions of Cuban citizens.[31] A notable upward trend of incentive payments in convertible pesos was another important factor. In 2005, after years of steady growth, remittances to Cuba suffered a decline (arguably as a result of

Bush's restrictions on Cuban-American travel and money transfers to the island) even though sales in hard currency stores rose slightly. But remittances appear to have expanded again since then. In general, in the way that Cuban-American arrivals on the island most likely increase when arrivals of Cubans living abroad increase, remittances to Cuba (primarily sent from the United States) most likely grow when sales in hard currency stores are on the rise.

Table 5.4 offers a time series of sales in hard currency stores and remittances to Cuba from 1995 to 2007. Figures from ECLAC are included for comparison. Since the legalization of dollar holdings in 1993, money remittances to Cuba have increased significantly. The ECLAC reports that individuals of Cuban descent sent more than $500 million to their relatives on the island in 1995. That figure topped out at $740 million in 2000. Almost 90 percent of remittance dollars reaching Cuba came from the United States (Orozco 2003, 1). Sales in hard currency stores expanded as well, but at much higher rates. Between 1997 and 2001, in particular, they grew from $867 million to $1,035 million. This suggests that the actual amounts of remittances to Cuba might have been higher than those reported by ECLAC. Whereas remittances, as calculated by ECLAC, increased only 9 percent during 1997–2001, sales in dollar stores rose by almost 20 percent.

I estimate that remittances to Cuba from abroad were $750 million in 1997, $900 million in 2001, and more than $1 billion a year between 2003 and 2007. The assumption of sizable undercounts in the calculation of remittances is also consistent with the growth of Cuban-American visits to the island after Clinton's inauguration of the people-to-people contact policy in early 1999. We should remember that a large part of money transfers is undertaken in the "gray area" of the informal tourism sector. Cuban official data put total sales in hard currency stores at $1,391 million (or millions of CUCs to be more precise) in 2005, $1,459 million in 2006, and $1,605 million in 2007, suggesting that remittances to Cuba have continued to grow despite U.S. attempts to curtail these financial flows. Based on sales volumes of CUC-only stores, remittances in 2007 might have actually been higher than ever before. Only CIMEX, the corporation that runs more hard currency outlets in Cuba, announced sales of $557 million that year, followed by other major Cuban corporations such as TRD-

Table 5.4. Sales in Hard Currency Stores and Remittances to Cuba, 1995–2007 ($U.S. Millions)

	1995	1996	1997	1998	1999	2000	2001	2002	2003	2004	2005	2006	2007
Sales in hard currency stores	537	744	867	902	941	986	1,035	1,055	1,232	1,379	1,391	1,459	1,605
Net current transfers	646	744	792	813	799	740	813	820	915	974	-367	278	-199
ECLAC estimates of remittances	537	630	670	690	700	740	730	—	—	—	—	—	—
Author's estimates of remittances	537	645	750	782	815	855	900	915	1,053	1,180	1,070	1,172	1,285

Sources: Oficina Nacional de Estadísticas (ONE) 2008b and previous editions; Banco Central de Cuba (BCC) 2002; Comisión Económica para América Latina y el Caribe (CEPAL) 2002, 2008; Estimates of the author.

Caribe ($377 million) and Cubalse ($288 million). The retail indicators of all three companies, which account for about 75 percent of total transactions in hard currency stores, improved in 2007 (ONE 2008b). Cuban authorities revealed that sales of CUC-only stores grew by an additional 8 percent in 2008.[32]

Accurate estimates of remittances to Cuba are inevitably complicated by the existence of well-developed informal mechanisms for money transfers. Instead of making use of formal wire transfer services, many U.S. citizens of Cuban descent rely on relatively inexpensive and more user-friendly informal remittance channels (Eckstein 2003, 15). It is well known that a huge flow of remittances arrives on the island in the luggage of friends, relatives, or entrusted agents. The latter, usually referred to as "mules," are entrepreneurs who travel frequently to Cuba as tourists and without a license to operate as a business. They carry both money and packages of goods to Cuban relatives of the senders for cheaper fees than the ones charged by official agencies.

A survey of November 2001 carried out by the Inter-American Development Bank (IADB) showed that 32.1 percent of Cuban Americans used Western Union to remit to Cuba, while more than 46 percent preferred to send money with persons traveling to the island.[33] More recent surveys of Cuban remitters in the United States found that the percentage of people using informal networks to transfer money to Cuba was less than 20 percent of the total in February 2005 and about 44 percent in January 2009 (Bendixen and Associates 2005; Orozco 2009, 6). Mules, in particular, became more active after President Bush enacted more stringent rules on remittances in 2004 and stepped up enforcement of U.S. law. In any case, the share of survey respondents who allegedly remit through mules or other travelers is in no way indicative of the economic magnitude of informal activities. A study in 2003 calculated that informal mechanisms captured up to 80 percent of the total flow of remittances to Cuba from the United States even though less than 50 percent of survey respondents claimed to make use of such networks (Orozco 2003, 4).

Some analysts have attempted to estimate the amount of remittances sent to Cuba by tracking the activities on the island of money transfer companies based in the United States and other countries and carrying out interviews with officials of those companies, travel agents, and other entrepreneurs. Figures from the IADB put the total amount of remittances to Cuba at $930 million in 2001 (similar to the author's estimate) and $1,138 million in 2002, an increase of approximately 22 percent over the previous year (IADB 2003). These findings are very surprising in light of the economic downturn of the U.S. economy following the terrorist attacks of September 2001. The IADB also reported that remittances to Cuba were $1,194 million in 2003, up around 5 percent from 2002 (IADB 2004).

There is some evidence that money transfers from the United States oftentimes violated the limit of $1,200 per year on remittances to Cuba. Whereas more than 50 percent of Cuban respondents in the IADB's survey of November 2001 said they sent less than $100 per transaction, interviews with mules showed that, on average, they carried more than $200 per individual package.[34] Given that most mules traveled twice a month using different routes, it is likely that transactions with these entrepreneurs frequently exceeded the $1,200 annual cap on remittances for U.S. citizens. A Bendixen survey of 2005 found that 13 percent of Cuban-American respondents were able to send more than $300 dollars per trimester to relatives in Cuba, mostly relying on informal networks (Bendixen and Associates 2005). As further proof of illegal activities, Cuban sources indicated in 2001 that the number of U.S. citizens of Cuban descent sending money back home could have been as high as 520,000 (Aguilar Trujillo 2001, 98). If we divide my remittance figures (with a 10 percent deduction because not all money came from the United States) by the estimated number of Cuban-American remitters, we can see that money transfers to Cuba from the United States were on average $1,558 per person in 2001, $1,584 in 2002, $1,822 in 2003, and $2,042 in 2004. Confirming these results, some experts argued in 2004 that Cuban Americans sent an annual average of $2,000 per person to Cuba using nontraditional channels like mules or other entrusted agents.[35]

Orozco reported that more than 80 percent of remittances to Cuba still came from the United States in 2005 but claimed that the U.S. share relative to other countries (especially Spain) had dropped to about 53 percent by January 2009. Yet, it remains unclear how 23 percent of money transfers to Cuba in early 2009 could originate from Spain and nearly half from locations outside the United States if, as specified by Orozco, only 7.1 percent of Cuban migrants resided in Spain and nearly 80 percent lived in the United States (Orozco 2009, 2). Growing remittances from Europe and other places might have been triggered in part by U.S. citizens using businesses located in third countries to circumvent U.S. restrictions. In August 2004, the Castro government launched a new service (SerCuba) allowing people in the United States or elsewhere to forward remittances to Cuban nationals via Spain and Italy or through the company's Web site.[36] In late December 2004, the Swiss firm AWS Technologies inaugurated its own online business for money transfers to the island from all over the world by any customer with a credit card.[37] Canadian-based services like Transcard, Duales, and Cash2Cuba have also facilitated unregulated remittance practices with respect to Cuba.

Overall, apart from a short-term negative impact, there is no evidence that President Bush's measures of 2004 curbed the flow of remittances to Cuba. On the contrary, remittances to the island seem to have reached unprecedented levels in 2007 and possibly 2008, raising doubts about the effectiveness of U.S. policy toward the Castro government. The Economic Commission for Latin America and the Caribbean (ECLAC 2004, 128) suggested that remittances increased in 2004 by reporting that net current transfers in Cuba's balance of payments were about $1 billion that year, up almost 10 percent from 2003 ($915 million). As for 2005, ECLAC (2006, 1) stated that money transfers to Cuba from abroad were down notably even though sales in hard currency stores had expanded by 6 percent. My estimates in table 5.4 highlight a similar trend. Since then, ECLAC has made no reference to the evolution of remittances in its annual reports on the status of the Cuban economy, probably because Cuban official figures on net current transfers showing sharp swings in 2005–2007 are even more difficult to interpret than previous ones. While a dramatic expansion of Cuban donations to other countries in the form of medical services might have had something to do with these large fluctuations, the latter remain largely unexplained.[38] On this last point, the Economist Intelligence Unit (2007) wrote, "An analysis of trends in the components of current transfers—remittances, earnings from the informal sector and donations—suggests that there is either an error in the accounts or a major accounting adjustment." Thus, considering the puzzling figures on net current transfers, sales in hard currency stores are undoubtedly the best reference source for a meaningful assessment of remittances to Cuba.

There are at least three plausible explanations for the potential increase of remittances to Cuba in 2004 and, more generally, for their apparent recovery after the drop in 2005. First, many U.S. citizens of Cuban descent anticipated Bush's restrictions, which were announced in early May 2004 but went into effect two months later, by delivering more money to their relatives on the island. For instance, it is conceivable that most Cuban Americans who traveled to Cuba in the early summer of 2004, to beat the deadline of June 30, carried enough remittances to satisfy their family members' needs for the rest of the year. Prior to the deadline, U.S. authorized travelers to Cuba could carry as much as $3,000 in remittances. The cap was then reduced to just $300.

Second, those Cuban Americans who had planned family visits to Cuba in 2004 but were unable to travel because of the new rules found themselves with additional money to remit to their relatives. It cannot be excluded that some exiles tried to remit both the amount of dollars they could usually afford to transfer and part of the money they had saved for a trip that never came. And since U.S. regulations allowed American citizens to send only $300 every quarter to immediate family members in Cuba, stiffened rules on travel and money transfers might have stimulated illegal remittances through unofficial mechanisms.

Third, the potential growth of remittances to Cuba between 2006 and 2008 is consistent with the sizable increase of Cuban-American trips to the island during this period. Furthermore, as noted before, substantial funds sent by Cubans residing in Europe and, perhaps more importantly, by U.S. citizens using the services of third countries might have accelerated such an upward trend. Unofficial estimates of money transfers to Cuba should be taken with caution but, if confirmed, they would underscore a very disappointing outcome for the United States. If remittances were indeed higher in 2006–2008, then U.S. policy would have succeeded neither in keeping Cuban families apart nor in stemming the hard currency flowing into the hands of Cuban nationals, and from there into the coffers of the Castro government.

Limitations on remittances were perhaps the most contradictory element of U.S. policy toward Cuba in the post–cold war era. While being part of a series of U.S. restrictions intended to squeeze the Castro

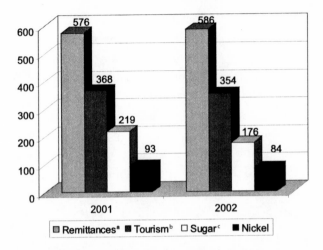

Figure 5.3. Rough Estimates of Cuba's Main Sources of Hard Currency in 2001 and 2002 (Net Revenues in $U.S. Millions).
Sources: Oficina Nacional de Estadísticas (ONE) 2003; Armando Nova González, "Continuará la Dolarización?" Economics Press Service, February 15, 2001; Declaration of Carlos Lage on Cuban National Television, March 18, 2001; "Cuba: Economía y Turismo," Economics Press Service, May 31, 2001; Declaration of Carlos Lage in Julia María Mayoral, "El País Tiene Confianza en Su Avance Social y Económico," *Granma Internacional*, April 5, 2003; Declaration of Marta Maíz in Gilda Fariñas and Susana Tesoro, "Turismo: Monedas al Aire," *Bohemia*, May 16, 2003; Interviews with Cuban economists in 2003 and 2004.
Notes: a. Net revenues are calculated as 64 percent of total transfers from abroad ($900 million in 2001 and $915 million in 2002).
b. Assuming the cost per dollar of gross income from tourism activities is $0.80.
c. Considering average costs and international market prices, net revenues from sugar are estimated as 40 percent of gross revenues.

government economically, remittances were Cuba's fastest growing source of hard currency during the 1990s. To put things into perspective, figure 5.3 provides rough estimates of Cuba's four largest sources of hard currency revenues (net figures) in 2001 and 2002. The total amounts are based on my data, figures released by Carlos Lage, Cuba's vice president, and Marta Maíz, Cuba's vice minister of tourism, and calculations of Cuban economists.

Remittances are a source of fresh capital for the Cuban population but, in terms of revenues, they do not constitute a net benefit for the Castro government. The latter obtains access to remittances mostly through sales in hard currency stores, and obviously there are costs involved in procuring the goods exchanged in these transactions. Products sold in state-run convertible peso stores carry an ideal markup (hidden tax) of 240 percent. This means that the retail price of each item is, on average, 2.4 times higher than the cost to produce it domestically or import it (Eckstein 2003, 17). Thus, net income of hard currency outlets is about 58 percent of total sales. Some remittances also end up in CADECA, farmers' markets, and hoarded stashes. Armando Nova González, an economist from the island, estimated that net revenues from remittances are about 63–64 percent of the total amount of money sent to Cuba.[39]

From figure 5.3, we can see that in 2002 net hard currency revenues to the Cuban government from family remittances ($586 million) were greater than its profit from tourism activities ($354 million), sugar ($176 million), and nickel ($84 million) exports. Remittances were actually just shy of accounting for more net revenues than the other three major sources combined. Although the limited accuracy of these estimates must be acknowledged, the importance to the Cuban economy of money sent from abroad is undisputable. Mainly intended to provide Cuban citizens with much needed additional income, remittances end up in the hands of their government, allowing the latter to meet the most urgent needs of the country and pay unavoidable short-term debts with high interest rates.[40] While gross revenues and net profits from tourism and nickel exports (but not sugar) have increased since 2002, remittances most likely remained the Castro government's top source of net hard currency revenues until the dramatic surge in 2005–2007 of exports of professional services in partnership with Venezuela.

Finally, currency changes enacted in Cuba between 2004 and 2005 boosted the foreign exchange earnings of the Castro government and helped it minimize the negative impact of Bush's economic measures against the island. In order to avoid the 10 percent fee on dollar/CUC exchanges, which took effect on November 14, 2004, but was announced a few weeks in advance, Cubans rushed to exchange large amounts of dollars they hoarded at home for CUCs. Some people opened accounts in local banks as hard currency deposits made prior to the November deadline could be withdrawn at any time either in dollars or convertible pesos without having to pay the 10 percent commission.[41]

The reevaluation in April 2005 of the CUC against all international currencies meant automatically an 8 percent growth of the Cuban government's net revenues from remittances and tourism activities. Based on gross earnings from international tourism and the estimated flow of remittances from abroad, such an increase might be worth almost $300 million a year, to which we must add extra profits coming from the penalty on U.S. dollar conversions. Moreover, the raised value of the convertible peso stimulated many Cubans who still hoarded U.S. dollars at home to purchase CUCs before the new exchange rates kicked in. Those who had not turned in their dollars in November 2004 probably decided that an additional 8 percent reduction in their purchasing power was too much to ignore. In sum, as Washington introduced tougher restrictions on U.S.-based travel and remittances to Cuba to deny hard currency resources to the Castro regime, the latter moved quickly to squeeze more profits out of these resources.[42]

U.S. Telecommunications Payments to Cuba

The development of the telecommunications sector has been a high priority for the Cuban government since the early 1990s. Cuba's telecom industry, which had received only minimal investment since 1959, was in need of modern digital technology and foreign capital as the entire phone network on the island still operated on analog systems. This sector became the target of some of the biggest investments by foreign companies. Two major joint ventures with foreign partners were established to expand and digitalize fixed-line service and develop a dollar-priced cellular phone service. But telecommunications services remain state monopolies. Cuba simply allowed foreign investors to participate in those monopolies (Peters 2001b, 4).

In mid-1994, Mexico's Grupo Domos and Italy's Telecom Italia (through its subsidiary STET International) entered into a joint venture (ETECSA) with the Cuban telephone company EMTEL for the modernization and expansion of Cuba's telephone system. The joint venture has a monopoly on Cuba's fixed-line communications and international switching. Mostly due to financing problems, Grupo Domos withdrew from its investment in 1997, while Telecom Italia increased its stake in ETECSA to 29 percent.

The remaining four shareholders were three separate corporations owned or controlled by the Cuban government with a combined 59 percent share and a Panamanian-registered corporation, Utisa, with a 12 percent share. At the end of 2002, Telecom Italia's shares in the company were valued at $469 million (USCTEC 2004).

In February 1998, Sherritt International Communications, a wholly owned subsidiary of Canada's Sherritt International, purchased a 37.5 percent interest in the Cuban cellular carrier Teléfonos Celulares de Cuba (Cubacel) for approximately $38.25 million.[43] During the first quarter of 2000, the Canadian corporation paid an additional $4 million to increase its ownership to 40 percent.[44] Until 2003, Cubacel and another small Cuban carrier, the state-owned Celulares del Caribe (C-Com), had exclusive rights to frequencies in Cuba's dollar-priced cellular phone market, which was only available to tourists and other foreign visitors. However, in late 2003 ETECSA took over both Cubacel and C-Com in a major business operation aimed to create an integrated fixed-mobile telecommunications operator and expand the wireless service to the local population. Sherrit International sold its 40 percent interest in Cubacel for $45.1 million. As a result of the merger, Telecom Italia's investment was reduced to 27 percent of the share capital of the new integrated operator.[45] The joint venture ETECSA now has a monopoly on Cuba's entire telecommunications sector.

Cuba's telecommunications indicators have improved significantly in recent years, although they are still among the lowest in Latin America.[46] Phone density increased from 3.18 telephone sets per 100 inhabitants in 1994 (when ETECSA was established) to 9.85 in 2008.[47] While in 1995 only 4 percent of all lines were digital, today about 96 percent of Cuba's telephone network is digitalized. In addition, the communist island had 330,000 cellular phone subscribers, 630,000 personal computers, 2,168 Internet sites, and more than 1.4 million Internet users at the end of 2008.

It should be emphasized that the United States played an important role in financing the development of Cuba's telecommunications sector. Ignacio Gonzáles Planas, a former minister of information technology and communications, maintained in January 2004 that "a portion of the revenues derived from telecom services is being systematically set aside for investments that enhance this infrastructure."[48] Basic residential phone service in Cuba is relatively inexpensive as consumers pay in regular pesos. But ETECSA collects hard currency revenues from two additional areas: business and tourism activities, and international service. A significant share of ETECSA's earnings that were used to upgrade the island's telecommunications industry has indeed come from dollar charges applied to incoming calls from the United States. Curiously, it happened against the backdrop of U.S. regulations prohibiting U.S. companies from investing in the improvement of that same industry.

Prior to the enactment of the Cuban Democracy Act (CDA) in 1992, phone service between Cuba and the United States was available, but U.S. payments to the island were made to a blocked account pending future changes in U.S. embargo policy. As the CDA authorized the U.S. president to allow payments to Cuba under specific licensing on a case-by-case basis (a change that took effect in late 1994), a number of U.S. carriers negotiated agreements to provide telecommunications services between the two countries, consistent with policy guidelines developed by the Department of State and the Federal Communications Commission (FCC). While none of the existing licenses permit payments from a blocked account, there are currently at least eight licensed U.S. carriers engaged in transactions incident to the receipt or transmission of telecommunications between Cuba and the United States: Sprint/Nextel, AT&T Corporation, Verizon Communications, Tricom USA, Teleglobe America, Telefonica Larga Distancia de Puerto Rico, iBasis Inc., and Americatel. There are also other carriers like Telecom New Zealand that reroute U.S. telephone calls to Cuba.

The Cuban and U.S. governments agreed to pay each other $0.60 for every minute of traffic originating in their respective territories (Peters 2001b, 7). The net revenue impact of this "settlement rate" would not be significant if phone traffic between the two countries was balanced in terms of minutes flowing in each direction. In other words, the amount U.S. carriers owe ETECSA and the amount the latter owes U.S. companies would simply even out. However, there are far more minutes of phone calls originating in the United States than those originating in Cuba.[49] Therefore, U.S.-based carriers end up paying Cuba a sizable amount of money every year to settle charges under traffic agreements. As established by Section 6004(e)(6) of the CDA: "The [U.S.] President shall submit to the Congress on a semiannual basis a report detailing payments made to Cuba by any United States person as a result of the provision of telecommunications services authorized by this subsection." Although they contain unclassified information on payouts to Cuba and no data on U.S.-Cuba phone traffic, most of these reports (especially recent ones) have not been made public. But all relevant information is compiled and released by the Federal Communications Commission in its *International Traffic Data* annual reports (Peters 2007).

Based on FCC statistics and my calculations, table 5.5 provides data on U.S.-Cuba telecommunications traffic (telephone service) and payments from 1995 to 2007. During this period, more than 1.3 billion minutes of phone traffic were billed in the United States as compared to just 30.2 million minutes billed in Cuba. There were on average approximately 44 minutes of conversations originating in the United States (mostly calls from Cuban Americans to family members on the island) for every minute from Cuba. The cumulative amount owed by U.S. carriers to ETECSA was $876.5 million versus a meager $15.8 million owed to them by ETECSA. Thus, U.S. firms ended up paying Cuba an astonishing $860.7 million to complete long-distance phone calls to the island. In 2007, U.S. payments peaked at $156.3 million with a traffic ratio of 496 minutes from the United States for every minute from Cuba. These payments surpassed those of 2006 when some U.S. carriers apparently handled a much larger number of calls to Cuba in the aftermath of Fidel Castro's illness and the transfer of power to his brother Raúl in late July of that year (Radelat 2007).

Another significant piece of information emerging from table 5.5 is that U.S. carriers generally paid a higher rate per minute of phone traffic than the one paid by ETECSA.[50] Between 1995 and 2007, the average U.S.-owed amount per minute billed in the United States was $0.67 (with annual rates as high as $0.80) as compared to a Cuba-owed amount of $0.52 per minute. The difference is far from being irrelevant. If U.S. companies had paid the same rate per minute that ETECSA paid, that would have saved the United States about $190 million in telecommunications payments to Cuba during 1995–2007.

Calls coming from abroad, mainly from the United States, are a precious source of hard currency for Cuba to continue upgrading its telephone

Table 5.5. U.S.-Cuba Telecommunications Traffic and Payments, 1995–2007 (Telephone Service)

	1995	1996	1997	1998	1999	2000	2001	2002	2003	2004	2005	2006	2007	Total
Traffic originating in the U.S. (millions of minutes)	89.2	103.0	121.3	141.2	80.6	90.4	36.4	49.3	77.5	110.8	87.1	130.4	197.7	1,314.9
Traffic originating in Cuba (millions of minutes)	5.8	0.8	1.1	1.2	7.4	3.2	1.9	0.1	4.6	3.0	0.6	0.1	0.4	30.2
U.S./Cuba traffic ratio	15:1	135:1	109:1	117:1	11:1	28:1	19:1	371:1	17:1	37:1	154:1	1,933:1	496:1	44:1
Amount owed by U.S. to Cuba ($U.S. millions)	53.8	64.2	73.5	84.6	47.2	52.1	21.6	35.0	51.5	81.8	50.1	104.5	156.6	876.5
Amount owed by Cuba to U.S. ($U.S. millions)	3.4	0.5	0.7	0.7	3.9	1.8	1.0	0.02	0.9	2.1	0.4	0.05	0.3	15.8
U.S.-owed amount per minute billed in the U.S. ($)	0.60	0.62	0.60	0.60	0.59	0.58	0.59	0.71	0.66	0.74	0.57	0.80	0.79	0.67
Cuba-owed amount per minute billed in Cuba ($)	0.58	0.60	0.60	0.60	0.53	0.57	0.53	0.16	0.20	0.69	0.73	0.79	0.81	0.52
U.S. payments to Cuba ($U.S. millions)	50.4	63.7	72.8	83.9	43.3[a]	50.3	20.6[a]	35.0	50.6	79.7	49.7	104.5	156.3	860.7

Sources: Federal Communications Commission (FCC), 2007 International Telecommunications Data, and previous editions; Calculations of the author from FCC data.
Note: a. ETECSA suspended direct dial service between the United States and Cuba in response to U.S. attempts to withhold payments and use the funds to settle legal claims against the Cuban government. As U.S carriers began to reroute telephone calls to Cuba through third countries, ETECSA continued to receive revenues from calls originating in the United States even though incoming traffic and receipts suffered a contraction.

system. Between 1995 and 2003, U.S.-based carriers' payouts to Cuba amounted to $470.6 million, representing nearly 60 percent of the island's total realized investments in its telecommunications sector ($786.2 million), almost entirely to modernize the fixed-line phone system. Furthermore, total U.S. payments from 2004 to 2007 were even higher than ETECSA's planned investments (in both fixed-line and cellular services) for this period as disclosed by the company's executive president in late 2003.[51] No one can deny that U.S. financing boosted the development of Cuba's telecommunications industry.

Cuba's recent strategies aimed at expanding the number of cellular users on the island highlight the importance of hard currency revenues from incoming international calls. In early March 2004, ETECSA announced its intention to offer cellular phone service in regular pesos to up to three hundred thousand local residents as new technology made it easier and quicker to install wireless rather than fixed-line systems.[52] Cellular phones were supposed to be distributed to Cubans through a joint venture between a Chinese firm and the Swedish Ericsson group. Although the plan never came into fruition, the idea behind it was clear. Like the fixed-line network, the peso-priced wireless system was going to be subsidized, for the most part, through expensive dollar charges placed on incoming calls from the United States, where many Cuban residents have relatives.[53]

The cellular business in Cuba is still priced only in convertible pesos, but the Castro government has stepped up efforts to increase the overall number of customers and its hard currency revenues. As Hoffmann (2004, 196) aptly stated, "Mobile phones will come as an addition to their already existing main line telephone connections, not as an alternative to it." Indeed, ETECSA's figures show that the share of investments in the cellular system over total investments in telecommunications was projected to grow from just 8 percent in 2002 to 37.7 percent in 2007.[54] During this period, the number of cellular subscribers in Cuba grew tenfold from twenty thousand to about two hundred thousand even though many Cubans had mobile phone service in the names of foreigners or their work places.

In late March 2008, Raúl Castro permitted all Cubans to buy and use cellular phones and put contracts in their own names. Official media also revealed that "priority will be given to the municipalities with the lowest phone density and to areas with more than 300 inhabitants that are still lacking a telephone service."[55] Besides the CUCs collected from new cellular contracts, the growing number of phone users receiving international calls will help the Cuban government obtain the hard currency needed to modernize its telecommunications sector, increase telephone density, and provide a better service to the Cuban population. Despite Cuba's concerns over the flow of information, it is also quite possible that President Obama's easing of restrictions on U.S. telecommunications services to the island might lead to roaming agreements between Cuban and U.S. cellular providers, especially in light of the rising number of Cuban-American family visits. This would allow most people coming from the United States to use their U.S.-based mobile phones in Cuba and generate substantial economic gains for all parties involved.

U.S. Indirect Investments in Cuba

The presence of U.S. investors in foreign firms that trade with or invest in Cuba is a very important and largely unexplored aspect of U.S.-Cuban economic relations that defies the logic of economic sanctions and undermines their main goals. Under the embargo, direct investments in Cuba are prohibited for U.S. entities. But the U.S. Department of the Treasury authorizes individuals and firms subject to U.S. law to invest in a third-country company that has commercial activities in Cuba as long as they do not acquire a controlling interest and provided that a majority of the revenues of the third-country company are not produced from operations within the communist island (USCTEC 2000). Thus, if the investment is an indirect one, a U.S. entity should have no problem in building a Cuba-related stock portfolio.

Table 5.6 provides data on U.S. investments in selected foreign firms operating in the Cuban market. It is just a sample based on public information, and the presence of U.S. shareholders in some companies could be even higher than reported. The key aspect is that, in an increasingly globalized world, the nationality of certain firms may become almost irrelevant. John Kavulich, then the president of the U.S.-Cuba Trade and Economic Council (USCTEC), noted in 2001: "U.S. companies have

Table 5.6. U.S. Investments in Selected Foreign Companies Operating in Cuba

Year	Company	Country	Type of Operations in Cuba	Presence of U.S. Investors (%)	Major U.S. Investors
2000	Hotetur	Spain	Management contracts in 4 hotels	26%[a]	Florida-based Carnival Corporation
2000	Iberia Airlines	Spain	Two joint ventures in cargo terminal + aircraft maintenance	2%	Texas-based American Airlines Inc.
2000	Mitsubishi Motors	Japan	Exporter of vehicles	10.41%	California-based Capital Research and Management Co.
2000	Sol Meliá	Spain	26 management contracts and 4 equity interests in tourism sector	16%	—
2001	Alcan	Canada	Exporter of aluminum products	23%	—
2002	Fiat Group	Italy	Exporter of vehicles	20%	Michigan-based General Motors Corporation
2002	Leisure Canada	Canada	Developer of luxury multi-destination resorts	30%	California-based Robertson Stephens Inc.
2002	LG Electronics Investment	South Korea	Exporter of refrigerators, washing machines, air conditioners, televisions	6.6%	New-York based Goldman Sachs Group
2003	Repsol YPF	Spain	Oil exploration in Gulf of Mexico waters	21.7%	New York-based J. P. Morgan Chase and Co.
2004	Altadis	Spain/France	Joint venture in tobacco sector (cigars)	30%	Massachusetts-based Fidelity Investments
2004	Sinopec	China	Oil production in Pinar del Río Province	14%	Texas-based Exxon Mobil Corporation
2004	Souza Cruz	Brazil	Joint venture in tobacco sector (cigarettes)	5.5%[b]	—
2006	Pernod Ricard	France	Rum distribution joint venture	4%	California-based Franklin Templeton Investments
2007	Accor	France	Several management contracts in tourism sector	22.1%	California-based Colony Capital LLC
2007	Nestlé	Switzerland	Mineral water and soda-bottling joint venture	32.7%	—
2007	Telecom Italia	Italy	Joint venture in telecommunications	8%	California-based Brandes Investment Partners L.P.

Sources: Compilation of the author based on data from U.S.-Cuba Trade and Economic Council 2000, 2001, 2002, and financial reports of selected companies.

Notes: a. In 2000, Carnival Corporation owned 26% of U.K.-based Airtours PLC, which owned 50% of Hotetur.

b. In March 2004, U.K.-based British American Tobacco (BAT), which also has U.S. capital, held 75.3% of the shares of Souza Cruz.

affiliations with and U.S. citizens have investments in Sol Meliá, Unilever, Accor, Alcan, Fiat, Daimler Chrysler, and Nestlé among many other companies, which have commercial activities within Cuba." He also pointed out that major U.S. financial institutions and investment banks were offering services to foreign companies doing business on the island.[56]

Here are some details of U.S. indirect business connections with Cuba as disclosed by USCTEC and financial reports of selected companies. The potential application of the Helms-Burton law against several foreign firms that invest in Cuba could affect U.S. entities holding publicly traded shares of those firms.

In 2000, individuals subject to U.S. law held approximately 16 percent of the shares of Sol Meliá, the largest hotel company in Spain and the leader in Cuba's tourism sector with equity interests in four hotels and twenty-six management contracts. In addition, Texas-based American Airlines Inc. owned about 2 percent of Spain-based Iberia Airlines and California-based Capital Research and Management Co. owned 10.41 percent of Japan-based Mitsubishi Motors (USCTEC 2000). Iberia Airlines has a joint venture (Empresa Logística de Carga Aérea S.A.) with the Cuban company Aerovaradero S.A. in a new freight terminal in the vicinity of the José Martí International Airport and another joint venture (Empresa Cubano-Hispana de Mantenimiento de Aeronaves IBECA S.A.) for aircraft maintenance.[57] Mitsubishi sells automobiles, spare parts, and accessories to Cuba through the Panamanian company Motores Internacionales del Caribe S.A.

Also in 2000, Carnival Corporation of Florida increased its indirect minority presence in Cuba with the purchase by the United Kingdom's Airtours PLC of 50 percent of the Spanish hotel chain Hotetur. Carnival Corporation owned 26 percent of the shares of Airtours PLC (USCTEC 2001). Hotetur has management contracts in four hotels in Cuba: Blue-Bay Cayo Coco in the province of Ciego de Ávila, Deauville in the city of Havana, and Hotetur Palma Real and Hotetur Sunbeach in Varadero.[58] In 2001, U.S. investors held approximately 23 percent of Alcan of Canada, which exports aluminum products to Cuba.[59]

In 2002, the Goldman Sachs Group of New York had a 6.6 percent interest in LG Electronics Investment of South Korea, General Motors Corporation of Michigan had a 20 percent interest in the Fiat Group of

Italy, and Robertson Stephens Inc. of California owned about 30 percent of the shares of Leisure Canada (USCTEC 2002). LG Electronics has a strong presence in the Cuban market. A variety of its products, including refrigerators, washing machines, air conditioners, and televisions, are assembled and sold in Cuba. The Fiat Group established a dealership on the island in 1995 (Agencia Cubalse Fiat) in conjunction with the Cuban corporation Cubalse. Since then, the Italian company has sold a large number of vehicles to Cuba, including automobiles, industrial vehicles, and agricultural machinery. Leisure Canada is developing five-star hotels, timeshare condominiums, and golf courses in three different Cuban locations, with an estimated investment plan of $400 million. Curiously, Leisure Canada announced in one of its brochures that the company is positioned to capitalize on the current growth of Cuban tourism and the future growth fueled by the United States following the inevitable normalization of U.S.-Cuba relations. It also specified that it is perfectly legal for U.S. potential investors to purchase shares of the Canadian firm and that U.S. investment banks already control over 20 percent of Leisure Canada.[60]

In recent years, U.S. indirect business links with Cuba have become even more significant, in part because of new operations on the island by multinational oil companies. In 2004, U.S. entities owned about 14 percent of communist China's Sinopec,[61] a substantial amount of shares of Brazil's Petrobras,[62] and 5.5 percent of Brazil's Souza Cruz. The U.K.-based British American Tobacco (BAT), which has considerable U.S. capital, owned 75.3 percent of Souza Cruz. In April 1995, Souza Cruz signed a joint venture (BrasCuba S.A.) with Cuba's Unión del Tabaco. With an initial investment of $7 million, BrasCuba renovated an existing cigarette factory in Havana and started producing and selling several brands of cigarettes for the domestic and international markets.[63] BrasCuba has today a virtual monopoly of cigarettes in Cuba's hard currency stores and for exports (Spadoni 2002, 167). In early 2005, Sinopec, China's second-largest oil firm, signed an agreement with Cuba's government-operated Cuba Petróleo (CUPET) to jointly produce oil on the coast of the western province of Pinar del Río. The Brazilian state-run energy giant Petrobras signed a deal with CUPET in October 2008 to explore for oil in Cuba's offshore waters in the Gulf of Mexico.

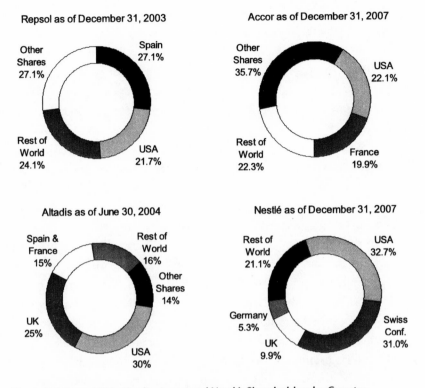

Figure 5.4. Repsol YPF, Altadis, Accor, and Nestlé: Shareholders by Country.
Source: Compilation of the author from financial reports of selected companies.

Furthermore, Franklin Templeton Investments of California held 4 percent of the shares of Pernod Ricard of France in 2006 and Brandes Investment Partners L.P. of California had an 8 percent interest in Telecom Italia in 2007. Pernod Ricard formed a joint venture with Cuba Ron S.A. in November 1993 to develop the Havana Club rum brand internationally. Telecom Italia is the foreign partner in the Cuban telecommunications monopoly ETECSA.

Finally, the share capital structure of four major overseas corporations should receive special emphasis because of the significance of their business activities in Cuba and the sizable presence of U.S. investors. Figure 5.4 offers data on shareholders (by country) of the Spanish Repsol YPF, the French-Spanish conglomerate Altadis, the Swiss Nestlé, and the French group Accor.

At the end of 2003, U.S. shareholders owned 21.7 percent of Repsol YPF and represented the second largest group of investors after Spaniards. Between June and July 2004, Repsol spent about $50 million drilling for oil in Cuba's deep-water areas and found signs of high-quality reservoirs, but its first well was not commercially viable.[64] Despite repeated delays, Repsol is planning to drill again in partnership with two other companies, Norway's Norsk Hydro and India's ONGC Videsh.[65] In mid-2004, individuals subject to U.S. law also held 30 percent of the shares of the French-Spanish group Altadis. French and Spanish investors held only a combined 15 percent of the company's shares.[66] Altadis has invested almost $500 million in a 50–50 joint venture (Corporación Habanos) with the Cuban state for the exclusive right to market Cuban cigars internationally.

In December 2007, U.S. entities held more shares (22.1 percent) of the French Accor than any other group of institutional investors, including French shareholders (19.9 percent). Similarly, U.S. shareholders owned 32.7 percent of the Swiss Nestlé at the end of 2007 while Swiss investors held 31 percent of the company's shares. The Accor group manages several hotels in Cuba with establishments that operate under the Sofitel, Coralia, and Mercure brands. Nestlé owns a number of mineral water bottling plants in Cuba and has a joint venture (Los Portales S.A.) with the Cuban company Coralsa that produces and markets the highest selling soft drinks and mineral waters on the island (Pérez Villanueva 2004, 188).

It is quite difficult to offer a comprehensive analysis of U.S. indirect business connections with Cuba given that private companies are not required to make public the list of their shareholders. Additionally, with millions of dollars moving around the world via electronic transactions, the real origin of financing for specific business operations is often unknown. The Cuban economist Omar Everleny Pérez Villanueva observed: "There are many companies in Cuba that are based in the Bahamas, other Caribbean islands, Spain or Britain, and you really can't tell if these companies receive U.S. funds attracted by the high interest rates we [Cubans] pay."[67]

Nevertheless, the information presented above shows that U.S. entities hold publicly traded shares of several major foreign firms engaged in business dealings with the Castro government. While profits from the Cuba-related stock portfolio may not be particularly significant for some

U.S. investors in terms of their global revenues, U.S. investments in foreign companies with commercial operations on the island are just another example of gaping holes in Washington's effort to isolate Cuba economically. Due to embargo restrictions, U.S.-based corporations cannot search for oil in Cuban waters, manage hotels on the island, or establish joint ventures with the Cuban government in any production activity to serve the domestic market or for exports. As multinational corporations headquartered in a foreign country can rely on U.S. capital to do just that, one is left wondering if it makes any sense for the United States to keep using economic sanctions as a tool to achieve ambitious foreign policy goals. Cuba's front door may be closed to U.S. investors, but the back door is wide open.

U.S. Food Sales to Cuba

Economic sanctions against Cuba have been under fire in the U.S. Congress at various times since the late 1990s. As a result of growing skepticism on the utility of economic coercion as well as lobbying efforts by U.S. business and agricultural communities (in particular food exporters), an increasing number of lawmakers have pushed for a relaxation of the embargo and the beginning of a new trade relationship with the Castro government. In October 2000, the U.S. Congress passed the Agriculture, Rural Development, Food and Drug Administration, and Related Agencies Appropriations Act, 2001. Title IX of the bill (the Trade Sanctions Reform and Export Enhancement Act, or TSRA), quickly signed into law by President Clinton, included provisions that allowed sales of U.S. food and agricultural products (and medicines) to Cuba for the first time in nearly forty years. Yet, a clause inserted in the final version of the bill prohibited U.S. companies and financial institutions from providing credits for such transactions, thus obligating Cuban authorities to complete their purchases only with cash payments or through financing provided by a third-country firm. Enraged by that restriction, the Cuban government initially said it would not buy any food until the embargo was completely lifted.

In fact, for about a year after the passage of the TSRA, Cuba refused to buy "a single grain of rice" from the United States.[68] But after hurricane

Table 5.7. Cuba's Food Imports from the United States and All Countries, 2001–2008 ($U.S. Millions)

	2001	2002	2003	2004	2005	2006	2007	2008
From the United States (USCTEC)[a]	4.3	138.6	256.9	392.0	350.2	340.4	437.6	710.1
From the United States (ONE)[a]	4.4	173.6	327.2	433.9	476.3	483.6	581.7	801.1
From All Countries	823.5	800.1	950.6	1,120. 9	1,435. 1	1,329. 4	1,646. 9	2,421. 3
Imports from U.S. vs. Total Imports	0.5%	21.7%	34.4%	38.7%	33.2%	36.4%	35.3%	33.1%

Sources: U.S.-Cuba Trade and Economic Council (USCTEC) 2009; Oficina Nacional de Estadísticas (ONE) 2009.

Note: a. USCTEC reports that data from Cuban sources may present multi-year cumulative values and incorporate transportation, insurance, and financial costs. Both USCTEC and ONE data include forest products. ONE's figures on imports from the United States also include a very small percentage of other U.S.-authorized goods.

Michelle caused widespread damage to the island in November 2001, the Castro regime began to take advantage of the law and buy U.S. food to replenish its reserves. The first contract between a U.S. company and the Cuban government, worth approximately $40 million, was signed on December 16, 2001. By the end of 2008, Cuba had signed deals with more than 150 U.S. firms from 35 different states and purchased about $2.6 billion worth of U.S. food products.[69] Leading U.S. exporters are Archer Daniels Midland (ADM) of Illinois, Cargill of Minnesota, and FC Stone of Iowa. Table 5.7 reports the values of Cuba's food imports from the United States and all countries during 2001–2008.

The United States has become a very important trading partner for Cuba, ranking first among the island's sources of imported food since 2002, the first full year of U.S. sales under the TSRA.[70] According to the U.S.-Cuba Trade and Economic Council, U.S. food sales to Cuba increased from only $4.3 million in 2001 to $392 million in 2004 and, after a couple of years of slight downward trend, peaked at $710.1 million in 2008 (USCTEC 2009). Cuban official figures, which apparently include transportation charges, taxes, and other additional costs (and a very small percentage of other U.S.-authorized goods), indicate that Cuba's food imports from the United States rose steadily from $4.4 million in 2001 to $801.1 million in 2008. Cuba's dependence on imported food, traditionally high, has reached record levels in recent years amid a declining domestic agricultural output and soaring prices of food products in the international markets. The island bought $2,421 million worth of food from abroad in 2008, more than double its level of spending in 2004 ($1,120 million). Imports from the United States accounted for one-third of those purchases. Havana's authorities estimated that the U.S. share could rise to about 60 percent with a complete lifting of the embargo.[71]

The United States sells to Cuba primarily corn ($195.9 million worth of transactions in 2008), wheat, chicken, and soybean products. As illustrated in table 5.8, by 2008 U.S. firms had captured an overwhelming share of Cuba's soybean (96.8 percent), corn (94.4 percent), and chicken (80.6 percent) markets and a sizable one of its wheat (49.5 percent) and soybean oil cake (39.9 percent) markets. The Castro government's decision to buy products from multiple U.S. states was clearly a deliberate political strategy to encourage U.S. farm groups with sizable economic

Table 5.8. Cuba's Main Food Imports from the United States in 2008 ($U.S. Millions)

Product	Imports from the United States (USCTEC)	Imports from All Countries (ONE)	Imports from U.S. vs. Total Imports
Corn	195.9	207.5	94.4%
Wheat	134.9	272.7	49.5%
Chicken	133.8	165.9	80.6%
Soybeans	66.6	68.8	96.8%
Soybean Oil Cake	46.2	115.9	39.9%
Soybean Oil	21.9	123.6	17.7%
Total (ONE)	801.1	2,421.3	33.1%

Sources: U.S.-Cuba Trade and Economic Council (USCTEC) 2009; Oficina Nacional de Estadísticas (ONE) 2009.

interests at stake to lobby Congress for the lifting of the embargo (Mesa-Lago 2005, 21). Even so, Cuba's economic considerations in terms of price competition were also a factor in the decision to import food from the United States. As recognized by a senior official in Havana, "The proximity of U.S. Gulf ports saves freight and warehousing storage costs, which give U.S. exporters the equivalent of up to 20 percent price advantage."[72] In 2008, Cuba was the sixth largest food export market for the United States in Latin America, and probably the safest one in the world because of the cash-in-advance provision.[73]

Food sales to Cuba by the United States have negatively affected some of the island's key trading partners, among them Canada, France, and Spain. Canada's official statistics reveal that wheat and frozen chicken exports to Cuba plummeted dramatically after 2001. Canadian sales of frozen chicken, in particular, dropped from $11.6 million in 2001 to just $0.4 million in 2008. Canada's wheat exports to Cuba also plunged from $14.9 million in 2001 to nearly zero in 2003 but have recovered strongly since then.[74] The French government announced that food and agricultural sales to the island, dominated by wheat sales, decreased from 117.2 million euros in 2001 to a meager 8.4 million euros in 2007 before experiencing some notable expansion in 2008.[75] Finally, Spanish authorities reported that Cuba's purchases of food products from Spain plunged by more than 40 percent in 2002.[76]

The passage of the TSRA in 2000 punched a significant hole in the U.S. embargo against Cuba. The United States is now the main supplier of foodstuffs to the island and U.S. sales reached record levels in 2007–2008. This is all the more significant if we consider that the Bush administration, defying the will of Congress, enacted more restrictive rules for such transactions in March 2005 by establishing that Cuba's payments must occur before U.S. goods leave U.S. ports rather than before they are delivered to the Cuban purchaser. But we should avoid concluding that the U.S. embargo has far less economic impact than before because of the opening of food exports from the United States to Cuba.

Above all, trade remains unidirectional as Cuban exports to the United States are prohibited. Tapping the U.S. market would make a huge difference for key Cuban goods such as rum, cigars, sugar, nickel, and some others. Furthermore, the Castro government must pay cash for its food purchases and receives no U.S. credit, with economic benefits being mostly limited to lower transportation and storage costs and perhaps access to better quality products. Lastly, the vast majority of U.S. commodities sold to Cuba are distributed to the population through the rationing system in regular pesos. Only a tiny share of them ends up in local hard currency shops where the steep markup in prices lines the regime's pocket.[77] Financial flows into Cuba sustained by activities of U.S.-based transnational actors have helped prop up the Cuban economy since the mid-1990s. Growing sales of U.S. goods to Cuba played only a very small role.

Cuba's New Economic Lifeline

Considering the stated goals of Washington's foreign policy toward Havana in the post–cold war era, it is worth discussing briefly Cuba's deepening economic ties with Venezuela and U.S. efforts to disrupt those ties. Until around 2004, revenues from international tourism and especially remittances captured through sales in state-owned dollar stores were the most important sources of hard currency for the Cuban government. However, booming revenues under bilateral agreements with the government of Hugo Chávez have now converted Venezuela into Cuba's new economic lifeline and engine of growth.

Since 2000, Cuba has been paying for vital imports of cut-rate Venezuelan oil (ninety-eight thousand barrels of high quality crude per day) with medical and educational services. Almost thirty-seven thousand Cuban doctors, nurses, and other healthcare personnel were stationed abroad in 2008, mostly staffed in medical clinics and other social programs in Venezuela.[78] Moreover, Cuba has greatly benefited from the launch in late 2004 of the program Operation Miracle, financed by Hugo Chávez, under which Cuban doctors are providing free eye surgery to patients from several Latin American and African countries.

The Cuban economy experienced a crucial structural transformation throughout the 1990s from an economy centered on agriculture and particularly sugar production to one based on services such as international tourism. It witnessed yet a new dramatic change in the post-2004 period principally as a result of Venezuela's financial largesse and its booming ties with Cuba.[79] Figures 5.5 and 5.6 highlight this latest change.[80]

Leaving aside the substantial amount of family remittances from abroad estimated at more than $1 billion per year, gross revenues from tourism activities represented 42.6 percent of Cuba's total exports of goods and services in 2004 according to official data of the Cuban Central Bank. In 2004, other major sources of hard currency revenues for the island were nickel exports (19.4 percent of the total), transportation services (6.3 percent), sugar (5 percent) and tobacco (4 percent) exports. But almost everything has changed since then due to the Venezuelan factor. Just to give an idea about Venezuela's crucial role in the Cuban economy, exports of professional services, primarily medical ones under special deals with Caracas, generated $2.9 billion or about 39 percent of Cuba's total hard currency revenues in 2005.[81] They replaced tourism as the island's top foreign exchange earner and brought in more revenues than exports of all goods combined.

In 2007, foreign exchange income from exports of professional services accounted for 44 percent of Cuba's total exports of goods and services. Revenues from international tourism dropped to 21.2 percent of the total, about half their level in 2004. The relative contribution of nearly every other sector of the Cuban economy underwent a similar downward trend. Nickel exports generated 17.6 percent of the island's hard currency revenues in 2007, followed by telecommunications services (3.6 percent), pharmaceuticals (2.4 percent), tobacco (2 percent), and sugar (1.7 percent) exports.

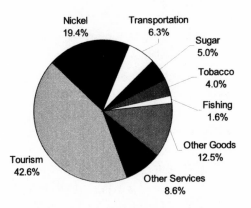

Figure 5.5. Cuba's Total Exports of Goods and Services by Sector in 2004 (Percentage Distribution). *Source*: Banco Central de Cuba (BCC) 2005.

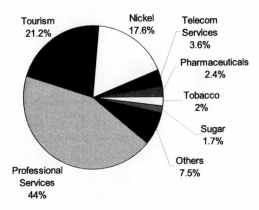

Figure 5.6. Cuba's Total Exports of Goods and Services by Sector in 2007 (Percentage Distribution). *Sources*: Calculations of the author from Oficina Nacional de Estadísticas (ONE) 2008a and data provided by Centro de Estudios de la Economía Cubana (CEEC) April 2009.

Cuba's earnings from the sale of professional services could have been as high as \$5.2 billion in 2007. Given this situation, the Bush administration launched a controversial program in August 2006 that offered asylum in the United States to Cuban doctors, nurses, and other healthcare personnel on assignments abroad.[82] Earning "political mileage" by luring Cuban doctors to escape communist Cuba and its oppressive system while ensuring orderly migration in the aftermath of Fidel Castro's illness of July 2006 might have been potential reasons for Bush's action. But the timing and focus of his new program were highly suspicious considering that Cuba had dispatched its doctors and nurses overseas for decades, albeit in lower numbers that in the period after 2004. A clear goal was to encourage large-scale defections among the massive contingent of Cuban medical workers stationed in Venezuela and nearly forty other developing countries, thus disrupting Cuba's productive partnership with the Chávez government that had turned the island's healthcare services into a crucial source of revenues for the Castro regime. Curiously, U.S. officials were increasingly worried about a possible mass exodus from Cuba as Fidel Castro's health conditions deteriorated, but they would welcome a wave of immigrants composed of Cuban doctors in order to intensify economic pressure on Havana.

This move was the latest in a long series of U.S. attempts to deny hard currency resources to the Castro regime that would allow the latter to maintain its grip on power, delay genuine changes, and facilitate its succession plans rather than progress toward democracy. However, by the time Fidel Castro fell ill and relinquished power temporarily to his younger brother Raúl in late July 2006, there was no evidence of a hastened democratic transition in Cuba. On the contrary, a process of re-centralization of the growing economy had gathered pace along with increased state control on the overall society. Even more important, apart from the introduction of various reforms in the agricultural sector and the removal of some restrictions for ordinary Cubans, no signs of major policy shifts have emerged in Cuba since Raúl Castro became president in February 2008. The long-standing U.S. strategy of cutting Cuba's economic lifelines to produce democratic changes on the island never worked.

When the Torricelli law of 1992 restricted trade with Cuba through U.S. subsidiaries located overseas, Fidel Castro stepped up the promotion of international tourism and foreign direct investment. When the Helms-Burton law of 1996 added secondary sanctions against third-country investors in Cuba, Havana's authorities had already developed a scheme to attract and capture remittances from abroad by legalizing the use of U.S. dollars and opening state-run hard currency stores. And when Washington began to crack down on foreign banks making transactions in U.S. dollars with the Cuban government, the latter responded by eliminating the commercial circulation of the U.S. currency on the island in order to build a new hard currency base (especially in euros) that could be deposited abroad more easily. Finally, when the Bush administration, in June 2004, decided to implement more stringent restrictions on Cuban-American travel and money transfers to Cuba, the island's economy was no longer as dependent on tourism and remittances as it was a few years before. Venezuela was becoming the main economic lifeline for the cash-strapped Castro regime.

In 2006, after several failed attempts to foster political changes in Cuba through economic pressure, Washington embarked on the unlikely mission of encouraging a large number of Cuban doctors working overseas to desert their posts and seek asylum in the United States. Cuban healthcare workers generally are not allowed to leave Cuba accompanied by their relatives. Even if they had the intention to defect, the fact of not being able to reunite with family members for a long time would certainly represent a major dissuading factor. Moreover, these doctors can earn enough money to help their families on the island as they receive significantly higher salaries than their counterparts at home. It is therefore not surprising that, by February 2007, only 480 or less than 2 percent of the estimated 28,000 Cuban doctors serving abroad had applied for entry to the United States under Bush's new program.[83] The program was just another misguided initiative.

Conclusion

From the analysis presented in this chapter, we can fairly argue that, in spite of the tightening of the embargo, the United States contributed in a notable way to the recovery of the Cuban economy following the deep recession of the early 1990s. While intended to stimulate democratic reforms and exercise pressure for regime change in Cuba by stemming the flow of hard currency to the island, U.S. economic sanctions achieved neither of these goals. Admittedly, the role of the United States in the Cuban economy would have been much more significant in the absence of sanctions. Yet, even with restrictions in place, sizable amounts of hard currency were channeled into Cuba through direct and indirect means of travel, remittances, and, to a lower extent, telecommunications payments and secondary investments. Washington's policy toward Havana ended up throwing a lifeline to the same government it was supposed to undermine.

Formal and informal activities by Cuban Americans were a major factor in keeping the Cuban economy afloat in the post–cold war period. Since the mid-1990s, the United States has consistently ranked among the top five providers of foreign visitors to Cuba, mainly because of Cuban Americans traveling to the island with or without their government's approval. In net terms, no other source generated more hard currency revenues to the Castro government than family remittances (primarily sent through informal mechanisms) from Cuban immigrants in the United States until special deals with Venezuela in late 2004 converted thousands of Cuban medical personnel into a key moneymaker. As argued by Eckstein (2003, 16), "The remittance economy reflects a society that is transnationally grounded, able, willing, and wanting to operate according to its own networks and norms, in defiance both of U.S. and Cuban official regulations that interfere." There is, in effect, little or no evidence that Bush's restrictions of 2004 on Cuban-American travel and remittances to Cuba had a sustained negative impact on these practices. Finally, between 1995 and 2007 U.S.-based phone carriers paid Cuba an average of about $66 million per year to handle incoming calls from U.S. territory, mostly placed by Cuban Americans to relatives on the island.

Conclusion

Throughout the cold war, the intent of the U.S. embargo to cause Cuba economic pain and the embargo's ability to produce political changes on the island were greatly inhibited by the fact that Cuba conducted most of its trade with socialist countries and received massive financial aid from the Soviet Union. The true test for yet another round of U.S. economic sanctions came only after the Soviet Union and the socialist bloc collapsed in the early 1990s and the Cuban economy took a nosedive. Although Washington's moves were mostly driven by the imperatives of domestic electoral politics and served more the interests of hard-liners in the Cuban-American community than the cause of democracy in Cuba, the overall U.S. policy was designed to strangle the Castro government by denying it hard currency revenues. This is exactly where sanctions failed the test.

Practices by transnational players, above all multinational corporations and migrants, bolstered the Cuban economy in the post–cold war era and constituted one of the chief reasons why the U.S. embargo did not work. Even if Fidel Castro was sidelined by a serious intestinal illness in the summer of 2006 and Raúl Castro is ruling the country, the Cuban Revolution celebrated its fifty-first anniversary on January 1, 2010, and Cubans are calmly going along with their new president. This is a different scenario from the one many U.S. officials had envisioned, where the exit of Cuba's "maximum leader" would soon result in the collapse of the Cuban system and in the United States determining the conditions for the lifting of the embargo. While it remains to be seen what will happen when the ailing Cuban leader passes away, the idea that the Cuban Revolution is much more than Fidel Castro may no longer seem so farfetched in Washington.

Unilateral sanctions achieved very limited success during the 1970s and 1980s, but they are even less likely to be effective in today's global marketplace where a target country can readily obtain the wherewithal it needs by promoting foreign investment, stimulating remittances, and tapping other sources of external support. In an increasingly interconnected global economy, a coercer state's effective use of sanctions is undermined "from above" by multinational corporations' investment activities and "from below" by migrants' connections with their places of origin. Multinational corporations channel capital, technology, and managerial skills into embargoed nations as they search for the best returns on their investments and take advantage of the diminished international competition created by the imposition of sanctions. They also raise funds in capital markets to finance their investment operations anywhere in the world. Huge flows of cross-border remittances by migrants, typically centered on family ties, mitigate the economic impact of sanctions by reducing social suffering that might otherwise translate into pressures for political change.

Unable to rally other states to the defense of its national security interests, or so it claimed, the United States initiated several new cases of unilateral sanctions during the 1990s and significantly expanded existing sanctions programs against certain targets. When allies and commercial partners refused to cooperate with U.S. policies and increased business relations with these targets, Washington tried to extend the reach of its sanctions by threatening or imposing penalties against firms located in third countries. The long-standing U.S. embargo against Cuba is perhaps the most emblematic example of a failed U.S. attempt to achieve ambitious foreign policy goals through the use of comprehensive unilateral coercive measures.

The Helms-Burton law made it more difficult and potentially risky to invest in Cuba. It also produced a deterrent "chill" effect on potential new investment and raised the cost to the Cuban government of obtaining short-term external financing. However, the law was unable to prevent foreign investment from boosting the recovery of the Cuban economy in the post-Soviet period. More importantly, activities by U.S.-based transnational players made a remarkable contribution to that recovery by sustaining hard currency flows into Cuba in the form of travel-related expenditures, remittances, payments for telecommunications services, and secondary investments. It should be noted that Bush's restrictions of 2004 on Cuban-American travel and remittances to Cuba had little impact on both practices. Despite tightened U.S. enforcement, many Cuban Americans circumvented the rules by traveling to Cuba via third countries and delivering remittances through mules or other informal mechanisms. And on top of all this, the emergence of Venezuela as Cuba's main economic lifeline has made the task of U.S. economic sanctions even more daunting.

As Cuban planners must continue to take into account transnational economic actors in devising strategies for the country's development, U.S. officials should accept their very limited ability to influence these actors' practices and react accordingly. A potentially more effective course of action for the United States is to foster a rapprochement with Cuba and remove the major provisions of the embargo in recognition that economic sanctions have not achieved their main goals. It could be a true game-changer. The end of restrictions on trade, investment, and travel with respect to Cuba would serve U.S. political and economic interests by allowing U.S. firms and a very large number of U.S. citizens to enter the island's market and influence its society. It would also increase pressure on the Castro regime by preventing it from using its traditional argument that the United States promotes economic deprivation in Cuba and seeks to constrain Cuban sovereignty.

A truly proactive policy, not the old failed approach of seeking regime change through economic warfare, is what the United States needs when it comes to Cuba. Washington must realize that democracy and other liberalizing changes on the island will come from within, led by the people of Cuba, and that attempts to control such internal developments end up reinforcing the Castro government's grip on society and delaying genuine reforms. A policy of engagement at all levels may indeed prove itself far more effective than one of confrontation and hostility in producing positive outcomes from the U.S. standpoint and facilitating Cubans' access to independent information and ideas. And it would surely be more useful than President Bush's ill-conceived efforts to expand U.S. propaganda broadcasts into Cuba to penetrate the information blockade that apparently keeps many Cubans in the dark.

A frequent argument raised by supporters of the embargo in the United States is that other countries' engagement with Cuba, especially since the demise of the Soviet Union in the early 1990s, has not produced major changes on the communist island. In effect, leaving aside Fidel Castro's health troubles and a cabinet reshuffle undertook by his younger brother, the political landscape in Cuba has remained virtually unaltered and the government continues to enjoy a monopoly on all media outlets. But various kinds of people-to-people contacts promoted by foreign countries, including the United States, have had a profound and lasting effect on Cuban society by disseminating knowledge of the outside world and exposing the shortcomings of the Cuban system. Less than two decades of thriving international tourism, in particular, have contributed more to changing Cubans' minds and their attitudes toward the Castro government than almost fifty years of U.S. sanctions, often used by Havana's authorities as an easy scapegoat for their own failures. Cubans learned about the virtues of alternative systems neither from state media nor from U.S. broadcasting. This knowledge is a social resource that will serve them well as they struggle to break with key aspects of their past. Michael Parmly, the former chief of the U.S. Interest Section in Havana from 2005 to 2008, once said he frequently chatted with Cubans in his walks around the capital, at Sunday Mass, at concerts, and at local markets "to reach out to the Cuban people, not so much to carry a message, but to relate to them as human beings."[1] Then why not allow all Americans to do the same?

The Obama administration's decision to grant Cuban Americans unrestricted rights to visit and send remittances to Cuba and reopen communication channels with Cuban officials is a good start. Obama's "new beginning" with Cuba and his departure from the aggressive hard line of George W. Bush might lead in a relatively short time to notable progress in areas of vital interest to the United States such as migration, drug trafficking, and other security matters. Yet, further progress toward normal relations between the two countries will be improbable unless Washington stops demanding far-reaching political concessions from Cuba and abandons the misguided idea that the current embargo may serve as a bargaining tool. The crucial lesson to be drawn from the past is that the embargo has proved rather ineffective in exercising enough economic strain to significantly alter the behavior of the Castro government, let alone to hasten its collapse. President Bush's all-or-nothing approach on Cuba, centered on preconditions for rapprochement such as Havana's commitment to hold free and fair elections, respect human rights, release political prisoners, permit the creation of independent organizations, and adopt a market-oriented economic system, achieved nothing.

The lifting of the travel ban on Cuba would open a huge crack in the embargo and generate powerful incentives for the easing of other U.S. restrictions, which is the reason why both opponents and supporters of sanctions in the United States tend to direct their best efforts toward this prohibition. Some U.S. studies estimated that between 550,000 and 1.1 million Americans would visit Cuba in the short-run if travel restrictions were abolished and more than 3 million would go there annually once the market has fully adjusted (USITC 2007; Robyn et al. 2002; Sanders and Long 2002). With a very large number of Americans spending money on the island, pressures would mount on the United States to allow U.S. banks to establish direct relations with their Cuban counterparts, so U.S.-issued credit cards could be used on the ground. Aside from booming tourism packages and increased airline traffic, U.S. hotel chains would likely push to be able to enter the Cuban market rather than watching quietly as Spanish hotel groups reap much bigger economic benefits from the inflow of U.S. tourists. Other U.S. companies, especially in the construction area, would also want a piece of the pie given that Cuba would be forced to upgrade its tourism facilities and related infrastructures. Last but not least, growing business opportunities for U.S. food suppliers to Cuba would intensify lobbying efforts to permit private U.S. financing for these transactions and relax other kinds of trade barriers. Put simply, the days of certain important parts of the embargo, and perhaps the whole Cuba sanctions program, would be numbered once the travel ban is no longer in place.

Like Presidents Clinton and Bush did before him, Barack Obama should use his executive prerogatives to modify existing licensing arrangements for travel to Cuba by U.S. citizens and permanent residents. Along with a less rigid enforcement of current rules, he could, for instance, convert specific licenses for some categories of U.S. travelers into general ones to allow a larger number of Americans to visit the island for religious, educational, humanitarian, and cultural purposes. Without having to seek prior approval from the State Department for their trips, non-tourist U.S. travelers to Cuba (and Cuban-Americans' family visits) might increase to the point where the overall travel ban would lose most of its relevance. Arrivals in Cuba of Americans of non-Cuban descent almost doubled between 1998 and 2000 due to Clinton's people-to-people contact policy.

The U.S. government should also rely on political and diplomatic tools to promote constructive engagement with the Castro regime and work closely with other governments in the Western Hemisphere and Europe to play a more meaningful role in Cuba's future and influence democratic improvements. Obama's friendly overtures toward Cuba during his remarks at the Summit of the Americas in April 2009 were interpreted by many observers as a sign of U.S. willingness to seek a real thaw in relations. Two months later, the United States voted with all members of the Organization of American States to revoke Cuba's suspension dating back to the early 1960s and pave the way for its readmission into the regional group. Although mechanisms were set up for Cuba's return, including compliance with the OAS's conventions on democracy and human rights, the vote showed some degree of U.S. appeasement toward the island.

Since he granted special exemptions to Cuban Americans, however, Obama has not taken significant steps to further soften the embargo. There are a number of reasons for this. First, Cuba ranks quite low on the White House agenda if compared to the war in Afghanistan and other foreign policy imperatives. Second, during his electoral campaign Obama did vow to maintain economic sanctions against Havana. Third, and most important of all, the U.S. president can weaken the embargo but only Congress can rescind it. Besides relaxing regulatory restrictions on non-tourist travel, Obama could allow Cuban Americans to spend more money in Cuba and expand the value and list of items eligible for inclusion in gift parcels sent to the island. He could also facilitate trade by creating a general license authorizing entry into a U.S. port to cargo vessels that have docked in a Cuban port within the previous 180 days to load or unload approved shipments. A specific license is currently required to perform these operations (GAO 2009, 12). With regard to the other major components of the Cuba sanctions program, they are codified into law and thus bound to stay unless Congress takes action.

As one Cuban scholar put it, U.S. interference and the embargo keep fueling a "mentality of besieged fortress" in Cuba that negatively affects the internal debate over potential reforms, the ideological climate, and the island's vision about its position in the international system (Hernández 2009). Far from downplaying the Castro regime's own responsibility for triggering tensions with Washington and its questionable use of the concept of an external foe to mobilize popular support for its policies, the lifting of the embargo would certainly take U.S.-Cuba relations to a whole different level and pave the way for the two countries to treat each other, if not as friends, at least as adversaries rather than enemies. Hard-liners in the United States continue to overlook the ineffectiveness of draconian economic sanctions against the island and justify them mostly by assuming what would happen if they were removed. Of course, the Cuban government would receive tangible economic benefits and no one knows for sure how it would react. But how worse could it be if Cuba is already, in the eyes of those hard-liners, a repressive totalitarian state with one of the worst human rights record in the world? Opponents of sanctions can count on the evidence of a unilateral embargo that not only has failed to hasten democracy in Cuba but also has strengthened the hands of the very government it was supposed to destabilize. And if we add its harmful effects on the Cuban population, even the alleged moral basis of U.S. policy seems doubtful.

More than anything else, the embargo has survived the end of the cold war as a domestic electoral issue linked to the votes of a sizable Cuban-

American constituency in South Florida and campaign contributions from anti-Castro exile groups aimed at influencing political outcomes. Nevertheless, recent polls of Cuban Americans reveal a shift away from isolationist policies toward Cuba in favor of closer ties, mainly triggered by younger generations of immigrants who left the island for economic reasons instead of political ones. Many moderate Cuban Americans welcomed Obama's move to eliminate restrictions on family visits and remittances to Cuba. In what amounted to a clear rejection of a foreign policy approach it helped to shape, the Cuban American National Foundation also supported the change, yet clarified: "Both President Obama and Vice-President Biden have made it abundantly clear that there will not be any unilateral lifting of the embargo absent significant moves on the part of the Castro regime towards freedom and democracy for the Cuban people. The Cuban American National Foundation concurs with the Obama Administration's position" (CANF 2009, 4). In short, while these reactions signaled to the U.S. president and Congress that sanctions-easing measures will encounter less strident opposition from Cuban exiles than in the past, serious obstacles remain in the path to deeper engagement with Cuba.

Lifting codified sanctions against Cuba will require political will and broad support from several interest groups within the United States besides moderate Cuban Americans. The key battle will take place in the U.S. Congress, which is more susceptible than the executive branch to the influence of lobbying pressures. Seeking to boost profits and galvanized by the growing unpopularity of the embargo, U.S. business organizations are stepping up lobbying efforts for a loosening of sanctions on behalf of agriculture, tourism, oil, and export industries. Religious, humanitarian, and academic groups are helping solidify a pro-normalization front in the ongoing debate over Cuba policy. But the conservative Cuban-American lobby and its congressional allies will do everything within their power to keep the status quo.

It seems reasonable to assume that the embargo will not be lifted all at once but rather gradually, bit by bit. After all, it is not a monolithic legislation but a set of economic sanctions impinging on the interests of many actors. Although the Castro brothers' definitive exit from the scene could speed up the process, the relaxation of the embargo will depend to a great extent on U.S. domestic dynamics. Given the vigorous lobbying by U.S. business groups and the conciliatory stance on Cuba of certain segments of the Cuban-American community, the most likely measures to be implemented in the near future should be the following: authorization of direct transfers from Cuban banks to U.S. financial institutions to execute sales of agricultural products to the island; permission granted to U.S. firms to explore and drill for oil in Cuban waters and export the oil to the United States; and unrestricted travel to Cuba for all American citizens. These measures are included in three separate bipartisan bills currently under consideration in the Democratic-run Congress. They all make good economic and strategic sense.

Lower transaction costs associated with food trade and streamlined operations would increase the competitiveness of U.S. agricultural producers and potentially boost their sales to Cuba. Exempting oil from the embargo might lead to the direct presence of U.S. investors in Cuba's offshore areas. They would manage the environmental aspects related to the exploration, drilling, production, and transportation of Cuban crude. And if large deposits are found, they would be able to serve their own market and reduce America's thirst for oil. As for the elimination of the travel ban, it would have a positive impact on a number of U.S. industries and outweigh the other bills. Overall, each measure is bound to generate impetus for additional easing of the embargo and create better conditions for a possible rapprochement between the United States and Cuba.

Long at loggerheads with each other, the United States and Cuba face a tough road toward finding a common ground. Five decades of animosities and mutual distrust are not so easy to erase. Havana has made abundantly clear that it will not make any unilateral concessions to improve relations with its powerful northern neighbor. Washington is still defending the embargo as a useful instrument of economic coercion. In reality, the greatest accomplishment of the embargo was to undermine U.S. ability to influence positive changes on the island while failing to deprive the Castro government of the financial wherewithal to resist those changes. A fresh U.S. move to eliminate major barriers to Cuba is long overdue.

To conclude, let us consider a quote by George W. Bush that helps highlight the core argument of this book. In July 2001, Bush stated, "The sanctions the United States enforces against the Castro regime are not just a policy tool, but a moral statement. It is wrong to prop up a regime that routinely stifles all the freedoms that make us human."[2] If this is the case, then U.S. policy toward Cuba in the post–cold war era has been nothing other than a "wrong" policy. Only time will tell if the new U.S. administration of Barack Obama and a Democratic-controlled Congress will finally make it right.

Notes

Chapter 1. Transnationalism in the Context of Economic Sanctions

1. The differentiation between transnationalism "from above" and "from below" has been criticized because it fails to recognize that certain agents may act simultaneously from above and from below depending on the nature of their actions (Schein 1998), downplays the role of states in co-opting and advancing transnational practices (Itzigsohn 2000), and privileges organized activities over more diffuse forms of mass action with no collective purpose (Mahler 1998, 72). In order to describe the variations in the intensities, frequencies, and the scope of cross-border linkages, international relations scholars have introduced several different typologies of transnationalism as referred to continuous or occasional practices (Itzigsohn et al. 1999), the level of state and economy or the intimate level of family and household (Gardner 2002), and global networks or kinship and diasporic ties (Faist 2000).

2. The political power and the low degree of accountability of U.S. corporations are mostly due to their economic power. In 2000, a total of fifty-nine of the global top two hundred TNCs were U.S.-based enterprises, including AT&T, Boeing, Lockheed-Martin, BellSouth, Kmart, Chase Manhattan, GTE, Mobil, and Texaco (Anderson and Cavanagh 2000).

3. The United Nations Conference on Trade and Development (UNCTAD 2004, 5) reported that between 1990 and 2002 the FDI performances of sanctioned countries like Sudan and Myanmar were among the best in the least developed world.

4. In his historical overview of immigration in the United States, Tilly (1990, 84) emphasized that, to a large degree, the actual units of migration are not individuals but groups of people connected by acquaintance, kinship, and work experience.

5. Official development assistance (ODA) consists of loans or grants administered with the objective of promoting sustainable social and economic development and the welfare of the recipient country. Official development assistance resources must be contracted with governments of foreign nations with whom the recipient has diplomatic, trade relations, or bilateral agreements or which are members of the United Nations, their agencies, or multilateral lending institutions.

6. While migrants' remittances to their countries of origin certainly benefit recipient families (Siddiqui and Kemal 2002; Adams and Page 2003; Maphosa 2007; Acosta et al. 2008), the issue of whether these financial flows contribute to economic development has elicited both positive (Stahl and Habib 1989; Adams 1991, 1998; Nishat and Bilgrami 1991; Glytsos 1993; Brown 1994; Alderman 1996; Durand et al. 1996; Ratha 2003; Carling 2004; León-Ledesma and Piracha 2004; Orozco 2007) and negative (Wiest 1984; Rubenstein 1992; Nyberg-Sorensen et al. 2002; Gubert 2002; Ballard 2003; Chami et al. 2003) responses.

7. When the U.S. Congress passed the Helms-Burton law and threatened sanctions against foreign firms investing in Cuba, the European Union vowed to fight the legislation at the World Trade Organization. Mexico and Canada passed antidote laws preventing their citizens from complying with U.S. regulations.

8. In 1980, after thousands of Cubans rushed into the Peruvian embassy in Havana in search of asylum, the Castro government opened the port of Mariel to permit anyone who wanted to leave the island to do so in an orderly fashion. While the exodus proceeded rather chaotically, approximately 125,000 Cubans left, most of them reaching the United States.

9. Brundenius (2002, 378) estimated that the Gini coefficient in Cuba grew from 0.22 in 1986 to 0.41 in 1999 as a result of unequal access to hard currency sources, with remittances representing one of the factors that contributed to increased inequality.

Chapter 2. Relations between Cuba and the United States, 1959–2009

1. For a review of U.S.-Cuba relations from the early nineteenth century until the revolution of 1959, see Pérez 2003.

2. The Monroe Doctrine, issued by President James Monroe of the United States in December 1823, proclaimed U.S. opposition to further European expansion in the Western Hemisphere and rejected any transfer of colonial possessions among European powers while pledging Washington's respect for existing possessions and borders in the region.

3. In late October 1962, the Khrushchev-Castro attempt to deploy nuclear missiles on Cuban soil brought the world to the brink of a nuclear war. The crisis ended with the Soviet Union agreeing to remove its missiles from Cuba in exchange for the U.S. commitment not to invade Cuba and to withdraw U.S. missiles from Turkey (Nathan 2001, 95). The removal of American missiles in southern Italy was also completed in 1963 even though they had been installed in 1959 and already proven obsolete (Nuti 1994).

4. Jimmy Carter did not renew the ban on travel to Cuba by U.S. citizens that was supposed to be renewed every six months. American visitors to the island were now allowed

to bring back up to one hundred dollars' worth of Cuban merchandise duty-free. They could also bring back more, but with a normal duty imposed.

5. Although scholars disagree on the feasibility of positive U.S. overtures to the Castro government in the late 1970s (Schwab 1999, 17; Pérez 2000), it is generally believed that Carter has been the only U.S. president to make a concerted effort to normalize relations with Cuba.

6. The list of candidates who received Free Cuba PAC money included the Republican senator Paula Hawkins of Florida and the Democratic senator Ernest Hollings of North Carolina. Hawkins was the main sponsor of the Senate bill approving Radio Martí, and Hollings was a key supporter of TV Martí (inaugurated in 1988).

7. The State Department report of 1989 noted that the Castro government had permitted representatives of the International Committee of the Red Cross to visit Cuban jails, released a large number of political prisoners and allowed them to emigrate, and decriminalized many petty offenses with a reform of the penal code. See U.S. Department of State 1989.

8. Unlike cold-war enemies of the United States such as China, Vietnam, North Korea, and other socialist countries, during the 1990s Cuba remained immune from the logic of engagement as a first step toward normalization of bilateral relations.

9. Larry Rohter, "Clinton Sees Opportunity to Break G.O.P Grip on Cuban-Americans," *New York Times*, October 31, 1992.

10. Both Israel and Uzbekistan (like the United States) currently trade with Cuba. Israel is also a major investor in the island's citrus sector.

11. Many Cubans on the island refer to the Helms-Burton law as the "Bacardi law" owing to the involvement of the Cuban-American family in the passage of the bill.

12. Clinton's share (34 percent) of the Cuban-American vote in Florida in 1996 was much higher than the share claimed by the Democratic presidential candidate Michael Dukakis (15 percent) in 1988 and Clinton himself (22 percent) in 1992.

13. See Sec. 112, "Reinstitution of Family Remittances and Travel to Cuba," Cuban Liberty and Democratic Solidarity (Libertad) Act of 1996, http://www.treas.gov/offices/enforcement/ofac/legal/statutes/libertad.pdf.

14. The complete results of the FIU's poll are available online at http://www.fiu.edu/orgs/ipor/cuba2000/.

15. See Sec. 910, "Requirements Relating to Certain Travel-Related Transactions with Cuba," Trade Sanctions Reform and Export Enhancement Act of 2000, http://www.fas.usda.gov/itp/cuba/title_ix.html.

16. Nancy San Martin, "Bill Allowing Travel to Cuba Approved by Senate Committee," *Miami Herald*, November 11, 2003.

17. See White House press release "President Bush Announces Initiative for a New Cuba," Office of the Press Secretary, May 20, 2002, http://www.whitehouse.gov/news/releases/2002/05/20020520-1.html.

18. Cuba has been on the U.S. Department of State's list of countries that sponsor terrorism since March 1, 1982.

19. Abby Goodnough, "G.O.P. Legislators in Florida Criticize Bush on Cuba," *New York Times*, August 13, 2003.

20. John Thor Dahlburg, "Fla. Lawmakers Warn Bush on Cuba Policy," *Los Angeles Times*, August 12, 2003.

21. "Bush Tightens Rules on Travel to Cuba," Associated Press, February 27, 2004.

22. Marcy Gordon, "Federal Reserve Fines UBS $100 Million," Associated Press, May 10, 2004.

23. The Report to the President of the Commission for Assistance to a Free Cuba of 2004 is available at http://www.state.gov/p/wha/rt/cuba/commission/2004/.

24. Oscar Corral, "Bush Hispanics Wary over Cuba," *Miami Herald*, March 19, 2004.

25. "Among Hispanics in Florida, 2008 Voter Registration Rolls Swing Democratic," Pew Hispanic Center fact sheet, October 29, 2008, http://pewhispanic.org/files/fact-sheets/44.pdf.

26. In March 2000, Vice President Al Gore broke with Clinton and other members of his administration over the custody and immigration battle involving the little Cuban boy Elián González, who had been found at sea by two fishermen on Thanksgiving Day of 1999 and turned over to the U.S. Coast Guard. While the Clinton administration was committed to (and ultimately succeeded in) the return of the boy to his father in Cuba, Gore announced that he was in favor of making Elián a U.S. permanent resident and having his custody case decided by a family court. Tony Karon, "Why Gore's Move over Elián Could Backfire," *Time*, March 31, 2000.

27. Chris Kraul and Carol J. Williams, "U.S. Leaves Cuban Physicians in Limbo," *Los Angeles Times*, March 8, 2007.

28. The Report to the President of the Commission for Assistance to a Free Cuba of 2006 is available at http://www.cafc.gov/documents/organization/68166.pdf.

29. "U.S. Calls Cuba's Interim Leader 'Fidel Light,'" Agence France Press, August 19, 2006.

30. See White House press release "President Bush Discusses Cuba Policy in Rose Garden Speech," Office of the Press Secretary, October 10, 2003, http://www.whitehouse.gov/news/releases/2003/10/20031010-2.html.

31. Pablo Bachelet, "Cuban Dissident Biscet Receives Presidential Medal," *Miami Herald*, November 6, 2007.

32. David Jackson, "Bush Pitches 'Freedom Fund' for Cuba," *USA Today*, October 24, 2007.

33. Will Weissert, "Cuban Dissidents Ask Looser US Embargo after Storm," Associated Press, September 4, 2008.

34. Aaron Wiener, "Obama Suggests Cuba Policy Reform," *Washington Independent*, December 31, 2008.

35. Casey Woods, "Obama First Democrat to Win Florida's Hispanic Vote," *Miami Herald*, November 6, 2008.

36. See White House press release "Fact Sheet: Reaching Out to the Cuban People," Office of the Press Secretary, April 13, 2009, http://www.whitehouse.gov/the_press_office/Fact-Sheet-Reaching-out-to-the-Cuban-people/.

37. David Gollust, "U.S. Holding Talks with Cuba on Obama Outreach," Voice of America, April 27, 2009.

38. Will Weissert, "U.S. Should Do More to Woo Cuba, Castro Says," Associated Press, April 30, 2009.

39. An overview of U.S. sanctions against Cuba with the latest rules on travel, gifts, and cash to the island is available at http://www.treas.gov/offices/enforcement/ofac/programs/cuba/cuba. pdf.

40. On April 22, 2009, during a House Foreign Affairs Committee hearing, Secretary of State Hillary Clinton clearly dismissed the possibility of a presidential veto to a relaxation of sanctions. She stated: "As you know, the embargo is part of our law. I mean, a President cannot lift the embargo. That has to be done by an act of Congress. If the Congress decides that's in the America's best interest, obviously the Administration will abide by that." "The Veto Threat Is Gone," *The Cuban Triangle*, April 23, 2009.

41. Leslie Clark and Frances Robles, "Showdown on U.S.-Cuba Policy Not Over Yet," *Miami Herald*, March 11, 2009.

Chapter 3. Evolution and Results of Foreign Investment in Cuba

1. Cuba had allowed foreign investment since the enactment of Decree-Law 50 in 1982, but no convincing attempts to attract FDI were made during the 1980s. By 1989, only two joint ventures with foreign firms had been formed in Cuba.

2. The term *international economic association* (or simply *economic association)* refers to the following: joint action by one or more national investors and one or more foreign investors for the production of goods, the offering of services, or both, for profit, in its two forms, which consist of joint ventures and international economic association contracts. *Joint ventures* imply the establishment of a legal status distinct from that of any one of the parties; the proportions of capital stock that should be contributed by the foreign investor and the national investor are agreed upon by both partners and defined as part of the authorization. *International economic association contracts* do not imply a legal entity separate from those of the contracting parties; each contracting party makes separate contributions, which constitute a cumulative amount that it owns at all times, and even though the contributions do not constitute capital stock, it is in the parties' interest to establish a common fund, as long as the portion of ownership belonging to each of the parties is well defined.

3. Manuel Roig-Franzia, "Cuba's Call for Economic Détente," *Washington Post*, July 27, 2007.

4."Inversión Extranjera: Menos de lo Esperado, Pero . . . ," Economics Press Service, February 15, 2002.

5. "Number of Foreign Firms in Cuba Fell in 2006," Reuters, January 29, 2007.

6. Fidel Rendón Matienzo, "Cuba Busca Mayor Eficiencia en la Inversión Extranjera," *Granma*, June 26, 2007.

7. Marc Frank, "Foreign Investment Projects in Cuba Down: Official," Reuters, July 9, 2008.

8. See Pebercan, "Pebercan Will End Its Commercial Activities," February 20, 2009, http://www.pebercan.com/files/pdf/PBC_February_20_2009_-_EN.pdf.

9. See Pebercan, "Consolidated Financial Statements," September 30, 2008, http://www.pebercan.com/files/pdf/Q3_2008_EN.pdf.

10. Will Weissert, "Cuba to Pay $162M Debt to Sherritt Over 5 Years," Associated Press, February 25, 2009. Under the payment agreement of February 2009 that Sherritt finalized with Cuba, the latter will pay $126 million in oil and gas receivables and $36 million in power receivables over the next five years with certificates of deposit and interest rates guaranteed by the National Bank of Cuba.

11. See Sherritt International, "Annual Report 2008," http://www.sherritt.com/doc08/files/financials/2008%20Annual%20Report/Sherritt_AR08_full.pdf.

12. See Sol Meliá, "2006 Year-End Results," http://inversores.solmelia.com/en/informes_anuales.html?tab=past.

13. "Expertos Encuentran Obstáculos en Convivencia Peso-Dólar en Cuba," EFE, July 7, 2004.

14. Regarding the contribution of each sector and country to the total amount of foreign direct investment in Cuba, the only data available are those of the U.S.-Cuba Trade and Economic Council as of March 1999. The total value of committed/delivered FDI through AECEs was estimated at $1,767.2 million. Leading sectors were telecommunications ($650m), mining ($350m), and tourism ($200m). Leading countries were Canada ($600m), Mexico ($450m), Italy ($387m), and Spain ($100m). For further details, see U.S.-Cuba Trade and Economic Council, http://www.cubatrade.org/FORINVES.pdf.

15. "Cuba: Inversión Reorganizada y Con Record de Ingresos," Associated Press, June 26, 2007; "Cuba Registra un Record de Inversión Extranjera en Sus Ingresos en 2006 y Considera Así Reorganizada Su Inversión," Europa Press, June 26, 2007; "Aumenta Cuba Ingresos por Inversión Extranjera," June 27, 2007.

16. Pérez Villanueva 2008 also reported Lomas's figure as *ingresos directos al país*, not as foreign direct investment.

17. "La Inversión Extranjera Directa en Cuba," Asociación Nacional de Economistas y Contadores de Cuba (ANEC). Workshop: Inserción Internacional, Gestión Macroeconómica y Regulación, Cuba y la Experiencia Internacional, Havana, February 14, 2006.

18. Marc Frank, "China's Sinopec Signs Up for Oil Production in Cuba," Reuters, January 31, 2005.

19. Joshua Goodman and Jeb Blount, "Petrobras, Cuba to Explore for Oil Close to Florida," Bloomberg, October 31, 2008.

20. Patricia Grogg, "Nickel Still Number One for Cuba," Inter Press Service (IPS), December 29, 2006.

21. The text of the agreement of December 2004 between Cuba and Venezuela for the implementation of the Bolivarian Alternative for the Americas (ALBA) can be found at http://www.cubaminrex.cu/English/ALBA/Articulos/Agreements/2004/04-12-14.html.

22. Marc Lacey, "Cuban Refinery Inaugurated, with Chávez in Spotlight," *New York Times*, December 22, 2007.

23. Esteban Israel, "Venezuela Trumps China in Cuba Ferronickel Deal," Reuters, January 29, 2007.

24. Economist Intelligence Unit 2008a; Julio Martínez Molina, "Amplían Capacidad Productiva de la Refinería Camilo Cienfuegos," *Juventud Rebelde*, September 21, 2008.

25. Information provided by MINVEC, June 2004.

26. Cuba Transition Project (CTP), "Cuba's Investments Abroad," *Focus on Cuba*, issue 50, December 17, 2003.

27. Since the early 1990s, Cuba has invested heavily in the development of its biotechnology and pharmaceuticals industries. It is well known that the island's scientific knowledge base and the quality of its programs, laboratories, and products are extremely advanced by international standards. The Cuban state-controlled biotechnology industry manufactures a wide range of products, including vaccines (like the only recombinant vaccine for hepatitis B), reagents and diagnostic systems, enzymes, molecular biology products, interferons, and monoclonal antibodies.

28. Interview with a Cuban official in Havana, June 10, 2004.

29. Reuters, "Foreign Investment in Cuba Plummeted to $38.9 Million in 2001 from $488 Million the Year Before," July 8, 2002.

30. Pebercan, "2005 Annual Report," http://www.pebercan.com/en/financials/RA2005EN.pdf.

31. For further information, see the statement of July 2002 by the European Union embassies in Havana, "Europeans on Cuba's Foreign Investment Regime," http://www.lexingtoninstitute.org/europeans-on-cubas-foreign-investment-regime?a=1&c=1184.

32. "Cuba Responds to Complaints from Foreign Investors," Associated Press, July 17, 2002. Cuba's labor code for AECEs has been denounced by several international labor organizations. Criticism mainly focuses on the system of payment of Cuban workers hired by foreign companies along with discriminatory practices of recruitment due to patronage, cronyism, and the conformity of workers' ideas and behavior to official ideology. The issue has gained importance since the opening to foreign investment in the early 1990s and especially after the legalization of hard currency holdings in 1993, which allowed Cubans to shop at state-owned dollar stores previously reserved for foreigners. Cuban workers in AECEs receive their wages in domestic currency at the official exchange rate of one Cuban peso (CUP) per dollar. However, owing to generalized shortages of goods available through the normal distribution system, they are compelled to buy convertible pesos or CUCs (they used to buy dollars before the Castro government put an end to the circulation of the U.S. currency on the island in November 2004) at the current unofficial exchange rate of 25 CUPs per CUC in order to purchase the products they need in stores that deal only with the latter currency. Given this situation, two Cuban exile groups (the Cuban Committee for Human Rights and the Independent Federation of Electric, Gas, and Water Plants of Cuba) filed a lawsuit in 1999 against forty foreign companies accusing them of being part of an illegal scheme by the Cuban government to deprive Cuban workers of most of their salaries. According to the lawsuit, foreign companies pay up to $450 dollars a month for the wage of each of their workers to a state employment agency. But the employment agency pays the same workers an equivalent of $5 dollars a month, while the government keeps the rest. See Peter Morton, "Two Canadian Companies in Cuba Lawsuit," *National Post*, June 29, 1999. Cuban authorities defend their labor code and justify the high charge made to foreign investors

by claiming that: 1) direct dollar payments by foreign companies to their workers would create too much difference between the latter and the rest of the Cuban work force; 2) direct payments in domestic currency by foreign companies should also include the cost of benefits for medical assistance, education, and housing that is instead assumed by the Cuban government; 3) it is fair for foreign companies to pay their workers more than in other emerging markets because Cuban workers are more efficient and qualified. Interview with two Cuban economists in Havana, June 7, 2001.

33. Marc Frank, "Cuba Central Bank Chief Says Forex Control Working," Reuters, September 15, 2003.

34. Marc Frank, "Castro Reins in Cuban Tourism," Reuters, July 13, 2004.

35. Marc Frank, "Cuba Tightens Up on Tourism," Reuters, October 16, 2004.

36. Raúl Castro's speech of July 26, 2007, delivered in the city of Camagüey, is available at http://www.granma.cubaweb.cu/secciones/raul26/02.html.

37. Cuban agricultural production decreased by approximately 37 percent between 2004 and 2008. By early 2007, an astounding 84 percent of all rationed food on the island was imported. Associated Press, "Cuba Importa 84% de Sus Alimentos," February 26, 2007.

38. Rosa Tania Valdés, "Cuba Abierta a Inversión Extranjera en Agricultura: Ministra," Reuters, April 9, 2008.

39. "Cuba Desestima Abrir Inversión Extranjera en Agro: Funcionario," Reuters, May 13, 2008.

40. Raúl Castro's speech of July 26, 2008, delivered in the city of Santiago de Cuba, is available at http://www.granma.cubaweb.cu/marti-moncada/cel-26.html.

41. Anthony Boadle, "Cuba Allows Foreign Firms to Pay in Hard Currency," Reuters, December 7, 2007.

42. For a discussion of Cuba's new policy on hard currency payments to employees of foreign companies, see Philip Peters's comments in his blog, "The Cuban Triangle," at http://cubantriangle.blogspot.com/2007/12/two-economic-moves.html.

43. Article 32 of Law 77, which regulates foreign investment in Cuba states: "Joint ventures, the parties to international economic association contracts and totally foreign capital companies may be authorized to create an economic stimulus fund for Cubans or permanent residents in Cuba who are working in activities corresponding to foreign investments. The contributions to the economic stimulus fund shall be made out of earned profits. The amount of these contributions shall be agreed upon between the joint ventures, foreign investors and national investors who are party to international economic association contracts, and totally foreign capital companies, on the one hand, and the Ministry of Foreign Investment and Economic Cooperation, on the other hand."

44. Rodrigo Malmierca had already replaced Marta Lomas as the new minister of foreign investment in November 2008. As usually happens in Cuba, the government gave no official reason for its decision to liberate Lomas from the position. "Raul Castro Names New Foreign Investment Minister," Reuters, November 12, 2008.

45. For more on the Cuban armed forces' growing role in the economy in the post-1990 period, see Klepak 2005, 75–102.

46. In April 2009, Cuba's Council of Ministers designated the army colonel Armando

Emilio Pérez Betancourt as the new vice minister of economy and planning. Pérez Betancourt had served since 1988 as the head of a special commission leading the Cuban military's effort to make state-run firms more profitable.

47. At the end of 2008, only 860 Cuban state enterprises had applied *perfeccionamiento empresarial*, representing 31.5 percent of the country's total. Asamblea Nacional del Poder Popular, "Informe sobre los Resultados Económicos del Ano 2008 y Perspectivas para el 2009," December 8, 2008.

48. Gerardo Arreola, "Cuba Reparte a Ministerios el Gasto en Divisas para Aligerar la Centralización," *La Jornada*, July 19, 2009; Marc Frank, "Cuba Unfreezes Some Bank Accounts to Boost Trade," Reuters, July 22, 2009.

49. The Ministerio para la Inversión Extranjera y la Colaboración Económica (MINVEC) reported that the average time of negotiations for AECEs in 2003 was 10.3 months, as compared to 10.8 in 2001 and 11.1 in 2000. Even so, this is still longer than virtually anywhere else in Latin America.

50. Marc Frank, "Cuba Adopts Two-track Foreign Investment Policy," Reuters, August 26, 2001.

51. Raisa Pagés, "Light Industry: Not Just Conquering Markets, but Maintaining Them," *Granma International*, July 13, 2001.

52. Marc Frank, "Cuba Places New Hoops in Path of Small Investors," Reuters, February 2, 2005.

53. Statistics on cooperative production agreements were posted on MINVEC's official website (http://www.minvec.cu) and then removed.

54. "Cuba: Inversión Reorganizada y con Récord de Ingresos," Associated Press, June 26, 2007.

55. Cuba's Office of National Statistics (ONE) stopped reporting the number of Cuban workers in joint ventures in 2004.

56. Information provided by MINVEC, June 2004.

57. Marc Frank, "New Cuban Sugar Exporter Has Mystery Partner," Reuters, March 7, 2002.

58. Gross capital formation refers to capital used for the production of goods and services.

59. Cuba's Office of National Statistics (ONE) indicated that the island's total earnings from goods exports in 2007 were $3,701.4 million.

60. Larry Luxner, "Spain's Repsol-YPF Helps Cuba Search the Waters Off Its Coast for Oil," *Miami Herald*, June 28, 2004.

61. This information is based on my calculations from Sherritt's and Pebercan's annual financial reports of 2007, available at http://www.sherritt.com and http://www.pebercan.com.

62. Sherritt International, "Sherritt Reports Record Earnings in 2007," fourth quarter report for 2007, http://www.sherritt.com.

63. Growing revenues from exports of pharmaceuticals and biotechnology products are mostly the result of Cuba's new joint ventures with Asian firms aimed at building pharmaceutical processing labs that meet the demand of Cuban vaccines and other medical products in that region.

64. This information is based on calculations of the author from data of the Cuban Central Bank, Cuba's Office of National Statistics, and the Centro de Estudios de la Economía Cubana.

65. See Oficina Nacional de Estadísticas (ONE) 2009.

66. Although production was practically stagnant, revenues from nickel exports grew fivefold between 2002 and 2007 due to skyrocketing nickel prices in the international market.

67. "Cuba Produces Equivalent to Four Million Tons of Oil in 2007," Cuban News Agency, December 26, 2007.

68. For an analysis of international tourism in Cuba during the 1990s and its effects on the island's economy, see Figueras Pérez 2002.

69. Oficina Nacional de Estadísticas (ONE) 2008b.

Chapter 4. The Impact of the Helms-Burton Law on Foreign Investment in Cuba

1. Robert Muse, a Washington, D.C. lawyer whose clients have included European firms with investments in Cuba, said he expects 430,000 lawsuits if Title III of the Helms-Burton law is implemented. He believes Cuban Americans will bury U.S. courts in claims for lost homes, businesses, and farms. James Cox, "U.S. Ponders More Aggressive Cuba Policy," *USA Today*, October 25, 2001. A Cuban family that owned a sugar plantation in Cuba valued at $3,000 in 1962 is seeking compensation of close to $10 million from a Spanish firm (Sol Meliá) that has built a hotel on that property.

2. The amendment to FEMA allows Canadians who are sued in the United States to recover any amounts awarded if the other party has assets in Canada. Mexico passed a similar law in October 1996. The law establishes that Mexican companies can be fined if they comply with the extraterritorial provisions of Helms-Burton and provides for the non-recognition and non-enforcement of foreign judgments under such extraterritorial legislation.

3. Richard Lapper, "Ambiguous Stance Towards Attracting Big Guns," *Financial Times*, March 24, 1999.

4. Interview with a Cuban official in Havana, May 29, 2001.

5. Interview with a Cuban consultant in Havana, June 15, 2001.

6. Interview with a news correspondent posted in Havana, June 11, 2001.

7. Data from the 1997 and 1999 annual reports of Compañía Fiduciaria.

8. Philip Eade, "Bypassing Helms-Burton," *Euromoney*, November 1, 1996.

9. Interview with a news correspondent posted in Havana, May 31, 2001.

10. Patrick Worsnip, "More Sherritt Executives Face U.S. Travel Ban," Reuters, March 14, 1997.

11. "Canada's Sherritt to Build Power Plant in Cuba," Xinhua English Newswire, February 6, 1998.

12. Christopher Marquis, "Two Firms Face Helms-Burton Sanctions," *Miami Herald*, January 22, 1997.

13. See U.S.-Cuba Trade and Economic Council (USCTEC), "Grupo Domos Out of ETECSA," http://www.cubatrade.org/eyeone.html.

14. Interview with a Cuban economist in Havana, June 21, 2000.

15. Larry Rohter, "Mexican Conglomerate Pulls Out of Cuba," *New York Times*, June 30, 1997. The U.S. Department of State later reinstated visa privileges for the executives of Grupo Domos (Roy 2000, 165).

16. Juan O. Tamayo, "Phone Group Moves Ahead in Cuba," *Miami Herald*, March 6, 1997.

17. Christina Hoag, "U.S. Law Curtails Resort's Deals in Cuba," *Miami Herald*, June 17, 2004.

18. Interview with a foreign correspondent stationed in Havana, June 21, 2004.

19. Doreen Hemlock, "Jamaican Hotel Chain SuperClubs to Close 2 Resorts in Cuba under U.S. Pressure," *South Florida Sun-Sentinel*, June 18, 2004.

20. Daniel W. Fisk, "Advancing the Day When Cuba Will Be Free," remarks to the Cuban American Veterans Association, October 9, 2004, http://www.scoop.co.nz/stories/WO0410/S00171.htm.

21. Christopher Marquis, "Cemex se Va de Cuba," *El Nuevo Herald*, May 29, 1996.

22. In early 2007, Tate and Lyle sold Redpath to American Sugar Refining Inc. of Yonkers, New York.

23. "Embargo de EEUU Deja Perdidas en Cuba de Mas de US$1.900 Millones en 2000," Agence France Press, July 17, 2001.

24. "British Borneo Says Cuba Pullout Was Political," Reuters, March 4, 1998. Curiously, a week earlier British Borneo had stated that its abandonment of oil exploration activities in Cuba was for technical reasons and not because of political opposition from the United States. See "British Borneo Denies U.S. Cuba Warning," Reuters, February 25, 1998.

25. Statement of Michael Ranneberger (Coordinator for Cuban Affairs, Department of State) to the Subcommittee on International Economic Policy and Trade of the House International Relations Committee, March 12, 1998.

26. Pascal Fletcher, "UK Company Looks to Cuban Trade," *Financial Times*, June 16, 2000.

27. "Cuba Sees Cigar Exports Doubling by Year 2000," Reuters, February 13, 1997.

28. Paolo Spadoni, "Foreign Banks' Exposure in Cuba Unaffected by U.S. Pressures," *Orlando Sentinel*, February 14, 2005.

29. Anthony Boadle, "Cuba Finds Itself Isolated from Financial Systems," Reuters, July 25, 2007.

30. "ING to Close Banking Operations in Cuba," Reuters, July 6, 2007.

31. Frances Kerry, "Cuba Admits Helms-Burton Hurts, but Not Fatal," Reuters, March 11, 1997.

32. "EE UU Envió Carta Empresa Panameña Respecto Ley Helms-Burton," EFE, January 24, 1997.

33. "Panama Firm to Stay in Cuba Despite U.S. Warning," Reuters, February 22, 1997.

34. Marquis, "Two Firms Face Helms-Burton Sanctions."

35. Anthony DePalma, "Buscando Vías para Invertir en la Isla," *El Nuevo Herald*, March 6, 2000.

36. Leisure Canada has nonetheless an important layer of protection against potential sanctions under Title III of the Helms-Burton legislation because it has no assets in the United States.

37. Sol Meliá manages two hotels in the United States, the Hard Rock Hotel Chicago and the Paramount New York (with 17.4 percent equity interest). It also owns the Paradisus resort in Puerto Rico (U.S. territory).

38. Mauricio Vicent, "La Helms-Burton Amenaza Otra Vez a Sol Meliá," *El País*, November 8, 1999.

39. Jorge Ebro, "Nada Va a Cambiar Respecto a Cuba," *Opciones*, August 22, 1999.

40. According to Spanish sources, the letter of July 1999 announced an imminent notification to Sol Meliá of the forty-five-day deadline during which a company must either disprove the charge or abandon its investment. But the notification was never sent. "Siguen Amenazas Contra Sol Meliá," Economics Press Service, November 15, 1999.

41. Cox, "U.S. Ponders More Aggressive Cuba Policy."

42. "Spain's PM Chooses Hotel to Protest Helms-Burton Act, AFP says," Bloomberg, November 16, 1999.

43. Bruce Barnard, "Inside Europe (EU Protests US Sanctions on Terrorism)," *Europe*, September 1, 1996.

44. The United States agreed not to make expropriations prior to May 1998 the target of lawsuits.

45. Walter Oppenheimer, "Helms Reniega del Acuerdo entre Clinton y la UE," *El País*, June 22, 2000.

46. Marta Veloz, "La Inversión Extranjera No Se Ha Detenido," *Opciones*, April 18, 1999.

47. "Foreign Investment Increases in Cuba in Spite of U.S. Blockade," Prensa Latina, February 2, 2001.

48. Interview with a Cuban official in Havana, May 23, 2001.

49. Thomson Financial, "Japan Suspends Trade Insurance for Exports to Cuba—Report," August 18, 2008; Marc Frank, "Crisis Global y Huracanes Golpean las Finanzas de Cuba," Reuters, December 18, 2008.

50. "Brazilian President Meets with Cuba's Raul Castro," Reuters, January 15, 2008; "Iran Mulls Over Opening €500m L/C for Cuba," *Tehran Times*, June 16, 2008.

51. Doreen Hemlock, "Spanish Cigar Company Accused of Using Cuban Cigars as Bait for Business," *South Florida Sun-Sentinel*, November 2, 2000.

52. Larry Luxner, "Cuba Sues Bacardi over Havana Club Trademark," *Impact International*, June 15, 1997. Pernod Ricard is also engaged in a legal battle with Bacardi over the rights to sell Havana Club rum in the United States once the embargo against Cuba is lifted. A U.S. law of 1998, known as "Section 211," prohibits the U.S. government from honoring trademarks confiscated by the Cuban government.

53. Cuba's new "sustainable social" GDP formula recognizes the value added of subsidized social services (healthcare, education, sports) provided by the Cuban state to its population and to citizens from other countries.

54. In January 2001, asked to comment on the poor presence of Great Britain in the Cuban market, a British officer gave one of the rare admissions of this particular problem

for foreign companies. He revealed that Great Britain was the second biggest investor in the world and most of its investments were in the United States. He added that U.S. threats of possible sanctions had put a brake on the British participation in economic activities on the island. "Gran Bretaña: Funcionario Considera Factible Incremento de Relaciones Bilaterales," *Opciones*, January 28, 2001. More recently, Valentín Díez Morodo, the president of the Mexican Foreign Trade, Investment, and Technology Council (COMCE), said that Mexican firms have reduced their investments in Cuba in part because of fear of the Helms-Burton law. "Empresarios Mexicanos No Invierten en Cuba por Temor a EEUU," *EFE*, January 4, 2005.

Chapter 5. U.S. Financial Flows in the Cuban Economy

1. David D. Kirkpatrick, "U.S. Halts Cuba Access by Educational Groups," *New York Times*, May 4, 2003.

2. In 1990, Cuba ranked twenty-third among the twenty-five top tourist destinations in Latin America. At the end of 2008, the island occupied ninth place.

3. In August 1994, after a series of violent boat hijackings and unprecedented street riots, Fidel Castro declared that anyone who wanted to leave Cuba on his own could do so. In the following weeks, some thirty-five thousand Cuban rafters left the island for the United States in what became known as the *balsero* crisis.

4. Licensed U.S. travelers to Cuba can spend additional money for telephone calls and for transactions directly related to the activities for which a license was issued.

5. Eckstein and Barberia (2001, 13) argued that there is contradictory information about Cuban-American visits to Cuba. According to them, while Cuban sources report that individuals of Cuban descent visiting the island between 1994 and 1996 were about twenty thousand per year, U.S. sources estimate that the actual number was approximately forty thousand in 1994 and one hundred thousand per year between 1995 and 1998.

6. In 1995, Canada was the most important source of visitors to Cuba (143,541), followed by Italy (114,767), Spain (89,501), and the United States (59,972). In 1998, Canadian travelers to Cuba were 215,644, followed by Italians (186,688), Germans (148,987), and U.S.-based travelers (141,678).

7. Data on Cuban-American visits to Cuba for 2000–2001 included in table 5.2 are similar to those provided by Robyn et al. (2002) and Sanders and Long (2002). Robyn et al. estimated that 120,000 Cuban Americans visited Cuba in 2000. Sanders and Long put that number at 124,000 in 2001.

8. "Embargo or Not, U.S. Is Now Fidel Castro's Economic Partner," *The Economist*, January 4, 2003.

9. Andres Oppenheimer, "U.S. May Tighten Cuba Travel," *Miami Herald*, December 15, 2002.

10. Rafael Lorente, "Travel from U.S. to Cuba Drops Sharply Since New Travel Restrictions," *South Florida Sun-Sentinel*, December 20, 2004.

11. Also see Vanessa Arrington, "Cuban Official: Embargo Losses Are More Than $4 Billion," Associated Press, October 3, 2006.

12. Sundred Suzarte Medina, "The U.S. Policy of Aggression Is the Main Obstacle between Cuba and Its Emigrés," *Granma International*, March 19, 2008.

13. Kelly Sullivan, "Americans Defy Cuba Embargo," *Washington Post*, October 31, 2001.

14. Jenalia Moreno, "Americans Defy Ban in Droves—Travel to Cuba Clashes with Official U.S. Policy," *Houston Chronicle*, February 28, 2003.

15. "Americans Who Make Trips to Cuba without OK Could Be Prosecuted," *Houston Chronicle*, March 9, 2003. Further information on OFAC's civil penalties enforcement for violations of travel-related transactions with respect to Cuba is available at http://www.treas.gov/offices/enforcement/ofac/civpen/index.shtml.

16. Tracey Eaton, "8 Vow to Have U.S.-Style Meeting in Cuba," *Dallas Morning News*, March 11, 2003.

17. Oscar Corral, "Groups Warned to Obey Travel Limits," *Miami Herald*, April 8, 2005.

18. The OFAC's new rules on travel to Cuba by licensed U.S. religious organizations introduced in early April 2005 capped the number of people in any specific group of travelers at twenty-five and limited such trips to once every three months.

19. Carlos Lage, Remarks on Noticiero Nacional de la Televisión Cubana (a broadcast on Cuban National Television), March 18, 2001.

20. "Cuba: Economía y Turismo," Economics Press Service, May 31, 2001.

21. Gilda Fariñas and Susana Tesoro, "Turismo: Monedas al Aire," *Bohemia*, May 16, 2003.

22. "El Producto Bruto en 2003 y Algunas Consideraciones sobre 2004," Economics Press Service, December 31, 2003. The search for increased efficiency was a key reason for the nomination of the head of the Gaviota tourism group, Manuel Marrero Cruz, as Cuba's new tourism minister in 2004. Gaviota, which is linked to the Cuban Defense Ministry, allegedly managed to obtain in its establishments an average cost per dollar of gross income of $0.64 in 2003. Cuban authorities hoped to achieve similar efficiency levels in the other tourism groups, whether they owned three-, four-, or five-star hotels. Interview with a foreign correspondent stationed in Havana, May 26, 2004.

23. Nancy San Martin, "Rules Changed on Cuba Trips," *Miami Herald*, March 25, 2003.

24. Since the late 1990s, an ever increasing number of Cubans have turned to the Transcard (sold by a Canadian company) as a fast, efficient, and less costly alternative to receiving remittances via Western Union. Individuals outside of Cuba can establish accounts in any Transcard office throughout the world and designate a Cuban national as the beneficiary, who would then be issued a credit card to access the account and make purchases. U.S.-Cuba Trade and Economic Council (USCTEC), *Economic Eye on Cuba*, October 27, 1997. It must be noted that transactions with Transcard are routed via Canadian banks, thus avoiding control from U.S. authorities.

25. Interview with a Cuban economist in Havana, June 9, 2003.

26. Interview with a Cuban economist in Havana, May 20, 2003.

27. Tim Johnson, "U.S. Action after Cuba Crackdown Debated," *Miami Herald*, May 5, 2003.

28. Some Cuban economists argued that at least $500 million was hoarded in the homes of Cubans in 2003. Most of that money reportedly came from relatives in the United States. Interview with a Cuban economist in Havana, May 20, 2003. See Vanessa Arrington, "Cuban Businesses No Longer Accept Dollars," Associated Press, November 8, 2004.

29. It is reported that in 2003 there were 2,705 people with licenses who, charging dollars, rented rooms to foreigners in Havana, where 80–85 percent of all Cuba's dollar-based renters were located. In addition, there were an estimated 5,200 unlicensed renters around the country who charged dollars or other foreign currencies. Patricia Grogg, "Landlords on the Verge of a Nervous Breakdown," Inter Press Service, July 4, 2003.

30. Interview with a Cuban economist in Havana, June 3, 2003. If remittances represented about 75 percent of all hard currency sources for the Cuban population, then they would have been approximately $890 million in 2001.

31. Beginning May 1, 2005, the monthly minimum wage in Cuba rose from 100 regular pesos to 225 pesos, and the minimum pension from 55 pesos to 150 pesos. Paolo Spadoni, "Remittances Could Raise Cubans' Wages, Pensions," Orlando Sentinel, May 22, 2005.

32. Asamblea Nacional del Poder Popular, "Informe Sobre los Resultados Económicos del Ano 2008 y Perspectivas para el 2009," December 8, 2008.

33. Inter-American Development Bank, "Survey of Remittance Senders: U.S. to Latin America," November/December 2001 (as cited in Orozco 2003, 4).

34. Manuel Orozco, e-mail message to author, April 5, 2003.

35. "Remesas: La Primera Fuente de Ingresos?" Economics Press Service, February 29, 2004.

36. Pablo Bachelet, "White House Stemming Flow of Remittances," Miami Herald, October 26, 2004.

37. "Nuevo Servicio de Remesas para Cuba Inaugurado por Empresa Suiza," EFE, December 24, 2004.

38. Paolo Spadoni, "Have Cuban Donations Reached an All-Time High?" Orlando Sentinel, October 16, 2007.

39. Armando Nova González, "Continuará la Dolarización?" Economics Press Service, February 15, 2001.

40. Interview with a Cuban economist in Havana, June 5, 2003.

41. Interview with a Cuban economist in Havana, November 7, 2004.

42. In 2004, Cuba's balance of payments account (which refers to international trade in goods and services, transfer payments, and short-term credit) registered its first surplus since 1994. "Cuban Central Bank Chief Says Island Sees First Surplus in Decade," Associated Press, March 29, 2005.

43. "Canadian Firm Buys Stake in Cuban Cellular Phones," Reuters, February 28, 1998.

44. Sherritt International, "Annual Information Form," March 15, 2001.

45. Telecom Italia, "Third Quarter Report 2003," http://www.telecomitalia.it/trimestrale0309/English/B03.html.

46. Worldwide statistics on telecommunications indicators are available on the

website of the International Telecommunication Union (ITU) at http://www.itu.int/ ITU-D/ict/statistics/.

47. The development of the telecommunications sector in Cuba presents profound spatial disparities between the capital city and the rest of the island. Havana has the largest share of Cuba's telephone lines and a much higher phone density than the national average. Even within Havana, however, some municipalities had a phone density of more than 50 percent while others only 2 percent in 2008. "Mas de 13.000 Líneas de Telefonía Móvil Han Sido Dadas de Alta en Cuba Desde Que Se Eliminaron las Restricciones," Europa Press, May 18, 2008.

48. Heriberto Rosabal, "La Digitalización y el Acceso a Internet Seguirán Creciendo," *Juventud Rebelde*, January 18, 2004.

49. In 2007, U.S.-Cuba phone traffic was the most skewed among all Latin American routes.

50. Only in 2005 and 2007 did ETECSA pay higher rates ($0.73 and $0.81) per minute of phone traffic than those paid by U.S. carriers ($0.57 and $0.79).

51. The planned investments of ETECSA for 2004–2007 amounted to $333.5 million. See José Antonio Fernández Martínez, "Las Telecomunicaciones en Cuba: Presente y Retos del Futuro," Presentation at VII Cumbre de Presidentes AHCIET, Havana, November 2003 (available at http://www.ahciet.net). Figures on realized investments are not available.

52. Marc Frank, "Cubans Enter Wireless Age," Reuters, March 1, 2004.

53. Interview with a foreign correspondent stationed in Havana, May 26, 2004.

54. Fernández Martínez, "Las Telecomunicaciones en Cuba."

55. "Cuba to Extend Its Telecommunications Services," *Granma International*, March 28, 2008.

56. "U.S. Goods, People, Cash Pour into Cuba," Reuters, July 28, 2001.

57. Miguel Comellas, "Iberia and Aerovaradero Establish Joint Venture," *Granma International*, April 10, 2002.

58. Additional information on Hotetur hotels in Cuba is available at http://www.hotetur.com.

59. "U.S. Goods, People, Cash Pour into Cuba," Reuters.

60. Leisure Canada created a hotel brand (Mirus Resorts and Hotels) to use on properties within Cuba and was given the right in June 2003 to manage the Monte Barreto hotel in Havana under its own new brand. According to the company, "The development of a hotel brand that can quickly transfer to a North American hotel chain, once the doors to Cuba open, further establishes Leisure Canada's vertically integrated gateway to Cuba" (USCTEC 2003). Also see Leisure Canada's website at http://www.leisurecanada.com.

61. The largest U.S. investors in Sinopec in 2004 were Exxon Mobil Corporation of Texas, J. P. Morgan Chase and Co. of New York, and Wellington Management Company LLP of Massachusetts. Sinopec's annual report of 2004 is available at http://english.sinopec.com/investor_center/reports/.

62. In September 2004, Petrobras issued $600 million in global notes in the international capital markets. More than half (54 percent) of the issue was placed with U.S.

investors. See http://www2.petrobras.com.br/atuacaointernacional/petrobrasmagazine/
negoc_eng.html.

63. The Havana factory used by BrasCuba was nationalized in 1960 and belonged to
the American Tobacco Company. Executives of Souza Cruz said they are not worried
about the expropriation because in 1994 the American Tobacco Company was bought
by Brown Williamson, another subsidiary of BAT. "Capitales Extranjeros en Cuba, Pero
Todavía Manda el Socialismo," Associated Press, July 10, 2001.

64. Gary Marx, "Spanish Oil Well off Cuban Coast Comes Up Empty," *Chicago Tribune*, July 29, 2004.

65. Marc Frank, "Cuba, Socios Aplazan Planes Perforación Petróleo Golfo México,"
Reuters, July 7, 2009.

66. In late April 2004, Chase Manhattan Bank of New York held 15.057 percent of
the shares of Altadis. The U.S. investment funds Fidelity International Ltd. and Franklin Resources Inc. Delaware owned, respectively, 5.84 percent and 5.003 percent of the
French-Spanish group.

67. "U.S. Goods, People, Cash Pour into Cuba," Reuters.

68. Neil King Jr., "Fidel's Appetite for U.S. Food Is More Than a Hill of Beans," *Wall
Street Journal*, August 14, 2002.

69. Statistics on U.S. food exports to Cuba are available at http://www.fas.usda.gov.

70. Anita Snow, "United States Become Cuba's No.1 Source of Imported Food," Associated Press, March 2, 2003.

71. Pav Jordan, "U.S.-Cuba Trade Grows Despite Restrictions," Reuters, February 17,
2003.

72. Marc Frank, "Cuba Slashes Imports Amid Ongoing Cash Crunch," Reuters, October 15, 2002.

73. In Latin America, only Mexico, Colombia, the Dominican Republic, Guatemala,
and Venezuela purchased more food products from the United States than Cuba in 2008.
Cuba also ranked twenty-ninth in 2008 out of 228 countries in total purchases of U.S.
food products.

74. For further information, see Industry Canada Trade Data Online (TDO) at http://
strategis.ic.gc.ca.

75. Economic Mission of the French Embassy in Havana, "Echanges Bilatéraux
France Cuba 2007—1er Semestre 2008," August 11, 2008. Also see Economic Mission
of the French Embassy in Havana, "Echanges Bilatéraux France Cuba 2008," February
2009, http://www.dgtpe.fr/se/cuba/index.asp.

76. "La Balanza Comercial de España con Cuba Registró un Saldo Positivo de 316
Millones de Euros en 2002," Europa Press, June 13, 2003.

77. Marta Veloz, "En Ascenso Compras de Cuba a EE.UU.," *Opciones*, November 2,
2003.

78. "Cuba Is to Extend Services Provided by Its Medical Personnel to 81 Countries
During the Year," *Granma International*, April 3, 2008.

79. Whereas in 1989 exports of goods represented 90 percent of Cuba's total exports,
by 2006 they accounted for just 31 percent. By that year, services accounted for 76 per-

cent of Cuba's GDP, generated almost 70 percent of its foreign exchange revenues, and received 68 percent of all investments (Martín Fernández and Torres Pérez 2006).

80. Total exports of goods and services used as a reference in figure 5.6 are those reported by Cuba in its national income account because trade data in the balance of payments include only exports (and imports) of goods and the service balance. However, national accounts and trade series are not necessarily comparable.

81. Ariel Terrero, "Economía del Conocimiento: Inversión en Células Grises," *Bohemia*, May 12, 2006.

82. Lara Jakes Jordan, "Bush Administration to Relax Immigration Rules for Cubans," Associated Press, August 8, 2006.

83. Gary Marx, "Cuba Loses Doctors to Asylum Offer," *Chicago Tribune*, February 11, 2007.

Conclusion

1. Anita Snow, "Top U.S. Diplomat in Cuba Displays a Different Style," Associated Press, December 10, 2005.

2. James Gerstenzang, "U.S. Gets Tough on Its Cuba Restrictions," *Los Angeles Times*, July 14, 2001.

Bibliography

Acosta, Pablo, Cesar Calderón, Pablo Fajnzylber, and Humberto López. 2008. "What Is the Impact of International Remittances on Poverty and Inequality in Latin America?" *World Development* 36.1: 89–114.

Adams, Richard H., Jr. 1998. "Remittances, Investment, and Rural Asset Accumulation in Pakistan." *Economic Development and Cultural Change* 47.1: 155–73.

———. 1991. "The Economic Uses and Impact of International Remittances in Rural Egypt." *Economic Development and Cultural Change* 39.4: 695–722.

Adams, Richard H., Jr., and John Page. 2003. "International Migration, Remittances, and Poverty in Developing Countries." World Bank Policy Research Working Paper 3179, Washington, D.C.

Aguilar Trujillo, José Alejandro. 2001. "Las Remesas Desde el Exterior: Un Enfoque Metodológico-Analítico." *Cuba Investigación Económica* 7.3: 71–104.

———. 1998. *Repercusión de la Ley Helms-Burton en la Economía Cubana*. Havana: Instituto Nacional de Investigaciones Económicas.

Ahlburg, Dennis A., and Richard P. C. Brown. 1998. "Migrants' Intentions to Return Home and Capital Transfers: A Study of Tongans and Samoans in Australia." *Journal of Development Studies* 35.2: 125–51.

Aja Díaz, Antonio. 2002. *Tendencias y Retos de Cuba Ante el Tema de la Emigración*. Havana: Centro de Estudios de Migraciones Internacionales.

Alderman, Harold. 1996. "Saving and Economic Shocks in Rural Pakistan." *Journal of Development Economics* 51.2: 343–65.

Alvarez, A., and D. Amat. 1996. "El Mercado Emisor Turístico Estadounidense Hacia el Caribe." Unpublished diploma work, University of Havana.

Alvarez, José, and Lázaro Peña Castellanos. 2001. *Cuba's Sugar Industry*. Gainesville: University Press of Florida.

Alvarez Gonzáles, Elena, and Maria Antonia Fernández Mayo. 1992. *Dependencia Externa de la Economía Cubana*. Havana: Instituto Nacional de Investigaciones Económicas (INIE).

Anderson, Sarah, and John Cavanagh. 2000. "Top 200: The Rise of Global Corporate Power." *Global Policy Forum*. http://www.globalpolicy.org/socecon/tncs/top200.htm (accessed October 2009).

Arreola, Antroy A. 1998. "Who's Isolating Whom? Title III of the Helms-Burton Act and Compliance with International Law." *Houston Journal of International Law* 20.2: 353–79.

Askari, Hossein, John Forrer, Jiawen Yang, and Tarek Hachem. 2005. "Measuring Vulnerability to U.S. Foreign Economic Sanctions." *Business Economics* 40.2: 41–55.

Axelrod, Robert, and Robert O. Keohane. 1985. "Achieving Cooperation under Anarchy: Strategies and Institutions." *World Politics* 38.1: 226–54.

Baldwin, David A. 1999/2000. "The Sanctions Debate and the Logic of Choice." *International Security* 24.3: 80–107.

———. 1985. *Economic Statecraft*. Princeton, N.J.: Princeton University Press.

Baliamoune-Lutz, Mina N. 2004. "Does FDI Contribute to Economic Growth?" *Business Economics* 39.2: 49–56.

Ballard, Richard. 2003. "Migration, Remittances, Economic Growth, and Poverty Reduction: Reflections on the Basis of South Asian Experience." Report prepared for the Department for International Development (DFID), London.

Banco Central de Cuba (BCC). 2005. *Economic Report 2004*. Havana: BCC.

———. 2002. *Economic Report 2001*. Havana: BCC.

Barberia, Lorena. 2002. "Remittances to Cuba: An Evaluation of Cuban and U.S. Government Policy Measures." Rosemarie Rogers Working Paper 15, Massachusetts Institute of Technology (MIT), Cambridge, Mass.

Bardach, Ann Louise. 2002. *Cuba Confidential: Love and Vengeance in Miami and Havana*. New York: Random House.

Barro, Robert J., and Xavier Sala-i-Martin. 1995. *Economic Growth*. Cambridge: McGraw-Hill.

Basch, Linda G., Nina Glick Schiller, and Cristina Blanc Szanton. 1994. *Nations Unbound: Transnational Projects, Post-Colonial Predicaments, and De-Territorialized Nation-States*. Langhorne, Pa.: Gordon and Breach.

Becker, Gary S. 1974. "A Theory of Social Interactions." *Journal of Political Economy* 82.6: 1063–93.

Bendixen and Associates. 2005. "Remittances to Cuba from the United States." Survey presentation, Washington, D.C., May 25. http://www.bendixenandassociates.com/studies2005.html (accessed October 2009).

Blue, Sarah A. 2005. "From Exiles to Transnationals? Changing State Policy and the Emergence of Cuban Transnationalism." In *Cuba Transnational*, edited by Damian J. Fernández, 24–41. Gainesville: University Press of Florida.

Bock, Peter G. 1979. "Controlling the Transnational Corporation: The Issue of Codes of Conduct." In *Transnationalism in World Politics and Business*, edited by Forest L. Grieves, 40–56. New York: Pergamon Press.

Bourdieu, Pierre. 1986. "The Forms of Capital." In *Handbook of Theory and Research for the Sociology of Education*, edited by John G. Richardson, 241–58. New York: Greenwood Press.

Boyd, Monica. 1989. "Family and Personal Networks in International Migration: Recent Development and New Agendas." *International Migration Review* 23.3: 638–70.

Brenner, Philip. 1988. *From Confrontation to Negotiation: U.S. Relations with Cuba*. Boulder, Colo.: Westview Press.

Brenner, Philip, Patrick J. Haney, and Walter Vanderbush. 2003. "Intermestic Interests and U.S. Policy toward Cuba." In *The Domestic Sources of American Foreign Policy*, edited by Eugene R. Wittkopf, 67–84. Lanham, Md.: Rowman and Littlefield.

———. 2002. "The Confluence of Domestic and International Interests: U.S. Policy toward Cuba, 1998–2001." *International Studies Perspectives* 3.2: 192–208.

Brown, Richard P. C. 1994. "Migrants' Remittances, Savings, and Investment in the South Pacific." *International Labour Review* 133.3: 347–67.

Brundenius, Claes. 2002. "Whither the Cuban Economy after Recovery? The Reform Process, Upgrading Strategies, and the Question of Transition." *Journal of Latin American Studies* 34.2: 365–95.

Campos, Nauro F., and Yuko Kinoshita. 2002. "Foreign Direct Investment as Technology Transferred: Some Panel Evidence from the Transition Economies." Discussion Paper 3417, Centre for Economic Policy Research (CEPR), London.

Carling, Jorgen. 2005. *Migrant Remittances and Development Cooperation*. Oslo: International Peace Research Institute (PRIO).

———. 2004. *Policy Options for Increasing the Benefits of Remittances*. Oslo: International Peace Research Institute (PRIO).

Carter, Barry E. 2002. "Study of New U.S. Unilateral Sanctions, 1997–2001." Washington, D.C.: USA Engage. http://archives.usaengage.org/archives/2002sanctions/index.html (accessed October 2009).

Central Intelligence Agency (CIA). 2007. *The World Factbook*. Washington, D.C.: CIA.

Centro de Promoción de Inversiones (CPI). 2003. "Potencialidades para la Inversión de Cuba en el Exterior." Havana: CPI.

Chami, Ralph, Connel Fullenkamp, and Samir Jahjah. 2003. "Are Immigrant Remittance Flows a Source of Capital for Development?" International Monetary Fund (IMF), Working Paper N.03/189, Washington, D.C.

Chandavarkar, Anand G. 1980. "Use of Migrants' Remittances in Labor Exporting Countries." *Finance and Development* 17.2: 36–38.

Cohan, J. A. 2001. "Environmental Rights of Indigenous People." *UCLA Journal of Environmental Law and Policy* 20: 133–84.

Cole, Ken. 1998. *Cuba: From Revolution to Development*. London: Pinter.

Comisión Económica para América Latina y el Caribe (CEPAL). 2009. *Cuba: Evolución Económica Durante 2008 y Perspectivas para 2009*. Mexico City: CEPAL.

———. 2008. *Cuba: Evolución Económica Durante 2007 y Perspectivas para 2008*. Mexico City: CEPAL.

———. 2002. *Cuba: Evolución Económica Durante 2001*. Mexico City: CEPAL.

Commission for Assistance to a Free Cuba (CAFC). 2006. "Report to the President." Washington, D.C.: CAFC.

Confidential Report for the Embassy of Japan in Havana. 1999. "Investment Opportunities in Cuba." Unpublished, March 31.

Corrales, Javier. 2006. "Cuba's New Daddy." *Hemisphere: A Magazine of the Americas* 17: 24–29.

Cortright, David, and George A. Lopez. 2002. *Smart Sanctions: Targeting Economic Statecraft*. Lanham, Md.: Rowman and Littlefield.

Crawford, Charmaine. 2003. "Sending Love in a Barrel: The Making of Transnational Caribbean Families in Canada." *Canadian Woman Studies* 22.3/4: 104–109.

Cruz, Robert David. 2003. *Foreign Direct Investment in Post-Castro Cuba: Problems, Opportunities, and Recommendations*. Miami: Institute for Cuban and Cuban-American Studies, University of Miami.

Cuban American National Foundation (CANF). 2009. "A New Course for U.S.-Cuba Policy: Advancing People-Driven Change." Miami: CANF. http://fd04admin.securesites.net/canf/issues/a-new-course-for-u.s.-cuba-policy/ (accessed October 2009).

Domínguez, Jorge I. 1997. "U.S.-Cuban Relations: From the Cold War to the Colder War." *Journal of Interamerican Studies and World Affairs* 39.3: 49–75.

———. 1993. "The Secrets of Castro's Staying Power." *Foreign Affairs* 72.2: 97–107.

Drezner, Daniel W. 1999. *The Sanctions Paradox: Economic Statecraft and International Relations*. Cambridge, Mass.: Cambridge University Press.

Drury, A. Cooper. 1998. "Revisiting Economic Sanctions Reconsidered." *Journal of Peace Research* 35.4: 497–509.

Durand, Jorge, Emilio A. Parrado, and Douglas S. Massey. 1996. "Migradollars and Development: A Reconsideration of the Mexican Case." *International Migration Review* 30.2: 423–44.

Eckstein, Susan. 2009. "The Personal Is Political: The Cuban Ethnic Electoral Policy Cycle." *Latin American Politics and Society* 51.1: 119–48.

———. 2004. "Transnational Networks and Norms, Remittances, and the Transformation of Cuba." In *The Cuban Economy at the Start of the Twenty-First Century*, edited by Jorge I. Dominguez, Omar Everleny Pérez Villanueva, and Lorena Barberia, 319–51. Cambridge, Mass.: Harvard University Press.

———. 2003. "Diasporas and Dollars: Transnational Ties and the Transformation of Cuba." Rosemarie Rogers Working Paper 16, Massachusetts Institute of Technology (MIT), Cambridge, Mass.

———. 1994. *Back from the Future: Cuba under Castro*. Princeton, N.J.: Princeton University Press.

Eckstein, Susan, and Lorena Barberia. 2002. "Grounding Immigrant Generations in History: Cuban Americans and Their Transnational Ties." *International Migration Review* 36.3: 799–837.

———. 2001. "Cuban-American Cuba Visits: Public Policy, Private Practices." Cambridge, Mass.: Center for International Studies, MIT.

Economic Commission for Latin America and the Caribbean (ECLAC). 2008. *Economic Survey of Latin America and the Caribbean 2007–2008*. New York: United Nations.

———. 2006. *Cuba: Evolución Económica Durante 2005 y Perspectivas Para 2006*. Mexico City: ECLAC.

———. 2005. *Foreign Investment in Latin America and the Caribbean, 2004*. New York: United Nations.

———. 2004. *Preliminary Overview of the Economies of Latin America and the Caribbean, 2004*. New York: United Nations.

Economist Intelligence Unit (EIU). 2008a. *Country Report: Cuba*. London: EIU.

———. 2008b. *Country Profile Cuba*. London: EIU.

———. 2007. *Country Report: Cuba*. London: EIU.

———. 2004. *Country Report: Cuba*. London: EIU.

Elliott, Kimberly Ann. 1997. "Evidence on the Costs and Benefits of Economic Sanctions." Speech given before the Subcommittee on Trade, Committee on Ways and Means, U.S. House of Representatives, Washington, D.C., October 23.

Elliott, Kimberly Ann, and Barbara Oegg. 2002. "Economic Sanctions Reconsidered Again: Trends in Sanctions Policy in the 1990s." Paper presented at the International Studies Association Convention, New Orleans, March 23–26.

Erisman, Michael H. 1995. "Cuba's Evolving CARICOM Connection." In *Cuba in the International System: Normalization and Integration*, edited by Archibald Ritter and John M. Kirk, 130–44. New York: St. Martin's Press.

Esterline, John H. 1979. "Multinational Corporations and the Political Process: Looking Ahead." In *Transnationalism in World Politics and Business*, edited by Forest L. Grieves, 23–39. New York: Pergamon Press.

Faist, Thomas. 2000. *The Volume and Dynamics of International Migration and Transnational Social Spaces*. Oxford: Oxford University Press.

Fernández, Damián J., ed. 2005. *Cuba Transnational*. Gainesville: University Press of Florida.

Figueras Pérez, Miguel Alejandro. 2002. "El Turismo Internacional y la Formación de Clusters Productivos en la Economía Cubana." In *Cuba: Reflexiones Sobre Su Economía*, edited by Omar Everleny Pérez Villanueva, 99–118. Havana: Universidad de La Habana.

Findlay, Ronald. 1978. "Relative Backwardness, Direct Foreign Investment, and the Transfer of Technology: A Simple Dynamic Model." *Quarterly Journal of Economics* 92.1: 1–16.

Fisk, Daniel W. 2001. "Cuba: The End of an Era." *Washington Quarterly* 24.1: 93–106.

Franklin, Jane. 1997. *Cuba and the United States: A Chronological History*. New York: Ocean Press.

———. 1993. "The Cuba Obsession." *The Progressive* 57.7: 18–22.

Funkhouser, Edward. 1995. "Remittances from International Migration: A Comparison of El Salvador and Nicaragua." *Review of Economics and Statistics* 77.1: 137–46.

García Jiménez, Alfredo, Pilar Caballero Figueroa, Alfonso Nichar Gladys, and Maricela Esperón Zaldivar. 2006. *Turismo: Desempeño y Futuro*. Havana: Instituto Nacional de Investigaciones Económicas.

Gardner, Kati. 2002. "Death of a Migrant: Transnational Death Rituals and Gender among British Sylhetis." *Global Networks* 2.3: 191–204.

Gleijeses, Piero. 2002. *Conflicting Missions: Havana, Washington, and Africa, 1959–1976.* Chapel Hill: University of North Carolina Press.

Glick Schiller, Nina, Linda Basch, and Cristina Blanc Szanton, eds. 1992. *Towards a Transnational Perspective on Migration: Race, Class, Ethnicity, and Nationalism Reconsidered.* New York: Annals of the New York Academy of Sciences.

Glytsos, Nicholas P. 1993. "Measuring the Income Effects of Migrant Remittances: A Methodological Approach Applied to Greece." *Economic Development and Cultural Change* 42.1: 131–68.

Gmelch, George. 1992. *Double Passage: The Lives of Caribbean Migrants Abroad and Back Home.* Ann Arbor: University of Michigan Press.

Goulbourne, Harry. 2002. *Caribbean Transnational Experience.* London: Pluto Press.

Government Accountability Office (GAO). 2009. *U.S. Embargo on Cuba: Recent Regulatory Changes and Potential Presidential or Congressional Actions.* Washington, D.C.: GAO.

Groombridge, Mark A. 2001. *Missing the Target: The Failure of the Helms-Burton Act.* Washington, D.C.: Cato Institute.

Grossman, Gene M., and Elhanan Helpman. 1991. *Innovation and Growth in the Global Economy.* Cambridge, Mass.: MIT Press.

Guarnizo, Luis Eduardo. 2003. "The Economics of Transnational Living." *International Migration Review* 37.3: 666–99.

———. 1994. "Los Dominicanyork: The Making of a Binational Society." *Annals of the American Academy of Political and Social Science* 533: 70–86.

Guarnizo, Luis Eduardo, and Michael Peter Smith. 1998. "The Locations of Transnationalism." In *Transnationalism from Below*, edited by Michael Peter Smith and Luis Eduardo Guarnizo, 3–34. New Brunswick, N.J.: Transaction Publishers, 1998.

Gubert, Flore. 2002. "Do Migrants Insure Those Who Stay Behind? Evidence from the Kayes Area (Western Mali)." *Oxford Development Studies* 30.3: 267–88.

Haines, Lila. 1997. *Reassessing Cuba: Emerging Opportunities and Operating Challenges.* New York: Economist Intelligence Unit.

Haney, Patrick J., and Walt Vanderbush. 2005. *The Cuban Embargo: The Domestic Politics of an American Foreign Policy.* Pittsburgh: University of Pittsburgh Press.

Held, David, Anthony McGrew, David Goldblatt, and Jonathan Perraton. 1999. *Global Transformations: Politics, Economics, and Culture.* Stanford, Calif.: Stanford University Press.

Hernández, Rafael. 2009. "Estados Unidos en la Política Cubana." Paper presented at the international conference "El Caribe en Su Inserción Internacional," San José, Costa Rica, February 3–4.

Hernández-Catá, Ernesto. 2001. "The Fall and Recovery of the Cuban Economy in the 1990s: Mirage or Reality?" Working Paper WP/01/48, International Monetary Fund, Washington, D.C.

Hoddinott, John. 1994. "A Model of Migration and Remittances Applied to Western Kenya." *Oxford Economic Papers* 46.3: 459–76.

Hoffmann, Bert. 2004. *The Politics of the Internet in Third World Development: Chal-*

lenges in Contrasting Regimes with Case Studies of Costa Rica and Cuba. New York: Routledge.

Hufbauer, Gary Clyde. 1999. *Trade as a Weapon.* Washington, D.C.: Institute for International Economics.

Hufbauer, Gary Clyde, Jeffrey J. Schott, and Kimberly Ann Elliott. 1990. *Economic Sanctions Reconsidered: History and Current Policy.* Washington, D.C.: Institute for International Economics.

Hufbauer, Gary Clyde, Jeffrey J. Schott, Kimberly Ann Elliott, and Barbara Oegg. 2008. *Economic Sanctions Reconsidered.* Washington, D.C.: Institute for International Economics.

Inter-American Development Bank (IADB). 2004. *Sending Money Home: Remittances to Latin America and the Caribbean.* Washington, D.C.: IADB.

———. 2003. *Sending Money Home: An International Comparison of Remittance Markets.* Washington, D.C.: IADB.

Itzigsohn, José. 2000. "Immigration and the Boundaries of Citizenship: The Institutions of Immigrants' Political Transnationalism." *International Migration Review* 34.4: 1126–53.

Itzigsohn, José, Carlos Dore Cabral, and Esther Hernandez Medina. 1999. "Mapping Dominican Transnationalism: Narrow and Broad Transnational Practices." *Ethnic and Racial Studies* 22.2: 316–39.

Jatar-Hausmann, Ana Julia. 1999. *The Cuban Way: Capitalism, Communism, and Confrontation.* West Hartford, Conn.: Kumarian Press.

Jonge Oudraat, Chantal. 2000. "Making Economic Sanctions Work." *Survival* 42.3: 105–27.

Karliner, Joshua. 1997. *The Corporate Planet: Ecology and Politics in the Age of Globalization.* San Francisco: Sierra Club Books.

Kaufman Purcell, Susan. 2002. "Helms-Burton and the U.S. Embargo against Cuba." Paper presented at a conference sponsored by the Center for International Studies, El Colegio de Mexico, Mexico City, March 15.

———. 2000. "Why the Cuban Embargo Makes Sense in a Post–Cold War World." In *Cuba: The Contours of Change,* edited by Susan Kaufman Purcell and David J. Rothkopf, 81–103. Boulder, Colo.: Lynne Rienner Publishers.

Kearney, Michael. 1995. "The Local and the Global: The Anthropology of Globalization and Transnationalism." *Annual Review of Anthropology* 24: 547–65.

Keck, Margaret E., and Kathryn Sikkink. 1998. *Activists beyond Borders: Advocacy Networks in International Politics.* Ithaca, N.Y.: Cornell University Press.

Keohane, Robert O. 1983. *After Hegemony: Cooperation and Discord in the World Political Economy.* Princeton, N.J.: Princeton University Press.

Keohane, Robert O., and Joseph S. Nye. 1971. *Transnational Relations and World Politics.* Cambridge, Mass.: Harvard University Press.

Kiger, Patrick J. 1998. *Squeeze Play: The United States, Cuba, and the Helms-Burton Act.* Washington, D.C.: Center for Public Integrity.

Kivisto, Peter. 2001. "Theorizing Transnational Immigration: A Critical Review of Current Efforts." *Ethnic and Racial Studies* 24.4: 549–77.

Klepak, Hal P. 2005. *Cuba's Military 1990–2005: Revolutionary Soldiers during Counter-Revolutionary Times*. New York: Palgrave Macmillan.

Kline, John M. 2003. "Political Activities by Transnational Corporations: Bright Lines versus Grey Boundaries." *Transnational Corporations* 12.1: 1–25.

Knippers Black, Jan. 2005. "The United States–Cuba Standoff: A Double Con?" In *Foreign Policy toward Cuba: Isolation or Engagement?*, edited by Michele Zebich-Knos and Heather N. Nicol, 53–66. Lanham, Md.: Lexington Books.

Kohpaiboon, Archanun. 2006. "Foreign Direct Investment and Technology Spillover: A Cross-Industry Analysis of Thai Manufacturing." *World Development* 34.3: 541–56.

Kornbluh, Peter, and William M. Leogrande. 2009. "Talking with Castro." *Cigar Aficionado*, January/February, 86–96.

Krinsky, Michael. 1996. "La Ley Helms-Burton: Su Alcance y Limitaciones." Paper presented at the internacional seminar "La Ley Helms-Burton, Implicaciones para Cuba y la Comunidad Internacional," Havana, September 17.

Lacy, Allison J. 1996. "Damage Control by Canadian Business." In *Helms-Burton and International Business: Legal and Commercial Implications*. Proceedings of a conference organized by the Canadian Foundation for the Americas (FOCAL) and the Center for International Policy (CIP), Ottawa, May 16–17.

Landau, Anya K., and Wayne Smith. 2001. *Keeping Things in Perspective: Cuba and the Question of International Terrorism*. Washington, D.C.: Center for International Policy.

Leogrande, William M. 2007. "Cuba's Future Relations with the United States." In *Looking Forward: Comparative Perspectives on Cuba's Transition*, edited by Marifeli Pérez-Stable, 280–308. Notre Dame, Ind.: University of Notre Dame Press.

———. 2005. "The United States and Cuba: Strained Engagement." In *Cuba, the United States, and the Post–Cold War World: The International Dimensions of the Washington-Havana Relationship*, edited by Morris Morley and Chris McGillion, 12–58. Gainesville: University Press of Florida.

———. 1998. "From Havana to Miami: U.S. Cuba Policy as a Two-Level Game." *Journal of Interamerican Studies and World Affairs* 40.1: 67–86.

———. 1997. "Enemies Evermore: U.S. Policy towards Cuba after Helms-Burton." *Journal of Latin American Studies* 29.1: 211–21.

León-Ledesma, Miguel, and Matloob Piracha. 2004. "International Migration and the Role of Remittances in Eastern Europe." *International Migration* 42.4: 65–84.

Levitt, Peggy. 2001. *The Transnational Villagers*. Berkeley: University of California Press.

———. 1998. "Social Remittances: Migration Driven Local-Level Forms of Cultural Diffusion." *International Migration Review* 32.4: 926–48.

Leyva de Varona, Adolfo. 1994. *Propaganda and Reality: A Look at the U.S. Embargo against Castro's Cuba*. Miami: Endowment for Cuban American Studies.

Li, Xiaoying, and Xiaming Liu. 2005. "Foreign Direct Investment and Economic Growth: An Increasing Endogenous Relationship." *World Development* 33.3: 393–407.

Lipsey, Robert E., and Fredrik Sjoholm. 2005. "The Impact of Inward FDI on Host Countries: Why Such Different Answers?" In *Does Foreign Direct Investment Promote De-*

velopment?, edited by Theodore H. Moran, Edward M. Graham, and Magnus Blomström, 23–43. Washington, D.C.: Institute for International Economics.

López, Juan J. 2000. "Sanctions on Cuba Are Good, but Not Enough." *Orbis* 44.3: 354–60.

Lucas, Robert E. B., and Oded Stark. 1985. "Motivations to Remit: Evidence from Botswana." *Journal of Political Economy* 93.5: 901–18.

Macleod, Sorcha, and Douglas Lewis. 2004. "Transnational Corporations: Power, Influence, and Responsibility." *Global Social Policy* 4.1: 77–98.

Mahler, Sarah J. 1998. "Theoretical and Empirical Contributions toward a Research Agenda for Transnationalism." In *Transnationalism from Below*, edited by Michael Peter Smith and Luis Eduardo Guarnizo, 64–102. New Brunswick, N.J.: Transaction Publishers.

Maphosa, France. 2007. "Remittances and Development: The Impact of Migration to South Africa on Rural Livelihoods in Southern Zimbabwe." *Development Southern Africa* 24.1: 123–36.

Marquetti Nodarse, Hiram. 2004. *El Proceso de Dolarización de la Economía Cubana: Una Evaluación Actual*. Havana: Centro de Estudios de la Economía Cubana.

Martin, Lisa L. 1992. *Coercive Cooperation: Explaining Multilateral Economic Sanctions*. Princeton, N.J.: Princeton University Press, 1992.

Martín Fernández, Mariana, and Ricardo Torres Pérez. 2006. *La Economía de Servicios*. Havana: Centro de Estudios de la Economía Cubana.

Masud-Piloto, Felix. 1996. *From Welcomed Exiles to Illegal Immigrants: Cuban Migration to the U.S., 1959–1995*. Lanham, Md.: Rowman and Littlefield.

McKenna, Peter, and John M. Kirk. 1998. "Canada and Helms-Burton: The Politics of Extraterritoriality." Paper presented at the twenty-first international congress of the Latin American Studies Association (LASA), Chicago, September 24–26.

Mesa-Lago, Carmelo. 2008. "The Cuban Economy at the Crossroads: Fidel Castro's Legacy, Debate over Change, and Raul Castro's Options." Working Paper 19/2008, Real Instituto Elcano, Madrid.

———. 2005. *The Cuban Economy Today: Salvation or Damnation?* Miami: Institute for Cuban and Cuban-American Studies.

———. 2004. "Economic and Ideological Cycles in Cuba: Policy and Performance, 1959–2002." In *The Cuban Economy*, edited by Archibald R. M. Ritter, 25–41. Pittsburgh: University of Pittsburgh Press.

———. 1994. *Breve Historia Económica de la Cuba Socialista: Políticas, Resultados y Perspectivas*. Madrid: Alianza Editorial.

Ministerio para la Inversión Extranjera y la Colaboración Económica (MINVEC). 2009. "Panorámica de la Inversión Extranjera en Cuba." Powerpoint presentation, Havana.

———. 2008. *Informe de Balance Año 2007*. Havana: MINVEC.

———. 2006. *Informe de Balance Año 2005*. Havana: MINVEC.

———. 2005. *Informe de Balance Año 2004*. Havana: MINVEC.

———. 2004. *Informe de Balance Año 2003*. Havana: MINVEC.

———. 2002. *Informe de Balance Año 2001*. Havana: MINVEC.

———. 2000. "Resumen del Informe Pericial del MINVEC." Havana: MINVEC.

Monreal, Pedro. 1999. "Las Remesas Familiares en la Economía Cubana." *Encuentro de la Cultura Cubana* 14: 49–62.

Monshipouri, Mahmood, Claude E. Welch Jr., and Evan T. Kennedy. 2003. "Multinational Corporations and the Ethics of Global Responsibility: Problems and Possibilities." *Human Rights Quarterly* 25: 965–89.

Mora, Frank O. 2004. "The FAR and Its Economic Role: From Civic to Technocrat-Soldiers." Occasional Paper Series, Institute for Cuban and Cuban-American Studies (ICCAS), Miami.

Morales Dominguez, Esteban, and Gary Prevost. 2008. *United States–Cuban Relations: A Critical History.* Lanham, Md.: Lexington Books.

Morgan, Clifton T., and Navin A. Bapat. 2003. "Imposing Sanctions: States, Firms, and Economic Coercion." *International Studies Review* 5.4: 65–81.

Morgan, Clifton T., and Valerie L. Schwebach. 1997. "Fools Suffer Gladly: The Use of Economic Sanctions in International Crises." *International Studies Quarterly* 41: 27–50.

Morley, Morris. 1987. *Imperial State and Revolution: The United States and Cuba, 1952–1986.* Cambridge, Mass.: Cambridge University Press.

———. 1984. "The United States and the Global Economic Blockade of Cuba: A Study in Political Pressures on America's Allies." *Canadian Journal of Political Science* 17.1: 25–48.

Morley, Morris, and Chris McGillion. 2002. *Unfinished Business: America and Cuba after the Cold War, 1989–2001.* New York: Cambridge University Press.

Nathan, James A. 2001. *Anatomy of the Cuban Missile Crisis.* Westport, Conn.: Greenwood Press.

Nichols, John S. 1988. "The Power of the Anti-Fidel Lobby." *The Nation*, October 24.

Nien-he, Hsieh. 2004. "The Obligations of Transnational Corporations: Rawlsian Justice and the Duty of Assistance." *Business Ethics Quarterly* 14.4: 643–61.

Nishat, Mohammed, and Nighat Bilgrami. 1991. "The Impact of Migrant Workers' Remittances on Pakistan Economy." *Pakistan Economic and Social Review* 29: 21–41.

Nuti, Leopoldo. 1994. *I Missili di Ottobre: La Storiografia Americana e la Crisi Cubana dell'Ottobre 1962.* Milano: LED.

Nyberg-Sorensen, Ninna, Nicholas Van Hear, and Poul Engberg-Pedersen. 2002. "The Migration-Development Nexus: Evidence and Policy Options." *International Migration* 40.5: 49–71.

Oficina Nacional de Estadísticas (ONE). 2009. *Anuario Estadístico de Cuba 2008.* Havana: ONE.

———. 2008a. *Anuario Estadístico de Cuba 2007.* Havana: ONE.

———. 2008b. *Ventas de la Producción Nacional con Destino a Tiendas y Turismo.* Havana: ONE.

———. 2007. *Ventas de la Producción Nacional con Destino a Tiendas y Turismo.* Havana: ONE.

———. 2004. *Anuario Estadístico de Cuba 2003.* Havana: ONE.

———. 2003. *Anuario Estadístico de Cuba 2002.* Havana: ONE.

———. 2000. *Anuario Estadístico de Cuba 1999.* Havana: ONE.

———. 1998. *Anuario Estadístico de Cuba 1997*. Havana: ONE.

———. 1996. *Anuario Estadístico de Cuba 1995*. Havana: ONE.

Orozco, Manuel. 2009. *The Cuban Condition: Migration, Remittances, and Its Diaspora*. Washington, D.C.: Inter-American Dialogue.

———. 2007. *Central America: Remittances and the Macroeconomic Variable*. Washington, D.C.: Inter-American Dialogue.

———. 2003. *Challenges and Opportunities of Marketing Remittances to Cuba*. Washington, D.C.: Inter-American Dialogue.

Oye, Kenneth A. 1985. "Explaining Cooperation under Anarchy: Hypotheses and Strategies." *World Politics* 38.1: 1–24.

Pape, Robert A. 1998. "Why Economic Sanctions Still Do Not Work." *International Security* 23.1: 66–77.

———. 1997. "Why Economic Sanctions Do Not Work." *International Security* 22.2: 90–136.

Pedraza, Silvia. 2007. *Political Disaffection in Cuba's Revolution and Exodus*. New York: Cambridge University Press.

Pérez, Lisandro. 2000. *U.S.-Cuba Relations: Trends and Underlying Forces*. Ottawa: Canadian Foundation for the Americas (FOCAL).

Pérez, Louis A., Jr. 2003. *Cuba and the United States: Ties of Singular Intimacy*. Athens: University of Georgia Press.

Pérez-López, Jorge F. 2007. "The Rise and Fall of Private Foreign Investment in Cuba." Paper presented at "The Cuban Economy: Challenges and Options," an international policy forum organized by Carleton University, the North-South Institute, and the Centro de Estudios de la Economía Cubana, Carleton University, Ottawa, September 9–11.

———. 1999. "Foreign Investment in Cuba in the Second Half of the 1990s." Paper presented at an international symposium organized by Carleton University and the University of Havana, Ottawa, September 28–30, 1999.

———. 1995. *Cuba's Second Economy: From behind the Scenes to Center Stage*. New Brunswick, N.J.: Transaction Publishers.

Pérez-Stable, Marifeli. 2007. "Looking Forward: Democracy in Cuba?" In *Looking Forward: Comparative Perspectives on Cuba's Transition*, edited by Marifeli Pérez-Stable, 17–46. Notre Dame, Ind.: University of Notre Dame Press.

———. 1999. *The Cuban Revolution: Origins, Course, and Legacy*. New York: Oxford University Press.

Pérez Villanueva, Omar Everleny. 2009. "Cuba: Evolución Económica Reciente." Paper presented at the international conference "El Caribe en Su Inserción Internacional," San José, Costa Rica, February 3–4.

———. 2008. "¿La Inversión Extranjera Directa en Cuba: Vientos a Su Favor?" Havana: Centro de Estudios de la Economía Cubana.

———. 2006. ¿*La Inversión Extranjera Directa en Cuba: Avances o Retroceso?* Havana: Centro de Estudios de la Economía Cubana.

———. 2004. "The Role of Foreign Direct Investment in Economic Development: The Cuban Experience." In *The Cuban Economy at the Start of the Twenty-First Century*, edited by Jorge I. Dominguez, Omar Everleny Pérez Villanueva, and Lorena Barberia, 161–97. Cambridge, Mass.: Harvard University Press.

———. 2001. *Foreign Direct Investment in Cuba: Recent Experience and Prospects.* Havana: Centro de Estudios de la Economía Cubana.

———. 1999. *La Inversión Extranjera Directa en Cuba: Peculiaridades.* Havana: Centro de Estudios de la Economía Cubana.

———. 1998. "El Papel de la Inversión Extranjera Directa en las Economías Subdesarrolladas: El Caso Cubano." Ph.D. diss., University of Havana.

Pérez Villanueva, Omar Everleny, and Pavel Vidal Alejandro. 2008. *Situación Actual del Turismo en Cuba.* Havana: Centro de Estudios de la Economía Cubana.

Perl, Shoshana. 2006. "Whither Helms-Burton? A Retrospective on the 10th Year Anniversary." Jean Monnet/Robert Schuman Paper Series 6.5, University of Miami.

Peters, Philip. 2007. "Phone Calls to Cuba Keep the Dollars Flowing." *CubaNews* 15.7: 10.

———. 2001a. *State Enterprise Reform in Cuba: An Early Snapshot.* Arlington, Va.: Lexington Institute.

———. 2001b. *Cuba Goes Digital.* Arlington, Va.: Lexington Institute.

———. 2000. *A Policy toward Cuba That Serves U.S. Interests.* Washington, D.C.: Cato Institute.

Poirine, Bernard. 1997. "A Theory of Remittances as an Implicit Family Loan Arrangement." *World Development* 25.4: 589–611.

Portes, Alejandro. 2003. "Theoretical Convergencies and Empirical Evidence in the Study of Immigrant Transnationalism." *International Migration Review* 37.3: 874–92.

———. 1998. "Social Capital: Its Origins and Applications in Modern Sociology." *Annual Review of Sociology* 24.1: 1–24.

———. 1997. "Globalization from Below: The Rise of Transnational Communities." Working Paper WPTC-98-01, Princeton University, Princeton, N.J. http://www.transcomm.ox.ac.uk/working%20papers/portes.pdf (accessed October 2009).

———. 1996. "Transnational Communities: Their Emergence and Significance in the Contemporary World-System." In *Latin America in the World Economy*, edited by Roberto P. Korzeniewicz and William C. Smith, 151–68. Westport, Conn.: Greenwood Press, 1996.

Portes, Alejandro, Luis Eduardo Guarnizo, and Patricia Landolt. 1999. "The Study of Transnationalism: Pitfalls and Promise of an Emergent Research Field." *Ethnic and Racial Studies* 22.2: 217–37.

Quintana, Rogelio, Manuel Figuerola, Mariano Chirivella, Damarys Lima, Miguel Alejandro Figueras, and Alfredo García. 2004. *Efectos y Futuro del Turismo en la Economía Cubana.* Havana: Instituto Nacional de Investigaciones Económicas.

Radelat, Ana. 2007. "Treasury: U.S. Phone Carriers Paid Cuba $102m in 2006." *CubaNews* 15.5: 4.

Radu, Michael. 1998. "Don't Reward Castro, Keep the Embargo." *Orbis* 42.4: 545–52.

Ram, Rati, and Kevin Honglin Zhang. 2002. "Foreign Direct Investment and Economic Growth: Evidence from Cross-Country Data for the 1990s." *Economic Development and Cultural Change* 51.1: 205–15.

Ramamurti, Ravi. 2004. "Developing Countries and MNEs: Extending and Enriching the Research Agenda." *Journal of International Business Studies* 35.4: 277–83.

Ratha, Dilip. 2008. "Development Implications of Migration and Remittances: The International Remittances Agenda." Presentation at the annual meeting of the International Agricultural Trade Research Consortium (IATRC), Washington, D.C., January 7–9. http://aede.osu.edu/programs/anderson/trade/Ratha.pdf (accessed October 2009).

———. 2003. "Workers' Remittances: An Important and Stable Source of External Development Finance." In *Global Development Finance 2003: Striving for Stability in Development Finance*. Washington, D.C.: World Bank.

Ratha, Dilip, Sanket Mohapatra, K. M. Vijayalakshmi, and Zhimei Xu. 2008. "Revisions to Remittance Trends 2007." Migration and Development Brief 5, World Bank, Washington, D.C.

Rich Kaplowitz, Donna. 1998. *Anatomy of a Failed Embargo: U.S. Sanctions against Cuba.* Boulder, Colo.: Lynne Rienner Publishers.

Robyn, Dorothy, James D. Reitzes, and Bryan Church. 2002. *The Impact on the U.S. Economy of Lifting Restrictions on Travel to Cuba.* Washington, D.C.: Center for International Policy.

Romero, Carlos A. 2009. "Venezuela y Cuba: 'Una Seguridad Diferente.'" *Nuevo Mundo Mundos Nuevos*, March 27. http://nuevomundo.revues.org/index55550.html (accessed October 2009).

Rothkopf, David J. 2000. "A Call for a Post–Cold War Cuba Policy . . . Ten Years after the End of the Cold War." In *Cuba: The Contours of Change*, edited by Susan Kaufman Purcell and David J. Rothkopf, 105–25. Boulder, Colo.: Lynne Rienner Publishers.

Rouse, Roger. 1992. "Making Sense of Settlement: Class Transformation, Cultural Struggle, and Transnationalism among Mexican Migrants in the United States." In *Toward a Transnational Perspective on Migration: Race, Class, Ethnicity, and Nationalism Reconsidered*, edited by Nina Glick-Schiller, Linda Basch, and Cristina Blanc-Szanton, 25–52. New York: Annals of the New York Academy of Sciences.

Roy, Joaquin. 2000. *Cuba, the United States, and the Helms-Burton Doctrine: International Reactions.* Gainesville: University Press of Florida.

Rubenstein, Hymie. 1992. "Migration, Development, and Remittances in Rural Mexico." *International Migration* 30.2: 127–51.

———. 1982. "Return Migration to the English-Speaking Caribbean: Review and Commentary." In *Return Migration and Remittances: Developing a Caribbean Perspective*, edited by William F. Stinner, Klaus de Albuquerque, and Roy S. Bryce-Laporte, 3–34. Washington, D.C.: Research Institute on Immigration and Ethnic Studies, Smithsonian Institution.

Sagebien, Julia. 1996. "Foreign Trade and Investment in Cuba after February 24, 1996: Life Between a Rock and a Hard Place." In *Helms-Burton and International Business: Legal and Commercial Implications.* Proceedings of a conference organized by the Canadian Foundation for the Americas (FOCAL) and the Center for International Policy (CIP), Ottawa, May 16–17.

Sagebien, Julia, and Demetria Tsourtouras. 1999. "Solidarity and Entrepreneurship: The

Political-Economy of Mexico-Cuba Commercial Relations at the End of the Twentieth Century." Research Paper, Center for International Trade and Transportation, Dalhousie University, Halifax, Nova Scotia. http://citt.management.dal.ca/Files/pdf%27s/DP-170.pdf (accessed October 2009).

Sanders, Ed, and Patrick Long. 2002. *Economic Benefits for the United States from Lifting the Ban on Travel to Cuba.* Washington, D.C.: Cuba Policy Foundation.

Schein, Louisa. 1998. "Forged Transnationality and Oppositional Cosmopolitanism." In *Transnationalism from Below,* edited by Michael Peter Smith and Luis Eduardo Guarnizo, 291–313. New Brunswick, N.J.: Transaction Publishers.

Schott, Jeffrey J. 1998. "U.S. Economic Sanctions: Good Intentions, Bad Execution." Statement before the Committee on International Relations, U.S. House of Representatives, Washington, D.C., June 3.

Schwab, Peter. 1999. *Cuba: Confronting the U.S. Embargo.* New York: St. Martin's Press.

Seiglie, Carlos. 2001. "Cuba's Road to Serfdom." *Cato Journal* 20.3: 425–30.

Siddiqui, Rizwana, and Abdur R. Kemal. 2002. "Remittances, Trade Liberalization, and Poverty in Pakistan: The Role of Excluded Variables in Poverty Change Analysis." London: Department for International Development (DFID).

Sistema Económico Latinoamericano y del Caribe (SELA). 1997. *Implicaciones Jurídicas y Económicas de la Ley Helms-Burton.* Caracas: SELA.

Sklair, Leslie. 2002. "The Transnational Capitalist Class and Global Politics: Deconstructing the Corporate-State Connection." *International Political Science Review* 23.2: 159–74.

Smith, Wayne S. 1998. "Our Dysfunctional Cuban Embargo." *Orbis* 42.4: 533–44.

———. 1988. *The Closest of Enemies: A Personal and Diplomatic History of the Castro Years.* New York: W. W. Norton.

Solimano, Andrés. 2003. *Remittances by Emigrants: Issues and Evidence.* Santiago, Chile: Economic Commission for Latin America and the Caribbean (ECLAC).

Spadoni, Paolo. 2004. "The Current Situation of Foreign Investment in Cuba." In *Cuba in Transition* 14, 116–38. Washington, D.C.: Association for the Study of the Cuban Economy (ASCE).

———. 2003. "The Role of the United States in the Cuban Economy." In *Cuba in Transition* 13, 410–29. Washington, D.C.: Association for the Study of the Cuban Economy (ASCE).

———. 2002. "Foreign Investment in Cuba: Recent Developments and Role in the Economy." In *Cuba in Transition* 12, 158–78. Washington, D.C.: Association for the Study of the Cuban Economy (ASCE).

———. 2001. "The Impact of the Helms-Burton Legislation on Foreign Investment in Cuba." In *Cuba in Transition* 11, 18–36. Washington, D.C.: Association for the Study of the Cuban Economy (ASCE).

Stahl, Charles W., and Ahsanul Habib. 1989. "The Impact of Overseas Workers' Remittances on Indigenous Industries: Evidence from Bangladesh." *Developing Economies* 27.3: 269–85.

Stark, Oded. 1991. "Migration in LDCs: Risk, Remittances, and the Family." *Finance and Development* 28.4: 39–41.

Stone, Peter H. 1993. "Cuban Clout." *National Journal* 25.8 (February 20): 449–53.

Suchlicki, Jaime. 2007. "Implications of Lifting the U.S. Embargo and Travel Ban of Cuba." Testimony at the U.S. Senate Finance Committee, Washington, D.C., December 11.

———. 2000. *The U.S. Embargo of Cuba.* Occasional Paper Series, Institute for Cuban and Cuban-American Studies (ICCAS), Miami.

Sullivan, Mark P. 2008. *Cuba: U.S. Restrictions on Travel and Remittances.* Washington, D.C.: Congressional Research Service (CRS).

———. 2007. *Cuba: Issues for the 110th Congress.* Washington, D.C.: Congressional Research Service Report for Congress.

Suter, Keith. 2004. "Transnational Corporations: Knitting the World Together." *Social Alternatives* 23.4: 42–45.

Sweig, Julia E. 2007. "Fidel's Final Victory." *Foreign Affairs* 86.1: 39–56.

Thomas-Hope, Elizabeth M. 1985. "Return Migration and Its Implications for Caribbean Development: The Unexplored Connection." In *Migration and Development in the Caribbean: The Unexplored Connection*, edited by Robert Pastor, 157–77. Boulder, Colo.: Westview Press.

Tilly, Charles. 1990. "Transplanted Networks." In *Immigration Reconsidered: History, Sociology, and Politics*, edited by Virginia Yans-McLaughlin, 79–95. New York: Oxford University Press.

Torres Martínez, Julio, and Ricardo Torres Pérez. 2006. *Reflexiones sobre la Problemática Energética Actual en el Mundo y en Cuba.* Havana: Centro de Estudios de la Economía Cubana.

Travieso-Díaz, Matias F. 1993. "Requirements for Lifting the U.S. Trade Embargo against Cuba." In *Cuba in Transition* 3, 222–49. Washington, D.C.: Association for the Study of the Cuban Economy (ASCE).

Travieso-Díaz, Matias F., and Charles P. Trumbull IV. 2002. "Foreign Investment in Cuba: Prospects and Perils." In *Cuba in Transition* 12, 179–97. Washington, D.C.: Association for the Study of the Cuban Economy (ASCE).

Triana Cordoví, Juan. 2004. *Cuba 2003.* Havana: Centro de Estudios de la Economía Cubana.

———. 2003. *El Desempeño Económico en el 2002.* Havana: Centro de Estudios de la Economía Cubana.

Tsebelis, George. 1990. "Are Sanctions Effective? A Game-Theoretical Analysis." *Journal of Conflict Resolution* 34.1: 3–27.

United Nations. 2006. "Necessity of Ending the Economic, Commercial, and Financial Embargo Imposed by the United States of America against Cuba." Report of the Secretary-General, A/61/132.

———. 2002. *International Migration Report 2002.* New York: United Nations.

———. 2001. "Necessity of Ending the Economic, Commercial, and Financial Embargo Imposed by the United States of America against Cuba." Report of the Secretary-General, A/56/276.

———. 1998. "Unilateral Economic Measures as a Means of Political and Economic Coercion against Developing Countries." Resolution 52/181.

———. 1997. "Necessity of Ending the Economic, Commercial, and Financial Embargo Imposed by the United States of America against Cuba." Report of the Secretary-General, A/52/342.

———. 1996. "Necessity of Ending the Economic, Commercial, and Financial Embargo Imposed by the United States of America against Cuba." Report of the Secretary-General, A/51/355.

United Nations Conference on Trade and Development (UNCTAD). 2008. *World Investment Report 2008: Transnational Corporations and the Infrastructure Challenge.* New York: United Nations.

———. 2004. *World Investment Report 2004: The Shift toward Services.* New York: United Nations.

———. 1995. *World Investment Report 1995: Transnational Corporations and Competitiveness.* New York: United Nations.

United Nations World Tourism Organization (UNWTO). 2009. *Yearbook of Tourism Statistics.* Madrid: UNWTO.

———. 2003. *Yearbook of Tourism Statistics.* Madrid: UNWTO.

United States International Trade Commission (USITC). 2007. *U.S. Agricultural Sales to Cuba: Certain Economic Effects of U.S. Restrictions.* Washington, D.C.: USITC.

———. 2001. *The Economic Impact of U.S. Sanctions with Respect to Cuba.* Washington, D.C.: USITC.

U.S.-Cuba Trade and Economic Council (USCTEC). 2009. "Annual Report—2008 U.S. Export Statistics for Cuba." *Economic Eye on Cuba,* February.

———. 2004. "2004 Commercial Highlights." http://www.cubatrade.org/ (accessed October 2009).

———. 2003. "2003 Commercial Highlights." http://www.cubatrade.org/.

———. 2002. "2002 Commercial Highlights." http://www.cubatrade.org/.

———. 2001. "2001 Commercial Highlights." http://www.cubatrade.org/.

———. 2000. "2000 Commercial Highlights." http://www.cubatrade.org/.

———. 1998. "1998 Commercial Highlights." http://www.cubatrade.org/.

U.S. Department of State. 1989. *Human Rights in Cuba: An Update.* Washington, D.C.: U.S. Government Printing Office.

Van Bergeijk, Peter A. G. 1997. "Economic Sanctions, Autocracy, Democracy, and Success." Paper presented at the conference on the effectiveness and effects of UN sanctions, Tilburg, The Netherlands, November 27–28.

———. 1995. "The Impact of Economic Sanctions in the 1990s." *World Economy* 18.3: 443–55.

Vertovec, Steven. 2003. "Migration and Other Modes of Transnationalism: Towards Conceptual Cross-fertilization." *International Migration Review* 37.3: 641–65.

Vertovec, Steven, and Robin Cohen. 1999. *Migration, Diasporas, and Transnationalism.* Northampton, Mass.: Edward Elgar Publishing Ltd.

Wagner, Harrison R. 1988. "Economic Interdependence, Bargaining Power, and Political Influence." *International Organization* 42.3: 461–83.

Wang, Hong-zen. 2005. "Asian Transnational Corporations and Labor Rights: Vietnamese Trade Unions in Taiwan-invested Companies." *Journal of Business Ethics* 56.1: 43–53.

Weinmann, Lisa. 2004. "Washington's Irrational Cuba Policy." *World Policy Journal* 21.1: 22–31.

Werlau, Maria C. 2001. "A Commentary on Foreign Investment in Cuba." In *Cuba in Transition* 11, 290–91. Washington, D.C.: Association for the Study of the Cuban Economy (ASCE).

———. 1997. "Foreign Investment in Cuba: The Limits of Commercial Engagement." *World Affairs* 160.2: 51–69.

Wiest, Raymond E. 1984. "External Dependency and the Perpetuation of Temporary Migration to the United States." In *Patterns of Undocumented Migration: Mexico and the United States*, edited by Richard C. Jones, 110–35. Totowa, N.J.: Rowman and Allanhend.

Willmore, Larry. 2000. "Export Processing Zones in Cuba." Department of Economic and Social Affairs (DESA) Discussion Paper 12, United Nations, New York.

World Bank. 2008. *Global Development Finance 2008: The Role of International Banking*. Washington, D.C.: World Bank.

Zebich-Knos, Michele. 2005. "U.S.-Policy toward Cuba: Trends and Transformation during the George W. Bush Administration." In *Foreign Policy toward Cuba: Isolation or Engagement?*, edited by Michele Zebich-Knos and Heather N. Nicol, 31–52. Lanham, Md.: Lexington Books, 2005.

Zimbalist, Andrew. 1995. "Cuba, Castro, Clinton, and Canosa." In *Cuba in the International System: Normalization and Integration*, edited by Archibald R. M. Ritter and John M. Kirk, 23–35. New York: St. Martin's Press.

Index

102, 107, 108, 109, 110–11, 119, 124, 197n24;
major investors as targets, 97, 120, 124;
potential investors, xxiii, 98, 101, 102, 111, 112,
198–99n54; low profile, 101, 102; negotiating
power, 102, 105–6; creation of offshore companies, 19, 102, 105; incentives to overstate,
98; relocation of activities, 113–14; reorganization of activities, 19, 104, 112–13; spin-offs,
19, 102, 106
Hoffmann, Bert, 160
Hotetur, 163
Hufbauer, Gary Clyde, xx, xxii, 4, 6

IADB. See Inter-American Development Bank
Iberia Airlines, 163
Iberostar, 69
India, 6, 69, 72, 166
ING Bank, 104, 112, 113, 120, 122
Inter-American Development Bank (IADB),
149, 150
Interests sections, 30, 31
International economic associations (AECEs):
operating abroad, 71–73, 195n63; audits
of, 74–75; authorizations and dissolutions,
73–74, 118–20; by country, 68–69; decline
of, 61, 64, 65, 67, 69, 73, 82, 95; growth of,
60, 61, 64; indicators, 65, 87, 95, 96; biggest
joint ventures, 88–89; mostly joint ventures,
64; productivity and efficiency, 87–88; with
profits and losses, 75–76; by sector, 67; different types, 191n2
Iran, 6, 11, 72, 123
Iraq, 11, 49
Israel, 41, 106, 189n10
Issa, Zein, 110
Italy: banking exposure in Cuba, 123; investments in Cuba, 68, 69, 89, 107, 155, 164,
192n14; visitors to Cuba, 135, 199n6
ITT Corporation, 107, 108, 118

Jamaica, 32
Japan, 8, 9, 122, 124, 163
Jatar-Hausmann, Ana Julia, 140
Johnson, Lyndon B., 27, 28

Karliner, Joshua, 8
Kavulich, John, 161
Keck, Margaret E., 13

Kennedy administration, 26, 28
Kerry, John, 51, 52
Kiger, Patrick J., 99
Kissinger, Henry, 30

Lage, Carlos, 64, 80, 94, 141, 153
Leisure Canada, 103, 115, 164, 198n36, 202n60
Leogrande, William M., 45
LG Electronics Investment, 163, 164
Libya, 6, 11
Lieberman, Joe, 52
Lomas, Marta, 65, 68, 77, 79, 84, 87, 118,
192n16, 194n44
Lone Star Industries, 110
Los Portales S.A., 166
LTI, 103, 120
Lugo Fonte, Orlando, 79

Mack, Connie, 34, 38
Maíz, Marta, 141, 153
Malaysia, 69, 72
Malmierca, Rodrigo, 80, 194n44
Mariel Crisis, 22, 188n8
Marrero Cruz, Manuel, 77, 200n22
Martínez, Mel, 48, 50
Mas Canosa, Jorge, 33, 34, 37, 38, 46
McCain, John, 55
Menéndez, Bob, 58
Mesa-Lago, Carmelo, 37
Mexico: investments in Cuba, 106, 107, 108,
110, 155, 192n14, 199n54; joint ventures with
Cuba in, 72; refused to join embargo, 28;
response to Helms-Burton law, 42, 188n7,
196n2
MICSA. See Motores Internacionales del
Caribe S.A.
Migration: from Cuba to Europe, 133, 151;
from Cuba to U.S., xxiii, 21, 22, 48, 133, 151,
184, 188n8; global flows, xxv, 15; notion of
diaspora, 13; transnational phenomenon,
1–2, 13, 15–16
Ministry of Foreign Investment and Economic
Cooperation (MINVEC), 67, 71, 74, 76, 78,
80, 84, 87, 88, 118, 194n43, 195n49
MINVEC (Ministerio para la Inversión
Extranjera y la Colaboración Económica).
See Ministry of Foreign Investment and
Economic Cooperation

Paolo Spadoni is a post-doctoral research fellow in the Center for Inter-American Policy and Research (CIPR) at Tulane University in New Orleans. He has published extensively in scholarly and academic venues, and his numerous opinion pieces on Cuban issues have appeared in the *Los Angeles Times, Christian Science Monitor, Orlando Sentinel, South Florida Sun-Sentinel, Washington Times,* and *Tampa Tribune.*

CONTEMPORARY CUBA
Edited by John M. Kirk

Afro-Cuban Voices: On Race and Identity in Contemporary Cuba, by Pedro Pérez-Sarduy and Jean Stubbs (2000)

Cuba, the United States, and the Helms-Burton Doctrine: International Reactions, by Joaquín Roy (2000)

Cuba Today and Tomorrow: Reinventing Socialism, *by Max Azicri (2000)*

Cuba's Foreign Relations in a Post-Soviet World, by H. Michael Erisman (2000)

Cuba's Sugar Industry, by José Alvarez and Lázaro Peña Castellanos (2001)

Culture and the Cuban Revolution: Conversations in Havana, by John M. Kirk and Leonardo Padura Fuentes (2001)

Looking at Cuba: Essays on Culture and Civil Society, by Rafael Hernández, translated by Dick Cluster (2003)

Santería Healing: A Journey into the Afro-Cuban World of Divinities, Spirits, and Sorcery, by Johan Wedel (2004)

Cuba's Agricultural Sector, by José Alvarez (2004)

Cuban Socialism in a New Century: Adversity, Survival, and Renewal, edited by Max Azicri and Elsie Deal (2004)

Cuba, the United States, and the Post–Cold War World: The International Dimensions of the Washington-Havana Relationship, edited by Morris Morley and Chris McGillion (2005)

Redefining Cuban Foreign Policy: The Impact of the "Special Period," edited by H. Michael Erisman and John M. Kirk (2006)

Gender and Democracy in Cuba, *by Ilja A. Luciak (2007)*

Ritual, Discourse, and Community in Cuban Santería: Speaking a Sacred World, *by Kristina Wirtz (2007)*

The "New Man" in Cuba: Culture and Identity in the Revolution, *by Ana Serra (2007)*

U.S.-Cuban Cooperation Past, Present, and Future, *by Melanie M. Ziegler (2007)*

Protestants, Revolution, and the Cuba-U.S. Bond, by Theron Corse (2007)

The Changing Dynamic of Cuban Civil Society, edited by Alexander I. Gray and Antoni Kapcia (2008)

Cuba in the Shadow of Change: Daily Life in the Twilight of the Revolution, by Amelia Rosenberg Weinreb *(2009)*

Failed Sanctions: Why the U.S. Embargo against Cuba Could Never Work, by Paolo Spadoni (2010)